Odds Against Tomorrow
The Critical Edition

The Center for Telecommunication Studies
Film as Literature Series

Odds Against Tomorrow
The Critical Edition

by
Abraham Polonsky

Edited
—with Annotations and Critical Commentary—
by
John Schultheiss

The Center for Telecommunication Studies
California State University, Northridge

DEDICATION

This book is dedicated to all of those who were blacklisted—and who remained faithful to their art and their friends.
—Abraham Polonsky

The screenplay *Odds Against Tomorrow* is printed
with the permission of Maureen Daly McGivern and Abraham Polonsky

Pictures courtesy of Metro-Goldwyn-Mayer,
the Screen Actors Guild, and the individual artists featured

PRINTED IN THE USA
First Edition
1999

Published by
The Center for Telecommunication Studies
California State University, Northridge
18111 Nordhoff Street
Northridge, CA 91330
with assistance from
Sadanlaur Publications
Los Angeles, California

ISBN 0-9635823-4-8
Library of Congress Catalog Card Number 98-74816

Contents

Photo Credit: Mary McArthur

Abraham Lincoln Polonsky

"There is no idea, no theory, no way of life that cannot be reshaped, illuminated and made more human by being subject to the imagination and criticism of the artist."

—Abraham Polonsky

Odds Against Tomorrow

The Screenplay

Film Noir Without Linguistic Irony. Johnny Ingram (Harry Belafonte, right) and Earle Slater (Robert Ryan)—the film noir protagonist and his double.

Odds Against Tomorrow:
The Shooting & Continuity Texts

The following is a synthesis of Abraham Polonsky's authorship of *Odds Against Tomorrow*. It is a blending of his **shooting** script (written before the film was shot) and the **continuity** script (a transcription of the dialogue and visual/aural elements of the film itself.) The shooting script is dated 12 February 1959, with revisions of 19 February and 9 March 1959.

Shooting scripts are helpful artifacts for the critic, since they usually indicate moods and authorial intentions. The dialogue printed is, of course, a verbatim transcription of the words spoken in the film. And, whenever Polonsky's expository language from the shooting script is compatible with the actual material as shot (i.e., when his first intentions were not altered during production), his original descriptive passages are always utilized. Thus, the texture of Polonsky's writing is conveyed through the original wording of the shooting script, such as: "The music scoring carries an overtone of premonition, of tragedy—of people in trouble and doomed. The music will be a continuing and highly expressive voice in the story." . . . "The hotel lobby is old-fashioned, moderately down at heels, a sense of immemorial dust." . . . "The string breaks and leaves its mark while the pearls cannonade around everywhere, falling like glittering hail all over the room."

When the content in the film has no counterpart in the shooting script, the editor provides simple descriptions of the action ["The clock strikes the fifth time."], in order to complete a stenographic continuity record. [All instances of these editorial descriptions are enclosed in bold square brackets.] Significant variations from the shooting script—and from the source novel by William McGivern—are noted at appropriate points, along with additional commentaries, in the "Annotations" section.

This HarBel production was shot late February through late April 1959 at Gold Medal Studios, the Bronx, and on location at Hudson, New York; distributed by United Artists Corporation; theatrical opening in New York: 15 October 1959.

[Credits on Screen]

HARBEL

presents

HARRY BELAFONTE   ROBERT RYAN   SHELLY WINTERS

in

ODDS AGAINST TOMORROW

Co-starring

ED BEGLEY   GLORIA GRAHAME

with

Will Kuluva, Kim Hamilton, Mae Barnes,
Richard Bright, Carmen De Lavallade, and Lew Gallo

Screenplay by
ABRAHAM POLONSKY
[signed by
John O. Killens
and
Nelson Gidding][1]

From a book by
WILLIAM P. McGIVERN

Photographed by
JOSEPH BRUN

Music Composed and Conducted by
JOHN LEWIS

Manager of Production
FORREST E. JOHNSTON

Settings by
LEO KERZ

Film Editor
DEDE ALLEN

Assistant Director
CHARLES MAGUIRE

Sound
EDWARD JOHNSTONE
RICHARD VORISECK

Costumes
ANNA HILL JOHNSTONE

Set Decorator
FRED BALLMEYER

Makeup
ROBERT JIRAS

Script Supervisor
MARGUERITE JAMES

Camera Operator
SOL MIDWALL

Gaffer
HOWARD FORTUNE

Grip
EDWARD KNOTT

Sound Editor
KENN COLLINS

Title by
STORYBOARD

Associate Producer
PHIL STEIN

Directed and Produced by
ROBERT WISE

ODDS AGAINST TOMORROW

Screenplay by
Abraham Polonsky

FADE IN:

[Credits have been displayed against a background of abstract,
expressionistic patterns, suggestive of kaleidoscopic images, ranging in
coloration from grey to sharp black and white contrasts. Robert Wise's
credit DISSOLVES to water in a gutter, shimmering in the sun, the curb
forming a strong vertical line separating a fire hydrant on the left from
debris floating in the water on the right.

A wider shot of the street: buildings, trash cans, the fire hydrant, the
water in the gutter—and newspapers blown by the wind, one being
momentarily caught by the iron grillwork of a fence, then disappearing
behind.[2] It is . . .]

EXT. - NEW YORK - DAY

A sunny day, a windy one in the late winter of this year. One block
from the Hudson River on a cross street in the Nineties.

Underscoring music accompanies. It is in a modern, moody, sometimes
progressive jazz vein, carrying an overtone of premonition, of tragedy
—of people in trouble and doomed. The music will be a continuing and
highly expressive voice in the story.[3]

A close moving shot on EARLE SLATER. Rangy, powerful, a natural
athlete in his forties. His expression, taught to be impassive and
indifferent is now alive with pleasure in the wind which floods with
immense force between the rather expensive apartment buildings,

between clusters of old brownstones now homes for Negroes and Puerto Ricans. Beyond is the Drive, and the Palisades of Jersey behind the whitecapped river; beyond is space, open, an arena in which the wind can drive and shake the howl. The sky explodes with light.

Panoramic shot of the sky in which piping gulls ride the wind.

Now suddenly, a little black boy appears, five or six years old. He is holding his outstretched arms like bat wings, and he is running before the sweep of the wind, letting it carry him along so that he seems to himself to fly. He comes round in front of the CAMERA and flies off toward Earle. Other children follow, doing the same thing. They cry out in a frenzy of joy and motion.

The CAMERA PANS to reveal the Drive. There is the curve of the river, there are the far hills, the exquisite bridge, the foreground of autumn park and shaking trees, the traffic. There is the wind, and along the side a line of black and white children, one after another swooping along in the wind, their coats open like wings. One by one they bank around the corner. Their voices pipe high like gull cries.

The last flyer is a black girl, with pigtails, a red coat, white socks and slender legs. She seems to jump aloft, so lightly do her giant flying steps take her, and she tumbles into Earle.

Tight two shot of Earle and the girl, with her in his arms. When he smiles his face is naked, soft, yet touched with willfulness. He speaks with a drawling accent.

                    SLATER
          You lil pickaninny, you goin' to kill yourself flyin'
          like that, yes you are.

The child simply looks at him with astonishment, and then she smiles, a glitter of teeth and innocence.

Earle sets her down. She leaps away, going faster and faster after the long line of children.
Earle makes for a building entrance whose green canopy snaps and flutters in the wild wind. We read on it: HOTEL JUNO. Earle ducks into the hotel.

INT. LOBBY HOTEL - DAY

Old-fashioned, moderately down at heels, iron grillwork, marble floors, the thinnest and oldest carpets, a sense of immemorial dust.

Earle pushes past the glass doors into the lobby.

At that moment an olderly man crosses Earle. He leads a dachshund in a knitted coat. The man is mufflered, wears a homburg and gloves. He nods to Earle.

                    MAN
        Windy?

                    SLATER
        You bet.

The man passes by on his way out and Earle turns within.

This is a residential hotel and the lobby desk is only a short counter and cubbyhole, backed by letter shelves. A middle-aged man, his face splotched with a wine-colored birthmark, sits in front of a switchboard and reads the afternoon paper.[4]

Earle stops at the desk, waiting politely for the clerk to look up, but the man is lost in the sports section and shows no sign of Earle's presence.

Earl's face grows uneasy, angry. He slams his open palm on the counter. The man half jumps from his seat in a tangle of alarm.

                    SLATER
            (soft as a cottonmouth)
        I thought you was deef, pops.

                    CLERK
        I'm sorry, I didn't hear you speak.

                    SLATER
        Didn't say nothin'.

The clerk, almost a head shorter than Earle, is bewildered and doesn't know how to put the conversation back into normal gear. Earle outwaits him.

                    CLERK
               (almost inaudible)
          Didn't you?

                    SLATER
          Mr. David Burke.

                    CLERK
          607, sir.

The switchboard buzzes.

                    CLERK
          Excuse me.

But Earle is gone. The clerk looks after him as if a wild animal has suddenly sprung by.

INT. ELEVATOR

Earle walks past an African American operator, dressed in a badly fitted gray uniform with gold shoulder straps. The operator is a youngish man, short, slight, with a gay and clever face. He looks up with interest and is eager to serve and talk. . .

                    OPERATOR
               (smiling)
          Floor, mister?

Earle standing stiffly there, ignoring the operator.

                    SLATER
          Six.

The door closes and the car grinds up while the shaft howls with wind.

OPERATOR
                You hear that wind.

The car rattles and the wind screams. [There is a slight forward
tracking in by the camera to more emphatically observe Earle's muted
hostility.]

                           OPERATOR
                Man, I'm going to get myself grounded out of the air
                force. That's what I'm going to do. Ain't going to
                fly this kind of crate any more. Can you blame me?

The operator presents his humorous face to Earle for a laugh and
approval. [Earle silently stares at the operator with icy contempt.]
The operator feels rejected, and brings the car to a halt. The grilled
gate is pulled open by the operator, and Earle steps out, not looking
back, while the operator peeks curiously after him.

INT. HALLWAY

Slater moves off without answering or looking back.

The operator SLAMS the gate closed. The corridor has an endless green
carpet running past heavy tall doors. Under the dim bulbs Earle
approaches silently with his easy stride.

Pausing before 607 he [puts down his collar], takes off his hat and then
after a hesitation places it back on. He rings the bell. A dog barks
within in reply.

The opening door pours daylight into the hall, bright sun and the
SOUND of the wind hammering on two big windows which overlook
the river and the Jersey shore.

In the doorway is DAVE BURKE, a man in his fifties, heavy-set, with
big shoulders and big features. His head is balding, stub nose, thick
brows, crinkled eyes.

BURKE
(expansively)
Right on time, Slater, right on time. All right
there, Yuley.

He takes Earle's hand and shaking it heartily draws him within,
while he pushes the dog back [out of the doorway].

BURKE
Come in, come in.

INT. BURKE'S APARTMENT

One big room, shabby, comfortable. What dominates the room are the
windows which hold all the sky and the walls which are literally
covered with framed photographs, memorials, awards. There is also a
stuffed sailfish. It is all so much the place of a man living in the past.

BURKE
Here, let me help you off with your things.

Burke helps Earle off with his coat. The dog meanwhile sniffs at
Earle's legs. He lets the dog sniff at his hand.

SLATER
What you doing with such a big ol' dog in New
York?

BURKE
(grinning)
Never had a wife.

Burke is wearing an old cardigan sweater and smoking a short and
stubby pipe. [He places Earle's hat and coat on the studio couch.] Earle
is reserved, uneasy, and defensive.

BURKE
Right on the button. That's what I'm looking for,
Slater, someone serious, with a head for business.
(MORE)

                    BURKE (CON'T)
               (directing the dog to sit on the
               chair)
     All right, here, come on, over here, here, up.
                    (to Earle)
     Whiskey?

                    SLATER
     I don't mind.

The dog on its favorite chair watches the rest of the scene with
melancholy and disbelieving eyes.

                    BURKE
     Straight or with water?

                    SLATER
     With water.

Burke makes the drink.

                    BURKE
     I got ice if you want ice.

                    SLATER
     No, just water.

                    BURKE
     Make yourself comfortable, Slater. We got to talk.

Earle sits in a worn club chair across from the dog. The light from the
windows shatters on his face and he looks covertly around. The wind
bangs on the double windows.

BURKE goes to the sink and runs water into two glasses of whiskey.

                    BURKE
     Like the view?

Turning his head to observe it .

SLATER
You got a whole heap of it.

Taking him back to Earle.

BURKE
I used to be able to afford a little space inside, too.

He hands Earle a glass, surveys his room with bitterness, [goes over to the chair in which the dog lies] and pats the animal.

BURKE (CON'T)
But we call this dump home, don't we, old boy?

SLATER
Not bad.

BURKE
(raising his glass)
Well, here's to our mutual benefit. May it be considerable.

They both drink.

BURKE
I guess you know all you have to know about me, Slater.

SLATER
(hesitantly)
I know something.

BURKE
(with an engaging grin)
All right, you tell me what you know, go on.

Earle is uncomfortable in this situation, unable to handle it.

SLATER
You said you wanted to talk to me. Since we knew a few people in common, I naturally wanted to come and find out.

                              BURKE
                      (still smiling)
                  I mean the dirt.

Earle feels a little mockery in this, and starts to harden and resent it.

                              SLATER
                  I know you were on the police force. You had a
                  session with the State Crime Committee and you
                  got a year for contempt.

                              BURKE
                      [hardening]
                  Because I wouldn't talk. I was on the force thirty
                  years. I had my own squad and I knew everybody.

He waves his hand to the walls. Earle twists his head to look at the walls.

                              BURKE
                      (continuing)
                  Everybody was my friend until they needed a
                  patsy.
                      (pauses)
                  I know about you, Earle. Two stretches, one for
                  assault with a deadly weapon, one for
                  manslaughter. Every time you get a decent job . . .

Earle turns back to look at the speaker.

                              SLATER
                  Knock it off!
                      (violently)
                  What's so big about you, Burke?

He stands up, [glaring in Burke's face].

                              SLATER
                      (continuing)
                  How come you make so much noise?

SLATER
(continuing)
You've been sniffing around trying to find a hole in
the fence, just like everybody else. What makes
you so big you can call me up to this dump and shoot
off your mouth?

He goes quickly to the couch, grabs his hat and coat, [and moves to the
door].

BURKE
I got an idea; that's why, Slater. How would you
like to pick up fifty thousand dollars, all in small
bills, just for yourself?

Earle's hand on the door knob. He is feeling the immense weight of the
numbers.

Burke is smiles and comfortable confidence.

BURKE
(continuing)
How would you?

Earle studies the other man.

The telephone is RINGING now on the desk and Burke goes to it while
Earle waits impatiently.

BURKE
(continuing)
'Lo, Johnny. No . . . When? Sure, that's fine.

He replaces it in the receiver. [As in anticipation, the camera tracks in
slightly for Earle's reply.]

BURKE
(continuing)
Well?

                    SLATER
           What would I have to do?

                    BURKE
           Just walk into a bank and take it.

Earle's nerves jump with acceptance, with doubt. Whenever he stops
being angry uneasiness returns in him.

Burke [stands waiting], in command of the situation.[5]

                    SLATER
           ([moving forward], with difficulty)
           Maybe you got me wrong, Burke. I never stole
           nothing in my life, 'cept maybe a watermelon when
           I was a boy on the farm.

In a sudden burst of energy, Burke's voice is urgent, persuasive, eloquent.

                    BURKE
           I don't want a big Joe with more decorations than
           Dillinger. I want a safe thing. I want a man who
           needs some money to set himself up. I want a man
           with guts. I want a serious guy in trouble and that's
           you. That's me. That's the both of us. This is a one
           time job, one roll of the dice, and then we're
           through forever. Come on, Slater, what do you say?

Slater's mouth is dry, his manner hesitant. Very slowly, Slater sits
down to listen.

The music builds.

EXT. RIVERSIDE DRIVE - DAY

The traffic, the river, the wind tearing at the trees. In the hum and
flow of cars a little white Austin-Healy picks along trying to find a
parking place. It rolls down a block, makes a U turn and returns,
snooping between cars, searching for a place. Finally the car passes
again the front of Hotel Juno.[6]

It parks in the one free space just as the line of children, borne along on their winged coats, appears. A tall man slips gracefully out of the bucket seat while the children, distracted by this toylike and fascinating car, stop and make a semi-circle around, watching in silence.[7]

The driver is an African American, in fine, conservative, and expensive clothes, slim, easy. He moves toward CAMERA while behind him the [children are touching and playing on] the car.

The man is JOHNNY INGRAM. His face is delicate, calm, the face of someone who has learned to live within his weakness and strength, one who no longer tries. There is nothing restless or urgent about him.

Ingram turns around for a last look at his parked car and sees the children about to convert it into a launching platform for their game. He grins amiably and turns back.

He speaks in a soft, husky voice with no trace of southern accent. It isn't an educated speech, but it is relaxed and confident.

                    INGRAM
        Alright, who'd like to make themselves a fortune?

He jingles money in his hand and a barnyard of voices rise around him.

                    CHILDREN
            Me, me, me . . .

He examines the change and starts handing out the money.

                    INGRAM
        Everyone stays off this car. Do I have a deal . . . ?

                    CHILDREN
            Yes, yes, yes . . .

Some begin to run around the car, others just stand and look at it or the driver. The biggest child, a girl, accepts command.

                    GIRL
I'll watch them.

INGRAM
(laughing)
And who'll watch you?

He starts back for the hotel entrance.

Johnny Ingram walks to the entry just as Earle Slater comes out of the lobby. The men pass each other but Slater sees no one, only the dream created up in room 607.

Ingram enters the elevator from the lobby.

INGRAM
Six, please.

The operator smiles again, this time with more confidence, and slams the door closed. The elevator ascends and the wind shrieks in the shaftway. The operator darts glances of admiration at his passenger, at the neat blue coat, the muffler, the fine pigskin gloves, the brand new black shoes. Ingram's elegance is part of his character, also, the operator is impressed and loves the feeling.

OPERATOR
Just you hear that wind.

The car rattles and shakes and Ingram looks around with a certain pleasant doubt.

INGRAM
You sure we going to make it?

OPERATOR
(laughing)
Always made it before.

INGRAM
With my luck, daddy, this could be it.

The operator breaks into a peal of strong laughter as the elevator halts at six. He swings the door back.

                    OPERATOR
        Maybe on the way down.

                     INGRAM
        I'm walking down.

Ingram walks away while the operator sticks his head out of the car
and watches, whistles with appreciation.

INT. CORRIDOR - OUTSIDE BURKE'S DOOR

Ingram RINGS, the dog BARKS and Burke flings the door wide open.

                      BURKE
        Down, back. Shut up, you mutt.

He grabs Ingram's hand and pumps it.

                      BURKE
                   (continuing)
        Johnny, come in, come in.

                     INGRAM
        Hello, Dave.

The dog runs forward and Burke pushes the dog away.

                      BURKE
        Scram. She'll get hair all over you.

He turns on the dog.

                      BURKE
                   (continuing)
        Take off.

Ingram is laughing silently, and goes in.

INT. BURKE'S ROOM

Burke reaches to help his guest with his coat. But Ingram slips aside, avoiding him.

> BURKE
> (continuing)
> Here, let me help you.

> INGRAM
> Can't stay long, Dave.

> BURKE
> Well, it takes some explaining. How about a drink?

> INGRAM
> No, thanks.

He sits down on the arm of a chair and the dog leaps nuzzles his hand.

> INGRAM (CON'T)
> You got the floor.

Burke moves to Ingram.

> BURKE
> Here . . . he keeps shedding . . . those blue coats and. . .

> INGRAM
> That's all right, don't worry about it.

Burke directs the dog back to its own place on the studio couch. Ingram brushes off a few hairs after he slowly removes his gloves. Burke is standing squarely in front of him, estimating him.

> BURKE
> You don't look like I could sell anything to you. You look like you have it all, right now.

INGRAM
(politely smiling but uninterested)
Come on, fill me in, Dave.

BURKE
You're into Bacco for too much dough.

INGRAM
Now, tell me something I don't know.

BURKE
You owe him about six grand. Right?

INGRAM
(more interested now)
Wrong, seven and a half.

BURKE
It was six last week.

INGRAM
(without emphasis)
Well, the horses are still running and I'm still
losing.

BURKE
And Bacco's willing to wait?

INGRAM
What's the pitch, Dave?

BURKE
I know how you can pay it off.

INGRAM
And I know what's coming next. The fix is in. It's a
sure thing, right?

Ingram turns away from Burke, starting to walk.

                    BURKE
                 (entering shot)
            Now wait a minute—

                    INGRAM
             (reaching for the door)
        No thanks, Davey boy. I'll go down the drain on
        my own.

Burke begins to laugh and Ingram is at first astonished.

It breaks Burke up, the foolishness of it all. He can't stop and Ingram
begins to smile himself, taken over by the other man's merriment.

                    BURKE
        You're crazy.

                    INGRAM
        Alright, so I'm crazy.

                    BURKE
        You're counting your fingers and toes.
                 (dead serious)
        I'm talking about five oh oh oh oh.

                    INGRAM
             (moving from the door after a long
              pause)
        I'll try the drink. Straight.

As Burke pours a couple of drinks. Ingram once again is seated in the
chair. He has opened his coat.

                    BURKE
             (friendly and intimate)
        Just tell me one thing, Johnny. How come Bacco
        hasn't knocked your teeth in for not paying off?

                    INGRAM
        Because I'm paying him a hundred a week interest.

Burke hands a drink to Ingram.

BURKE

Well, that can't leave you much.

INGRAM

(gestures with the glass to Burke)

Just my teeth.

He drinks.

BURKE

You ever going to pay it off?

INGRAM

If I can wear out this streak.

(he shrugs his shoulders)

No use stopping now. I'm way past the liferopes
and praying for a miracle. What do you mean, fifty
grand?

BURKE

Just what I said, fifty to seventy-five thousand,
like that, all in small bills.

INGRAM

And you need Johnny Ingram? I'm just a bone picker
in a four-man graveyard.

BURKE

It's a bank job.

Ingram is really startled.

INGRAM

Aren't we social climbing, David?

Burke leans forward with confidence and feeling.

BURKE

This is easy money.

INGRAM
Man, you're drifting.

BURKE
I'm serious.

INGRAM
(vigorously)
It's not your line, Dave. That's the firing squad.
That's for junkies and joy boys. We're people.[8]

BURKE
(bitterly, resentfully)
Okay, what's my line?

INGRAM
(clamming up)
I'll forget you asked me.

BURKE
You don't even want to hear?

INGRAM
I did all my dreaming on my mother's knee.

Burke gives a last lingering estimate. His eyes are cool, his glance
objective, and now suddenly a warm smile floods back into his face.

BURKE
All right. Forget it. Forget it. You riding?

INGRAM
Downtown.

As Ingram prepares to leave, picks up his hat and gloves.

BURKE
I'll ride with you.

He sheds his old cardigan and gets a coat and overcoat from the closet,
an old snap brim hat. The dog begins jumping around him.

> INGRAM
> (half kidding)
> A man like you thinking thoughts like that, Dave.
> You're in trouble.

> BURKE
> (intensely)
> I've got to get out of this trap. They've kicked my
> head in. What can I do?

> INGRAM
> (sardonically)
> Find a hobby, man, anything. They sure changed
> your color when they rehabilitated you at Sing
> Sing.

> BURKE
> Fifty grand can change it back.

Burke opens the door, and the dog springs out.

> BURKE
> Here. Come back here, you. Get back in here. You
> heard me.

There is a challenge of looks and the dog returns, dropping its cocked
tail.

> BURKE
> (continuing; abruptly kind)
> Mind the store.

He closes the door.

EXT. SEVENTY-SECOND STREET

The car conspicuous among the taxicabs and trucks and buses on Seventy-
second Street.

INT. CAR

Ingram is smoking, Burke leans in his corner and covertly watches the other man's face.

BURKE
How are those two little women of yours?

INGRAM
The kid's fine but that ex-wife of mine, man, she's
worse than Bacco. If that alimony isn't there on
the first, her lawyer is there in the second.

EXT. STREET AND CAR

Ingram wheels the car over to the curb, across the street from the park.
Burke pushes open the door.

BURKE
Thanks for the lift. If you change your mind,
Johnny, I think I can get you the 7500 right away to
pay off Bacco.

INGRAM
I've got five hundred on the nose of Lady Care
today. Can't lose forever.

BURKE
You'd be surprised.

Burke closes the door of the car, which scoots down the street. Burke
watches after the car a moment and then looks toward the park.

EXT. PARK

There among the bushes and the tall trees a man in a dark coat and hat
stands like St. Francis among the beasts feeding a flock of pigeons.

About twenty yards from the pigeon feeder is a park bench inhabited by
two oddly assorted characters. One is very young, COCO, a dark and

almost beautiful youth, wearing a polo coat wrapped tightly around his slim waist. His black trousers are pencil thin, his feet small, elegant in Italian shoes. [A scarf is around his] throat and his hair is too long, yet beautifully set in place and somewhat curled. He has very long lashes and when he talks he flutters them for emphasis.

At a bench, Coco is sitting with a companion is reading the *Morning Telegraph,* and a POLICEMAN stands and chats with Coco.

COCO

(to policeman)
Just tell me, how come it isn't safe to walk in the park at night, a big city like this?

POLICEMAN

Ah, it's these wild kids.

Burke walks in and pauses before the bench. Coco looks up, batting his eyes in recognition and smiling.

COCO

Well, if it isn't the old clam himself.

His voice is soft, uneducated, even coarse in pronunciation.

MORIARITY, the man reading the paper, raises his eyes, almost white-blue in their white corneas, without recognition in them; but he nods to Burke and goes back to his paper. The policeman moves away unobtrusively, continuing his beat.

BURKE

This fresh air'll kill you, Coco.

COCO

(spitefully)
I know it, but this is pigeon time for the little king.

MORIARITY

(with another metallic look)
What's this, a press interview or something?

                    COCO
              (grinning, to Burke)
Go and talk to the old man if you want to. He wants
to do you a favor. What's the matter with this
Davey Burke, he says, I want to pay him off.

Burke strolls across the yellowed lawn up to the outskirts of the pigeon
flock, having stopped listening long ago.

A man in black holds a paper bag of cracked corn. His name is BACCO,
the loan shark. He is about fifty-five or sixty, sallow. His clothes are
utterly new and well fitting.

He looks up, and a pale smile ornaments his anemic face.

                    BACCO
     Hi, Dave.

                    BURKE
     Hello, Bacco.

The wind blows here, but it is high in the trees out of which from time
to time birds drop to the ground to join the feeders.

                    BACCO
     Join me.

He takes out a plump handful of feed which he hands to Burke. Now
the two men stand side by side and feed the birds.

                    BACCO
     Want me to open up something for you, Dave,
     something in the operation? I told you, whenever
     you're ready.

                    BURKE
              (grinning)
     You're outside the law.

                    BACCO
     A little inside, a little outside. More or less.
     Everything is more or less. Just name it.

> BURKE
> (casually)
> A fellow by the name of Ingram owes you .

> BACCO
> Sure, a very entertaining boy at Connoy's place.

Burke moves closer to Bacco with a sudden seriousness, while around the birds shatter the air with wings.[9]

> [DISSOLVE]

EXT. SIDE STREET IN THIRTIES - EAST SIDE

Quiet morning, around seven-thirty, the light slanting over the brownstones. The curbs are lined with parked and silent cars, but very little traffic. The light is pale, a little blue, shimmering with dust and haze.

A fairly new sedan pulls up in front of one of the brownstones. Burke climbs out.

Burke hurries up the stairs into the tiny vestibule and RINGS a bell inside. Then he comes out again, goes down a few steps and looks up.

Behind a second floor window Slater waves to Burke.

INT. SLATER'S APARTMENT - DAY

Two rooms, fairly large, opening into each other. The shades are drawn as are the drapes, but the breeze from the open window kicks up the cloth and light darts in and out. To one side is a door leading to a small efficient kitchen. The back room is a bedroom, its double doors wide open, and deep in the gloom, is a big double bed and the usual furniture.

The house is well furnished, but mostly with inexpensive pieces carefully selected, fixed up by the owners, the apartment made pretty and comfortable as if it were important to the people inside.

Slater is dressed, but tieless and coatless, and he moves softly into the bedroom, stopping in front of the dressing table. He picks up a tie and begins to knot it.

In the bed, the blankets piled high over the curled-up figure of a woman. She begins to stir and he turns his head to look back at her. Then her voice, clogged with sleep, comes to him. It is a very womanly voice, rather deep-toned and vibrant, even now.

> LORRY
>
> Hey, what time is it?

> SLATER
>
> (softly)
> I'm on my way, stupid, go back to sleep.

> LORRY
>
> What time?

> SLATER
>
> Seven-thirty.

> LORRY
>
> Why so early?

She begins to struggle up in the bed, to sit up. LORRY is in her thirties with a passionate face somewhat marred by experience and objectivity. She is a big woman with a very fine and graceful neck, very full shoulders and bosom.

Earle [is at the mirror]. His tie is made.

> SLATER
>
> Burke is waiting.

She [reaches over to the bedside table for a comb to fasten her hair].

> LORRY
>
> Earle, can you trust this Burke?

Earle's bony, distrustful face is now soft and open to this woman.

SLATER
Not like I can trust you, but enough.

Lorry's eyes are open wide, very dark and shining. She looks up at him.

LORRY
Come here, you big clown.[10]

He moves to the dresser where he stuffs his pockets with a wallet, handkerchief, keys, money.

SLATER
(not looking at her)
Now you go back to sleep.

LORRY
Let him wait.

SLATER
I'm off to make my fortune.

LORRY
What kind of a fortune?

SLATER
Just one of those fortune fortunes. I told you about it.
Burke got hold of some kind of concession.

Earle goes to the closet, takes out his jacket and puts it on.

LORRY
Burke—he's a friend of that Lefty Gowers isn't he?

SLATER
Yea, he's the one told Burke about me.

LORRY .
You knew Gowers in jail. Didn't you?

SLATER
No, at the millionaire's club. Where else?

LORRY

Earle, what does he want with you.?

She shivers and pulls the blankets over her shoulders.

SLATER

I'll tell you after I see the proposition.

LORRY

Do you have to stay over night, or do you just want
to stay over night?

SLATER

I have to see the concession.

He has stopped at a closet for his topcoat and hat. There is a small
leather suitcase packed and standing on a chair near the big old-
fashioned mahogany door that leads to the hall.

LORRY

You have enough money, sweetie?

SLATER

Plenty.

LORRY

How much is plenty?

SLATER

About fifteen dollars.

LORRY

You better take some more.

SLATER

Burke is paying.

LORRY

What do I care if he's paying? You take some more
then if you feel like paying you just pay.

There is almost a wounded look on Earle's face, very full of feelings, a sudden outgoing of his heart to the woman. He goes back into the bedroom to the dresser. In the mirror we see her on the bed while he goes to her purse and takes out a few bills. She sits looking at him. Suddenly he turns and moves quickly out of the SHOT but in the mirror we see him fall at the bed, kneeling, embracing her, burying his face against her breast. She holds him with strength and comfort.

She holds him as if she would like to absorb him within her flesh to protect him.

> LORRY
> I know. You don't have to take this deal if you
> don't like it. If this isn't what you want, you just
> don't take it. There's no hurry.

> SLATER
> (his face tight)
> There is a hurry. I have to make it, Lorry, and I
> have to make it now. It wasn't too bad when I was
> grubbing along by myself . . .

> LORRY
> I know. I know.

> SLATER
> It always was too tough . . . too greedy. But now,
> because of you . . .

> LORRY
> No, no.

> SLATER
> I have to make it on my own, Lorry, because of you,
> and I have to make it any way I can . . .

> LORRY
> (passionately)
> No, you don't. Not just any way. And you mustn't
> even try.

                    SLATER
I have to.

                    LORRY
Earle, listen. I have you, right? You have me.
What difference does it make where the money
comes from?

He rises.

                    SLATER
They're not going to junk me like an old car.

He starts out again, [and she rises, the blanket around her shoulders.]

                    LORRY
Earle . . .

                    SLATER
    (pausing)
Now, don't worry. If it isn't all right, I won't do it.

He hurries to his suitcase, picks it up, and goes out without looking
back. She stands, shivering with cold. But she walks into the living
room to the open window, pulls the curtain apart and looks out.

EXT. INTERCHANGES AND BRIDGES

Burke's car in the beltline. The geometry of traffic.[11]

EXT. HIGHWAY - LONG SHOT - DAY

Burke's car making a good sixty miles an hour on the fourlane parkway.

INT. BURKE'S CAR

Slater has a roadmap in his hands, raises it to look at it.

BURKE
It's about a hundred miles up the Hudson. I got it
marked there. Melton . . .

[Insert of map, zoom in to the name of Melton underlined in black.]

EXT. MELTON - DAY

SLOW PANS, SHOTS to reveal the town, nudged by hills, the few big
new industrial plants along the river, the bustling sense of a market
town, booming with an insurge of workingmen, shopkeepers and ex-
urbanites.

Down the street, is the old fashioned bank building, Main street, and
just beyond, the town square, town hall, the winter look, and beyond,
bare trees, the river, hills.

A street clock, an old, four face job, standing high above the curb on a
fancy cast iron pole, the whole thing ornate and rather charming. The
time is 2:48 PM, and the gold legend around the dial reads: First
National Bank of Melton, 1836.

EXT. MELTON - NIGHT

[Long shot of Main Street. The lights come on.] Close shot on the clock.
The dials are illuminated. The time is 6:03.

INT. OUTSIDE CORNER ROOM, MELTON HOTEL - NIGHT

[Tight shot of closed venetian blinds. Slowly, they begin to open. The
hands of Slater reach in and widen the opening in the slats on the right
side of the blinds. Burke's hands execute a similar action on the lower
left portion of the blinds. Both] peer tensely into the Main Street of
Melton, a narrow thoroughfare, lined with two-story, nineteenth
century buildings with twentieth century storefronts.

Directly across the street on the Northeast corner is a large drugstore.
The sign reads: MELTON DRUG COMPANY.

An African American in dark glasses, a slender man, tall, willowy, wearing a chef's hat, white coat, white trousers, white apron, appears in the drugstore entrance. He carries two cartons, rather narrow ones such as are used for delivering orders of sandwiches and containers of coffee.

He steps out onto the street, bearing his burden protectively.

BURKE (VO)

Now watch the waiter.

Burke's heavy head is on the left side of the frame.

The waiter heads for the corner and waits for the traffic light to change.

As the lights alter the waiter heads across the street, followed by the eyes of the watchers. He disappears, blocked off by the window

BURKE (VO)

Over here . . . [12]

Earle and Burke cross the room to the window on the other side. Here, too, the Venetian blinds are drawn. [Again, the two men separate] the strips to reveal the scene below.

Through the blinds, we are facing the side street and corner now. The waiter appears from the right, and heads down the sidestreet. The corner building is a bank. The bank clock reads a few minutes past 6:00.

It is the most unmodern thing in Melton, still with its great windows and ornate and carved granite facade. The windows are high, just above street level on this side, and some twenty yards down the street is a side door, [with a small security window at eye level].

The waiter stops at the side door, and KNOCKS on the [security window]. After a pause, the [security window opens, the waiter is recognized by the guard inside, and the window closes]. The door now opens about half a foot where it is stopped by a guard chain. The face of the guard appears, an elderly man with glasses. He smiles and takes the boxes which just fit through the aperture. Then the door is closed and the waiter starts back up the street.

                    BURKE (VO)
               (simultaneously with the above
               action)
Now here's the set up. That side door is the key to
the whole job. The bank stays open Thursdays till
six. Most of the factories pay on Friday, so the
bank is loaded with payroll cash and deposits from
the stores. Every Thursday night there's close to
two hundred thousand dollars in untraceable cash
sitting in there. A half dozen clerks stick around
for an hour totaling up and straightening out the
books. The assistant manager has a bad heart. Joe
Foss, the guard, is about to retire, has glasses and
arthritis. That's it. That colored waiter from the
drugstore brings them coffee and sandwiches just
after six. The rest of the town's home at supper.
You could take it with a water pistol.

His voice is soft, intensely feeling.

The waiter disappears into the side of the SHOT.

Slater and Burke move back to the first window, where again through
the slatter blinds they watch the scene. Once again the waiter
reappears in the crosswalk, and makes his way to the drugstore.

                    BURKE
               (hushed with excitement)
Well, what do you think?

                    SLATER
               (his voice cold, drawling)
There's just one thing wrong with it.

                    BURKE
               (all keyed up)
     What?

As the men face each other, Burke's face frustrated and impatient,
Earle Slater with that old uneasy look, beginning to back inside his
cold mask.

SLATER
You didn't say nothing about the third man being a
nigger.

INT. CANNOY'S CLUB - NIGHT

A close-up of Ingram fills the screen.

[The first two words of the following song's lyrics have played over the last frames of the previous shot.] [13] Ingram is spotlighted. Behind him the beat of the small combination, piano, drums, double-bass. The other players are also African Americans. Ingram is at the microphone, singing and playing his vibraharp.

INGRAM
(singing, his face strained)
At night I tell you people
When that cold, cold sun goes down,
At night I tell you people
When that cold, cold sun goes down,
I cry, I sigh, I want to die
'Cause my baby's not around.
What's the matter, pretty baby?
Tell me what's your daddy done.
Won't you tell me, pretty mama,
What's your daddy done?
You've got to come and hold me
Before the morning sun.

[Several SHOTS reveal this to be] the cellar of a brownstone turned into a bar and small dinner place. A dozen people in street clothes are there, intent on their own conversations which never cease. This is Cannoy's Club where serious gambling is done upstairs by racketeers, some show people, or big time spenders, everyone touching the seedy side of life, and no squares allowed.

Down the entrance stairs a sturdy man in a dinner jacket brings Bacco, Moriarity, and Coco. The captain sets them at a table while Coco heads for the bandstand.

As Ingram plays he watches the new arrivals closely.

Coco enters, exquisite in black, like a black snake. He wears no tie, but a black velvet shirt under his black jacket. He pauses in front of Ingram who is just touching harmonies on the vibes for the piano solo.

> COCO
> Hi, baby, what's shakin'?

Ingram [glowers].

> COCO
> Bacco wants to buy you a drink, and I want to buy you a shiny new car.

[Ingram smirks in contempt.]

Coco turns to go, pauses.

> COCO
> Too bad about Lady Care.

> INGRAM
> Yea, they bobbed her nose.

Ingram, suddenly gloomy, [resumes his singing].

> INGRAM
> Believe me, pretty mama,
> It's not just me, I know.
> Believe me, pretty mama,
> It's not just me, I know.
> I just can't make that jungle
> Outside of my front door.

The number winds up, and Ingram walks slowly toward the door, just passing Bacco's table. Coco stands up to make room for him, but Ingram just nods and walks by, going out into the foyer.

INT. FOYER

Ingram runs into a party of two men and a girl which is just entering.

The girl, quite tall and elegant, is the showgirlish type, somewhat too striking in clothes and figure. She stands back as the men hand their coats to a woman attendant. The men go upstairs to the gambling rooms, while the girl, KITTY, addresses Ingram.

                              KITTY
          Well, at last, the invisible man.

He looks trapped.

                              INGRAM
          I had a heart attack.

                              KITTY
          For a couple of horses.

                              INGRAM
          Don't be like that, baby.

A pained and suffering look touches her mouth.

                              KITTY
                    (lightly)
          I don't care if you want to drop me, Johnny, but send
          back the key.

He is caught there, unwilling to be present, trying to be polite, not really caring, yet attempting not to show it.

                              INGRAM
          Who said anything about dropping you?

                              KITTY
                    (without a flicker of an eyelash)
          Then you know where to find me.

Ingram takes Kitty by the arm and leads her away out of the light. Ingram takes her in his arms, kissing her. Her embrace is needful, his is dutiful but he does his best.

[She pushes him away.]

KITTY
That's good, but it was better when you wanted it.

She walks hurriedly into the club, passing Coco who leans in the doorway.

COCO
I told you Bacco has a message for you.

INGRAM
It's a long night, pretty boy, I'm not going anywhere.

Abruptly, Coco turns back in and Ingram heads for Cannoy's office.

GUARD
Johnny, maybe I should lend you a piece of iron.

Ingram hesitates, glances into the bar.

INGRAM
Maybe.

He reaches into his back pocket.

GUARD
I can let you have this juvenile delinquent.

And he produces a very small automatic that fits into his heavy palm. Ingram takes it from him.

INGRAM
I'm only playing with kids.

Ingram slips the gun into his coat pocket and [turns toward the office].

He KNOCKS on a closed door [marked NO ADMITTANCE] which is unlocked by a heavy-set man named GARRY.

GARRY
(smiling)
Johnny? Come in.

                    INGRAM
    Hi, Garry.

He closes the door behind them when Ingram enters.

INT. CONNOY'S ROOM

Sitting on the desk is a man, very neat, with a polished face and dark
hair. He is like a ball bearing, just as shiny and just as hard. This is
EDDY CANNOY and at the moment he is admiring a string of pearls
which he slips from hand to hand.

                    CANNOY
    Hello, Johnny.

                    INGRAM
    Can I see you, Ed?

                    CANNOY
    Why, sure.

[Cannoy gets up and walks around the desk to greet Ingram.]

                    GARRY
    Want me to cut out?

                    INGRAM
    No, not for me, Garry.

Cannoy hands Ingram the pearls.

                    CANNOY
    Well, Johnny, what do you think of these?

                    INGRAM
    Who are they for?

                    CANNOY
    My oldest. It's her sweet sixteenth. Those are real
    cultured pearls.

INGRAM
(shaking his head)
Sixteen already? Wow!

CANNOY
Yea, they don't stand still like we do, Johnny.

Ingram hands back the pearls which Cannoy puts down on the desk.

CANNOY (CON'T)
Well, what can I do for you?

INGRAM
Bacco just blew in. He called me earlier today.

CANNOY
Oh? What do you owe him?

INGRAM
Seven five double oh.

Cannoy slides off the desk [and walks around behind it]. He is very
quiet, thinking, and it is obvious he isn't just thinking about money.

Ingram's face is composed. He picks a cigarette, puts it in his mouth,
and snaps on a desk lighter whose flame he studies for a long moment.

The SOUND of the door opening behind Ingram, who turns to look.
Behind the flame in the foreground, the opening door, and the figure of
Bacco entering.

Bacco enters the room, followed by Moriarity and Coco.

BACCO
Hello, Ed.

CANNOY
Bacco.
Bacco saunters up to the desk where Ed is standing. The men shake
hands and Bacco almost unintentionally seems to find himself in
Cannoy's seat. [Bacco picks up Cannoy's string of pearls.]

                          BACCO
            I come down for my money, Johnny.

                          INGRAM
            I don't have it.

Moriarity looks on impassively but alertly. Ingram's voice is tense, yet
quiet and low pitched.

                          BACCO
            Maybe you're not looking hard enough, maybe you
            think I'm a jerk who can wait forever.

                          INGRAM
            Look, I lost again today. I've been losing steadily
            for a month. I just got to break his streak I'm in,
            Bacco. I can't let it knock me out.

                          BACCO
            Suit yourself, just get the money to me by tomorrow
            night. All of it.

Coco drifts to the wall behind Ingram where there is a mirror. He
produces an ivory comb and begins to comb and set his longish hair.

                          INGRAM
            Suppose I can't.

The uncontrollableness of emotion which is one of Bacco's main
characteristics leaps into his face.

                          BACCO
            There is no can't. I don't like the word can't. I say
            have it.

Bacco speaks angrily at the desk, Cannoy withdrawn and passive to
one side. Ingram after a calculating estimate of BACCO turns to
Cannoy.

                          INGRAM
            Can you bail me out, Ed?

Cannoy's first reaction is to say yes, and the yes is written over his face, but he darts a quick and careful glance past Ingram and to one side toward Bacco who almost imperceptibly lowers his lids and [turns his head away in disapproval].

Cannoy hesitates. When he speaks his voice is very friendly.

                    CANNOY
          I'm sorry, Johnny, I can't help you. Well, you
          already owe me a couple of thou anyway. Now, I
          asked you to stop with the horses. I remember I
          told you once and for all to stop.

                    INGRAM
               (shows no reaction as he turns back
               to Bacco)
          I can't get it for you tomorrow.

Bacco's brows join as if knitted, and the willful and passionately white face knots like a fist.

                    BACCO
          You're saying what to me?

Ingram is under perfect control.

                    INGRAM
          Look man I'm telling you in front. I don't have it
          now and I won't be able to get it by tomorrow.

[Bacco glances at Moriarity.]

Moriarity makes a move suddenly to grab Ingram. Ingram steps back and points the gun still in his pocket.

                    INGRAM (CON'T)
          I'm not dancing with you, Moriarity.

The gunsel slides back against the wall and waits, but Bacco is livid, jumping to his feet, and leaning forward over the desk.

BACCO
You mean you come here with a gun, when I
personally call you to talk to you, when I stretched
you six months with a debt someone else would be
dead for, and you come here and pull a gun on me . . .

INGRAM
The gun's in my pocket.

BACCO
(shouting)
The gun's at my head, that's where it is. I tell you,
Ingram, I want you to know. Have that dough at
my place tomorrow night or I'll collect it from you
or that ex-wife of yours or your kid.

The mention of his ex-wife and child chills his face with fury.

INGRAM
You'll do what?

He moves forward and pulls the little automatic from his pocket.
Behind him, the indolent Coco slides forward and with two swift steps
jams a gun in Ingram's back.

COCO
I'm sorry, Johnny, drop that gun.

But Moriarity hasn't been waiting. In one motion he grabs the gun from
Ingram's hand, pins his arms, and thrusts him forward, half-leaning
forward over the desk. There Bacco in a frenzy of rage slashes Ingram
across the face with the string of pearls. The string breaks and leaves
its mark while the pearls cannonade around everywhere, falling like
glittering hail all over the room.

Now there is a stillness in which Bacco's anger is in his breath and
Ingram, humiliated, outraged, and helpless, breathes with the
heaviness of a man who has just run the last race of his life. The two
breaths are the only sounds in the room. The loan shark's pale face is
like a mummy's.

                    BACCO
        Tomorrow night at eight or I'll kill you and
        everything you own.

Bacco continues on out of the room without looking back again.

INT. CONNOY'S CLUB/BANDSTAND

[The lights above the bandstand glare in the camera's lens. Music is
playing.]

The bartender is ANNIE, a buxom, middle-aged woman who can sing a
blues; her assistant, a beautiful young girl called FRA THE FLYER.
Annie is singing the lovesick words of a popular ballad, trying to make
them mean something while the band glitters behind her with bop
harmonies and the late hour lags in air.

                    ANNIE
                (singing)
        Well, it tells you in the good book
        And they teach the same in school
        Let a man get his hands on you
        And he'll use you for a mule.
        My mama gave me warning
        And now I know it's true.
        She said, "All men are evil."
        And daddy that's you.
        All men are evil . . .

Suddenly, Ingram's face in the SHOT, as the angle widens. He has been
drinking, his tie is loose, his collar open. He [joins in singing the lyrics].

                    INGRAM
        All men are evil . . .

                    ANNIE
        All men are evil . . .

                    INGRAM
        She said, "All men are evil . . ."

[He is no longer singing. He begins to provide personal commentary to
the music.

                    INGRAM
          They bobbed my nose. Annie, they bobbed my nose.
          Don't ever love nobody . . .]

He starts to get laughs, sings louder, wilder. Annie is struggling to
finish her song against Ingram's interference. He begins to say any
crazy thing that comes to mind.

Garry stands beside Kitty, and the pretty bargirl makes a third. Only
the bar girl is laughing, the others are serious, and Kitty is very upset.

                    FRA (THE BAR GIRL)
          He's been making crazy like that for hours, like
          someone slipped the leash or something.

Ingram continues saying gibberish. Annie from time to time shouts out
the real words and each time she does Ingram makes pirouettes of
verbal frenzy around her.

The song finishes in a crescendo of noise and nonsense and laughter.
[Annie, disgusted with Ingram, makes the last line of the song have
particular reference to him.]

                    ANNIE
          (looking with dismay and contempt
          at Ingram)
          All men are evil—and that's *you*!

She leaves the bandstand and goes over to the bar.

Ingram continues to bang frenziedly on the vibraharp.

Annie is at the bar with Kitty, observing it all sadly.

                    ANNIE
          That little boy is in big trouble.

Ingram's melancholy cacophony continues, playing off the big blow-up in him which is tearing him apart.

[DISSOLVE TO:]

EXT. SLATER'S HOUSE - DAY

Burke's sedan drives up to the curb and Slater jumps out.

INT. CAR

Burke slides over to the window and leans out toward Slater. Burke is very serious, Slater sullen.

> BURKE
> Is that your last word?

> SLATER
> I'll keep my mouth shut.

> BURKE
> (with an effort)
> Think it over, Earle.

> SLATER
> Nothing to think over. Just the idea of it makes me nervous. I wouldn't trust my own self on a deal like this with a colored boy.

> BURKE
> Okay.

He slides away to the seat and drives off.

Slater stands there watching the car drive off. The CAMERA MOVES IN ON HIM until we can see the grim disappointment in his eyes.

INT. HOUSING DEVELOPMENT - DAY

A polite but wary smile on the face of this young woman, as she steps back to let her ex-husband in. [This is] the foyer of a three-room apartment in one of New York's Housing Developments. RUTH is in her late twenties, a small woman with a delicate and refined face. Her facial characteristics are of her race, an oval head, a long and graceful neck, full mouthed, her hair tight with no signs of having been treated and straightened. Everything about her points to an almost excessive pride in self, an excess of dignity.

Whatever Ingram feels is hidden by his extreme formal politeness.

> RUTH
>
> Hi. You're late.

> INGRAM
>
> I'm always afraid to wake up on this once a week father's day.

> RUTH
>
> Johnny, what time will you get back?

> INGRAM
>
> Why?

> RUTH
>
> I've got a PTA meeting tonight. Should I get a sitter?

> INGRAM
>
> You got your sitter.

Suddenly there is a burst of footsteps and an exultant child's cry. A little girl comes springing out of the hall and kitchen and flings herself into Ingram's arms. He raises her, embracing her, beginning to laugh as she laughs. Ruth stands by with patience and diplomacy, letting these two have the joy of their meeting.

He lifts the little girl high above their heads.

INGRAM
What do you see up there?

EADIE
(shading her eyes and looking
around)
The park . . .

As he slowly turns with her while she surveys the vast expanses.

EADIE
(continuing)
. . . the lake. . . . I see a merry-go-round . . . I see a
red balloon . . . I see people skating . . .

But she is breaking up with laughter. Johnny smiles while Eadie
rushes off for her coat and hat.

INGRAM
Sounds like Central Park today.

As he turns he is suddenly face to face with a middle aged woman who
stands to the entry to the living room. As if caught in the trap of
circumstance Ruth moves forward into the living room.

RUTH
Oh, Mrs. Anker, this is Eadie's father.

MRS. ANKER
How do you do, Mr. Ingram?

INGRAM
Well.

RUTH
We're having a meeting of the PTA steering
committee here, some of my friends . . .

And Ingram follows after her and stands on the threshold of the long
room. He sees a group of eight, four women and four men, African
American and white. Someone obviously is worrying an agenda, the
ages are varied.

RUTH

This is Eadie's father, Mr. Ingram.

Ingram nods to everyone. They all murmur the usual pleasantries, and
he stands there and they wait there.

INGRAM

Well I . . . I hope you can steer your way out of it.

And he hurriedly backs out into the foyer, as Eadie appears dressed in
a matching coat and hat, her legs twinkling with haste.

INT. FOYER

EADIE

I'm ready, Daddy, let's go. I'll get the elevator.

The child opens the door and takes off down the hallway.

Ingram holds back, staying closer to his ex-wife, observing her with a
grave and hidden interest.

At the door, Ingram pauses beside his ex-wife. Behind them the
murmur of voices from the living room. She looks up at him, so clear
and simple in her truthfulness, that he leans forward and brushes his
lips against her cheek. She [initially] makes no motion to avoid him,
but she closes her eyes. [She slowly moves her face away from his kiss.]

INGRAM

What did I ever see in you?

EADIE'S VOICE
(off yelling)
It's here, it's here.

RUTH
(with a nod down the hall)
That.

And she closes the door.

With a crash of gay music,

SHOCK CUT TO:

INT. CAROUSEL - DAY

[Low angle close up of the head of a carousel wooden horse.]

The CAMERA PLACED IN THE INNER CIRCLE OF THE CAROUSEL wheels with the motion and spins the building, the faces of the parents and onlookers around. The MUSIC is bright, the sun is shining outside the entrances, and the walks are crowded with parents and their children. Eadie is rising and sinking aboard her wooden horse.

Again and again the CAMERA picks up and lets go of the images of the surrounding area, the walls, the faces, the entry, and up and down goes Eadie. She has a balloon tied to one of her fingers and it flutters in the wind of the motion. Johnny edges over and stands with one hand on the horse and the other on his daughter's shoulders. As she [rises and descends they exchange kisses]. It makes her laugh and they play the game.

Ingram watches the crowd as they whirl by. Suddenly his attention fixes and he frowns. He cranes his head back to look but the machine whirls impassively around.

Ingram moves away from his daughter to the edge of the carousel and leans out to see better. The whirling ride returns to the entry.

MOVING SHOT ON CROWD[14]

As CAMERA picks up Moriarity and a heavy set man watching Ingram intently.

CLOSEUP - ON INGRAM

The world whirling behind his head, his eyes hooded and his face tight. Once again he cranes to look.

BACK TO SHOT

The crowd sweeping by and the face of Moriarity and the man beside him. The MUSIC hops along but the carousel begins to slow up.

> INGRAM
> Here's another ticket, Eadie.

> EADIE
> How about you?

> INGRAM
> It makes me dizzy.

> EADIE
> (laughing)
> You're too old.

Moving shot on Ingram that takes him back to the entrance where he heads into the crowd and goes directly up to Moriarity.[15]

> INGRAM
> (low voiced, serious)
> What's the big idea?

> MORIARITY
> Bacco's afraid you might blow town.

> INGRAM
> You tell that [peckerwood] boss of yours that if he looks hard at my wife or baby, I'm blowing him a new one. I don't want to see you guys around here. You gum up the scenery.

> MORIARITY
> We like it here.

> INGRAM
> I'm telling you to fade or I'm turning you right in, now, to those cops.

Moriarity grins.

MORIARITY
That'll be the day.

Behind them the merry-go-round has begun again, the MUSIC is LOUD
and the voices are like a cageful of birds.

Ingram with a reckless anger starts elbowing his way through the
people, directly for the policemen. Moriarity and his partner exchange
first a glance of disbelief and then one of uneasiness. Just as Ingram
reaches the police, the gunmen push their way through the crowd in
the opposite direction.

LONG SHOT

The police and Ingram in the foreground. In the background Bacco's men
hurrying away, going up the little hill to the road.

INGRAM
Officer.

The policeman pulls his head out of the window through which he has
been talking to the men in the car. It is an African American policeman.

OFFICER
Yes, can I help you?

In the far distance, up the hill, the men are almost trotting away,
disappearing.

INGRAM
Can you tell me where I can find the zoo?

OFFICER
(pointing)
Just go through that tunnel and follow the signs.

INT. SNACKHOUSE - SKATING RINK - DAY

A tumult of voices, beyond the circle of skaters. In the foreground Eadie
is eating [a snack.] Ingram looks around for any sign of being followed

but there is none. A lady and a boy of eight [are eating at the same table.]

Ingram looks at his wristwatch.

> INGRAM
>
> You stay right here, Eadie. Daddy's got to make a phone call.

> EADIE
>
> I'm staying. I'm eating.

Ingram hesitates.

> INGRAM
>
> Don't you budge.

> LADY
>
> I'll see that she stays here, if you like.

> INGRAM
>
> Thank you, ma'am.

He leaves.

> LADY
>
> (smiling)
> And what's your name, little girl?

> EADIE
>
> Eadie. Eadie Ingram.

INT. TELEPHONE BOOTH

As Ingram dials a number.

> INGRAM
>
> Mr. Burke, please.

A sudden relief on Ingram's face. He waits.

                    INGRAM
Dave, Johnny. Yeah, yeah, I know you've been out.
Listen, Dave, I'll take out that deal . . . wait, wait,
wait . . . I need 7500 bucks right away to pay off
Bacco. Yeah . . . Yeah.
            (he waits)
All right. I'll call you back in fifteen minutes.
Yeah. Bye.

As if he had been holding himself up by sheer will alone, he [looks at
the receiver and hangs it up].

INT. BURKE'S APARTMENT

Close shot on Burke, dialing the telephone, an eagerness in his gesture.

                    BURKE
Hello, Bacco, Burke.
            (a pause)
Fine, fine. That's what I'm calling about. Call
those babies off.

INT. BACCO'S APARTMENT

Close shot of Bacco, head and shoulders in bed, as if naked.

                    BACCO
I told you, Davey, I got a problem. It got a little
rough. Now he has to make a deal. It was a public
thing. He's got to make a deal.

INT. BURKE'S APARTMENT

Burke is upset.

                    BURKE
That's what I'm telling you, he's got a deal. I'm
making it for him.
                                    (MORE)

                    BURKE (CON'T)
    I'll give you the dough in two weeks.
              (pause)
    He pulled a gun?
              (frowning at the unexpected
              complication)
    Look. It can still be straightened out . . .

His eyes go to the ceiling in frustration as the torrent continues.

INT. SLATER'S HOUSE - DAY

Close up on a piece of paper on which Lorry has written a note. At the
edge of the paper a thumb and finger can be seen.

              Earle darling,
              If you have time, run down to the cleaner and get
              my blue taffeta dress. I have to rush out tonight.
                            Love, Lorry.
              P.S. I hope everything was fine. I told Helen you'd
              baby-sit 'til I got back.

                    SLATER'S VOICE
    Baby sit.

Slater crumples the message. He has a tumbler half-full of whiskey in
his hands. [He takes a sip of the drink.]

Slater goes into the bedroom. He puts his drink down and enters the
bathroom. The sound of a shower running.

He returns, [and takes off his shirt]. There is a KNOCKING on the
door. He doesn't hear it at first because of the running water and then
when it repeats even more loudly, he takes his drink, bare-chested, and
goes to the door and opens it.

At the door, a woman, in her thirties, quite pretty with a neat and
tight little body, is standing there. She wears a sweater, slacks and
slippers. Her name is Helen Svenson. Earle just stands there looking
sullenly at her.

HELEN
What's going on in there, an orgy?

SLATER
What's on your mind, Helen?

HELEN
Can't I flirt with you a little?

SLATER
Some other day.

HELEN
Are you staying home tonight?

SLATER
Why?

HELEN
I can't get a baby sitter.

SLATER
Then stay home and take care of him yourself.

She looks a little hurt but tries to run it off lightly.

HELEN
Well, if you're busy. You see, Sam's boss gave him two tickets to this musical, and I'm to meet him in front of the theatre.

SLATER
Take the baby with you.

HELEN
(angrily)
What's the matter with you, am I bothering you or something? It's just because Lorry said that you would.

He closes the door in her face.

EXT. RIDING RING - DAY

Eadie is just mounting a pony cart while her father holds her red
balloon.

                    INGRAM
              (to attendant)
          Just keep taking her around for me, will you. I have
          to make a phone call.

He hands the man a fistful of tickets. Still holding the balloon Ingram
walks off.

EXT. TELEPHONE BOOTH - ARCADE/ZOO

The two booths are filled when Ingram comes up, trailing his
highflying balloon. He lights a cigarette and waits while in the
distance, [the roar of wild animals is heard].

A booth empties and Ingram enters.

The gas-filled balloon is large and clumsy so he simply holds the string
and closes the folding doors with the red balloon riding and tugging just
outside the door.

INT. OF BOOTH

Close shot across Ingram at instrument, to the closed door and the wind
agitating the red balloon, the people passing outside, the murmur off of
steps and voices and from time to time the sudden ancient roar of the
lion.

Ingram dials his number.

                    INGRAM
          Mr. Burke, please.
              (waits)
          Yeah. I'm listening, Dave.

His face shows his immediate relief.

                    INGRAM
                  (continuing)
Oh, stop crowing, man. There's nothing to
celebrate. That little [crumb] threatened my kid
and my ex-wife. Yeah, yeah, I know I got rid of a
headache. Now I got cancer.

Ingram grins without pleasure.

                    INGRAM
                  (continuing)
Yeah, I'll see you tonight . . . Wake up, Dave, we're
committing suicide . . . this is three o'clock in the
morning.

EXT. TELEPHONE BOOTH

As two boys and a girl, exaggeratedly dressed in jackets and pants,
with a rock and roll look, pass by. They are smoking and the girl, who
has the wild look of someone who never takes a step without making a
dare, touches the end of her cigarette to the balloon. It bursts with a
loud noise.

INT. TELEPHONE BOOTH

Ingram turns to look, surprised by the noise. His balloon is gone and no
one is there. He opens the door and the sounds rush in including the lion
roar. He stands there, listening, thinking, the tumult and the roaring of
animals and people drowning him.

EXT. THIRD AVENUE - DAY

Earle is walking, bearing in front of him on its hanger Lorry's blue dress
in a plastic bag. The wind catches at it and the dress flutters like a
banner. The camera pans Earle down the avenue past the butcher, the
baker, the candlestick maker, all the neighborhood stores, until he
reaches the corner where a brown, decaying bar-and-grill stands. On
the avenue the trucks are grinding along, the taxis, the shining new cars

in red and white. There is something very somber, a sense of isolation, in the way Earle walks.

He pauses at the corner, starts to make the turn and hesitates. He wheels and enters the bar.

INT. BAR - DAY

An island for the lonely, a few tables, a long polished counter, dark with age. The television screen is dark but a radio is humming old tunes.

Earle hesitates in the doorway for there are more people there than he expects. A soldier tanned, young, big, stands in the center of a circle of civilian friends demonstrating some judo holds and breaks.

                    SOLDIER
          (loudly)
     Just throw anything.

He stands with assumed casualness while one of his friends crouches in front of him and playfully throws a light slow punch. The soldier grabs his friend's wrist, makes the appropriate motions, and in a moment his friend is on his knees, crouching, his arm twisted behind his back. Then the soldier makes a chop at the man's neck, not hitting him, of course.

                    SOLDIER
     You're out.

                    GIRL
     That's pretty neat.

Naturally they are amused. The idlers form a group at the bar to drink.

                    SOLDIER
     It's all this new atom war stuff. It's the first thing
     they teach you now.

GIRL

I sure could use that technique from time to time.

Observing this. Earle has a look of irritated distaste on his face, but he enters anyway,

He moves a dozen feet away from the group at the bar. The bartender joins Earle who carefully puts the dress down on a chair, removes his light coat and hat and makes himself at home.

BARTENDER

The same, Earle?

SLATER

Hit me with a couple, Mac.

He pulls out his pack of cigarettes and lights up. But there is no peace here. The soldier is eager to demonstrate his skill again to the girl.

SOLDIER

You know, I'd like to teach you sometime.

GIRL

You mean a girl could do that?

SOLDIER

Well, sure. It doesn't matter how big the guy is. ·
Here, let me show you.

Earle is in the foreground watching the whole affair through the mirror while the bartender pours him a double rye and leaves the bottle there. He draws a beer for Earle's chaser.

SLATER

What's this, the kiddy hour?

BARTENDER
(grinning)
It's make-believe wartime, Earle, the hour of sweet romance.

The soldier has chosen one of his friends to be the masher. Now, laughing at his own role, he pretends to mince along.

> SOLDIER
> Okay, Georgie, rape me.

In a tumult of good humor, George comes up behind the soldier and grabs at him. The soldier with excellent skill grabs his friend's wrists, slips beneath them, twists, uses the leverage of his body and spins the man away, down the length of the bar [and bumps into Earle]. Earle's drink spills and splashes over the plastic garment bag.

Earle jumps up, pulls a handkerchief from his pocket and wipes the liquor off the bag.

> GEORGE
> (apologetically)
> I'm sorry, buddy, I hope I didn't get it on you. Here,
> he drink's on me.

> SLATER
> (icily furious)
> I buy my own drinks.

He [continues cleaning up].

> BARTENDER
> (to George)
> Look, kiddo, let's just take it easy.

[The girl walks over to the soldier.]

> GIRL
> Show me.

The soldier comes up behind the girl and begins to show her how to do it.

> SOLDIER
> Sure. What do you do when a guy grabs you this
> way?

GIRL

I give in.

SOLDIER

Relax, baby. Don't fight me.

GIRL

I thought that was what I was supposed to do.

SOLDIER

Not yet.

GIRL

Not yet! In a minute it will be too late.

SOLDIER

Come on, grab my wrist. Now, don't try to break the
hold. Put your right foot over in front of mine. Now
throw your hip out, then forward, and throw me.

The soldier is all prepared to let himself go, to exaggerate the effect.
The girl takes the right hold. Earle slowly faces them.

SLATER

(in a loud cold voice)
Honey, if you're goin' to throw that bum, throw
him the other way.

The little group is arrested in its play.

BARTENDER

(quickly)
All right, why don't we all just drink up and quit
fooling around.

The soldier is slowly walking up to Earle.

SOLDIER

You say something to me, bud?

Earle is immensely still, frustrated, ugly in feeling. But he knows he
mustn't do anything: he knows it from his past, from everything that
has ever happened to him.

SLATER
(softly)
That stuff belongs to my war. Take her to
Canaveral and launch her.

He drains his drink [and begins to make preparations to leave].

SOLDIER
Well, maybe you know something better.

The group is forming around them, curious, alert, excited by the conflict.
The soldier is big, young, in good shape, confident. The girls are
offended by Earle. Only the bartender is worried.

BARTENDER
Now look, fellows, let's all just settle down, shall
we?

SLATER
(putting on his hat)
I'm going.

SOLDIER
Maybe you'd like to try.

SLATER
Sonny, you better go back and play with the girls.
Tell them all about sputnik.

SOLDIER
I thought you were an expert or something. Come
on, throw a punch. I'll show you if it's bull.

BARTENDER
All right, soldier, let's break it up.

SOLDIER
(sarcastically)
It's not a fight. I just want to show this old veteran
how this thing works.

Earle's [head turns sharply to the soldier]. His face is dark, angry, baffled.

                    SOLDIER
               (continuing)
     Now come on. Don't you want to throw something?

                    SLATER
               (ready to explode)
     Get lost.

He wants to get out and away from all of this. But the soldier [refuses to let it go].

                    SOLDIER
               (taunting him)
     It's just a scientific experiment. We're just a couple of scientists. Now come on. Throw a punch. Try it.

The bartender comes out from behind the bar, and steps up to the soldier.

                    BARTENDER
     All right, Earle, let me take care of this. Now look, soldier . . .

The soldier pushes the bartender away.

                    SOLDIER
               (to Earle)
     Go on, try it.

                    SLATER
               (almost in a whisper)
     Any particular hand?

                    SOLDIER
               (now tense and alert)
     Any one you like, Pop.

Earle feints with his left and the soldier grabs but Earle arrests the blow, wheels and drives in with his right, a crushing blow into the soldier's body. The soldier crumples, twisting with agony, losing his breath, begins to keel over and suddenly flops to his knees, writhing, going over, down.

Everyone gets the message at the same time. There is a flurry around the boy but no attempt to get at Earle who stands there alert like some crazy animal let out of his cage and ready for anything.

> BARTENDER
> The kid was only showing off, Earle.

> SLATER
> (sullenly)
> I didn't mean to hurt him.

The boy is gasping on the floor and Earle is alone, the look on his face bewildered, lost. He picks up his dress and starts to leave.

> GIRL
> You slob, what'd you do?

Earle blindly goes out of the saloon, the dress fluttering from its hanger like a war flag.

INT. HALLWAY - SLATER'S APARTMENT

The hall light is burning, the old heavy door sits squarely there in the shadows and the history of the house.

Slater appears and goes to the door. The size, the heavy chiaroscuro, the light burning there, contribute to his mood, that he is alone, pushed inside, a man running within himself.

He opens the door with his key and warm electric light floods out upon him and with it Lorry's voice.

> [LORRY'S VOICE
> (on the phone)
> Are you sure he's not there? Well, did you look in
> the back booth?

Slater closes the door.

LORRY'S VOICE
(hearing him come in, hanging up
the phone)]
There you are. Sweetie, I've been calling all over,
where were you?

Slater has hidden his life behind the mask of his face, and there it is,
bony, grim, blank, and somehow a little frightening this way.
MOVING SHOT that carries him across the living room to bedroom
where Lorry appears. Her pale face is upset, hurried, distracted. He
hands her the dress.

LORRY
(continuing)
Sweetie, I knew your deal went wrong. I knew it
went wrong the minute that Helen phoned and she
said you'd insulted her. I apologized for you and I
said that I was sure you could baby sit for her later.

He passes her, pulling off his hat, which he places on the top of the
dresser, and his coat, flinging it on the bed. Earle just drops into the
bed, and lies down.

LORRY remains fixed for a long moment and then removes her skirt.
[She goes into the bathroom, fussing with her hair, spraying perfume,
engaged in the preparations for going out.]

LORRY
(continuing)
Honey, I want to hear everything that happened
when I get back, but right now I'm so late I got to
rush right back downtown.

Earle [continues to sit on the bed staring intently ahead].[16]

LORRY
(continuing)
Hey, guess what? My boss is going to buy a new
place and I'm going to manage it. How about that!
We're having dinner with the owner, and he wants
me there to . . .

He [remains] unresponsive. Suddenly she turns and comes toward him, [still in the process of getting ready].

> LORRY
> (continuing)
> Well, maybe I better call and say I can't make it.
> Maybe I better stay home tonight, huh?

> SLATER
> You don't have to hold my hand.

His voice is utterly bruised and antagonistic. It stops her and she turns back to the dresser.

> LORRY
> All right. Your dinner is on the stove. And there
> are some good programs on tonight. Sweetie? Hey.
> You'll be here when I get home, won't you?

> SLATER
> Where else would I go?

Earle is outstretched on the bed. Lorry is upset.

> LORRY
> Come on. I wish you wouldn't make a such a big
> thing out of this. Listen, with that deal it's just as
> well. I told you, honey, I don't care how long it
> takes for you to find the right thing to do. Sweetie,
> we're doing fine. And, you know, if my boss does
> take on this new shop, I'll be making much more
> money.

Now she is all dressed and returns to the bed. She stands over him looking quite elegant and attractive.[17]

> LORRY
> (continuing; in a coaxing voice)
> You might at least say that I look . . . good.

> SLATER
> If you're going why the hell don't you go?

She flashes with anger and [she needs to go], but this man holds her there by his mere hurt. [She sits down on the edge of the bed.]

                    LORRY
Earle . . . You know, I knew you were in trouble when
I fell in love with you. I knew it. I knew it would
be rough for us, honey, and would take time. But I
didn't care.

[Close up of Lorry.]

                    LORRY
          (continuing)
You don't have to be the great big man with me,
Earle. I don't care about things like that.
There's only one thing I care about.

                    SLATER
          (coarsely)
I know, but what happens when I get old?

It is a physical blow to her and she [stands up].

                    LORRY
          (bitterly)
You are old now.

She runs to the door. Earle sits up abruptly, frightened again by his own violence.

                    SLATER
     Lorry.

                    LORRY
          (opening the door)
You can go straight to hell.

And she runs out, the door slammed behind her. He turns a blind face this way and that, caged, frustrated, and then relief comes as always in anger, in fury, in striking out.

He grabs the telephone as if to choke it, holding the whole instrument in his raging hands, dialing.

SLATER
Hello—Dave Burke. Yeah, Burke.

INT. RUTH'S APARTMENT - NIGHT

A dark bedroom. Eadie is asleep in the bed, and Ingram is stretched out beside her sleeping, utterly fagged after this long day and even longer one before. His shoes are off, his shirt collar open.

Ruth enters and sees them. It's [an ambivalent] moment for her, seeing her ex-husband and child so much together with her in the apartment, part of it.

Tiptoeing over, she leans over Ingram, studying his face for a long and difficult moment, and then as if tempted to kiss him, bends closer, refrains, and wakens him gently.

Opening his eyes, he stares and then his head moves up.

Ingram catches her in his arms and kisses her. There is nothing sensual about this. It is simply full of longing. Once again there is that hesitation in her. She moves her face away, and he lets her go at once, as if shocked by himself. She hurries out of the room. Ingram gets up and follows.

INT. LIVING ROOM

Ruth still in her coat, waiting, trying to be impersonal as Ingram walks in.
RUTH
(a low, troubled voice)
You mustn't do that.

INGRAM
Sorry, I was dreaming.

[He puts on his shoes and jacket].

INGRAM
A man always dreams of what he wants or what
he's afraid of.

In the foyer he puts on his coat and holds his hat.

Ruth stands against the white wall, ill at ease, as if she were a
stranger in her own house.

They are both waiting, Ruth for what is happening in the room, Ingram
for what is happening in his mind, the terrible sense of the momentous
meaning of this day and night for him and the dangerous future.

Ingram makes an ineffectual motion to leave, the silence mounting
around them.

Then, as on a sudden intuition, he takes set of car keys which he puts on
the small table in the foyer.

INGRAM
Look, I'm going away for a couple of days. Maybe
you want to take Eadie for a drive or something.

The words are like stones in his mouth, hard to get out.

RUTH
Thanks, maybe I will.

It is a victory for him, her simple acceptance. It is also like writing a
will. She is waiting for his embrace, and when it comes she starts to
return it. Then:

RUTH
(twisting away)
No. No.

It's a hard thing to pull his eyes from her and force himself to go away.

INGRAM
(in a low, stifled voice)
How did this all happen to us?

Her answer comes out calm and reasoned.

> RUTH
> You know, Johnny, I didn't mind what you did to me
> . . . I mean I minded, but I would've gone on.

Ingram returns to her, hope in his face.

> INGRAM
> You 're saying I can come back?

> RUTH
> (swaying her head)
> The door's never been locked against you, Johnny.
> Not for my sake. But I couldn't do it to Eadie. A
> child can't have a father who lives your life.

> INGRAM
> (sardonically)
> Except on visiting days.

> RUTH
> (inexorably)
> Not even on visiting days, but that's the law.

> INGRAM
> You're tough.

> RUTH
> Not tough enough to change you.

> INGRAM
> (with searing bitterness)
> For what? To hold hands with those ofay friends of
> yours?

> RUTH
> (flaring)
> I'm trying to make a world fit for Eadie to live in.
> It's a cinch you're not going to do it with a deck of
> cards and a racing form.

INGRAM

But you are, huh? You and your big white brothers.
Drink enough tea with 'em and stay out of the
watermelon patch and maybe our little colored girl
will grow up to be Miss America, is that it?

RUTH
(coldly furious)
I won't listen when you talk like that. You'd better
go.

INGRAM
(grabbing her arm)
Why don't you wise up, Ruth. It's their world and
we're just living in it.

RUTH

Let go of me.

INGRAM
(gripping her)
Don't you ever let me catch you teaching Eadie to
suck up to those . . .

EADIE'S VOICE
(shocked, dismayed)
Daddy. . .

They freeze as they are. Ingram in the act of holding Ruth against her
will and she about to push him off—both appalled, ashamed.

EADIE
You woke me up.

Ingram is with her in two steps. He has her in his arms, embracing her,
kissing her, soothing her.

INGRAM

Oh, baby, I'm sorry. Sweetheart. Listen. I was just
telling your mommy how much I love you. And you
must never forget it.

EADIE
(looking to Ruth)
We had such a nice time today.

Ingram clinging to his daughter, walking with her to Ruth.

INGRAM
(softly, desperately)
I'm telling you how much I love your mama. You'll
always mind her and be good. We're counting on
you a lot in this family.

He [kisses his daughter on the cheek], hands her over and quickly
leaves the apartment. The door slams behind him; the mother [quickly
embraces the child] who is watching the blank door.

INT. SLATER APARTMENT - NIGHT

There is a knock on the apartment door. Slater swings it wide open.
Helen Svenson is there. She wears a wraparound housecoat, drawn
much too tightly about her body. When she sees Earle she speaks
coldly.

HELEN
I want to see Lorry.

SLATER
(grinning)
Lorry's out.

[She turns to go, but Slater grabs her by the arm.] His southern voice
gets thicker, softer, more caressing, charming her.

SLATER (CON'T)
Oh, come on now, don't be mad. I'm sorry about this
afternoon, I really am. Just me and my miseries you
walked in on.

The woman responds at once. He holds out his hand. She takes it, but
instead of shaking it, he kisses it.

HELEN
(smiling)
Oh you.

SLATER
(smiling)
I'm ready to kiss, make up, and say I'm sorry.

HELEN
Do you know what that louse of a husband of mine did? When I told him that I couldn't got a sitter he just decided to go there with one of the boys. How do you like it?

Earle takes her gently by the arm and pulls her in.

SLATER
I don't mind.

HELEN
The kid's sleeping upstairs.

SLATER
C'mon in and have a drink. I have to go by eleven. I should have told you that anyway. Was I really mean?

He leaves the door open and heads for the kitchen. Helen oscillates in intention there.

HELEN
Don't you remember what you said ?

Earle has disappeared into the kitchen and his voice comes back from inside.

SLATER (VO)
I'm scared to. What was it?

She fixes her hair, looks at herself, pulling her wraparound more tightly about her compact body.

HELEN

I forget.

He returns, easy and laughing, holding two drinks. Very gallantly he hands her one and offers a toast.

SLATER

To a much more affectionate future.

[She is charmed by anything he says now. They both drink.]

SLATER
(continuing)

Come on in and have a visit.

HELEN

I've got to keep an ear open for the baby.

SLATER

You can hear the baby plenty down here. Come on.

[Earle sits down in a chair.] She strolls into the room.

Helen is one of those women who naturally use their bodies too freely when they walk, and now feeling coquettish, happy to have made up, angry with her husband and charmed by Earle, she adds to her emotions.

HELEN

Would you do a thing like that?

SLATER

Like what?

HELEN

Like he did. Leave me alone this way.

SLATER

Not for a minute.

Her easy smile comes again. Everything he says tickles her. She strolls around sipping her drink.

HELEN
(continuing)
Can you really hear my kid down here?

SLATER
Honey, I've spent more sleepless nights with you
than you know.

Earle watches her as she ambles around the room. She is letting
herself be seen, with no particular intention in mind, but she is conscious
of his maleness and her femaleness at the moment. Now she makes her
turn. Her face becomes curious, almost greedy with curiosity.

HELEN
I'd like to ask you something, but you must promise
not to be angry.

SLATER
I promise.

[She takes a couple of steps towards him.]

HELEN
No, I mean seriously.

[Slater gets up from the chair.]

SLATER
All right. I promise.

She pauses, seems to take a deep breath and asks then in a small and
rather tentative voice.

HELEN
How did it feel when you killed that man?

Earle is surprised and upset. His mouth sets in that stubborn sullen look
of his. He turns away [and sits down on the arm of the chair].

HELEN
(continuing; regretting her words
already)
I'm sorry. I'm stupid.

He looks back to her, his face serious, but not hiding, and there is a
narrowness in his eyes, a kind of calculation at last in the way he is
looking at her.

SLATER
You want me to make your flesh creep?

HELEN
(upset herself now)
No, no, forget it.

SLATER
I enjoyed it. It scared me but I enjoyed it. I hated
that man so I could've killed him all over again
even though I didn't mean to.

HELEN
What did he do to you?

SLATER
He called me. He insulted me. He was a very
smart talking character and then he called me.

HELEN
What do you mean?

She is lost in his personality now, thrilled, clinging to his words, and
his eyes are bright, golden and fascinated by her.

SLATER
He dared me.

There is a silence now and a measuring glance from him to her until she
lowers her eyelids and doesn't look at him. [Extreme close ups of their
eyes.]

SLATER
(continuing)
Like you are . . . now.

She turns away. As she turns away his fingers catch at the tied bow
which holds her wraparound, and as she walks, the housecoat opens
away from her because he holds on. Now his hand is in the SHOT
AND WE CAN SEE ALL OF HER. She wears a half slip, and a
brassiere, stockings, but there is a shameful sense of nakedness there for
her. She pulls the housecoat around herself, staring at him.

He goes to the open door. Leaning against it he slowly closes it. He
waits briefly then approaches Helen, her hand still holding the
housecoat closed. Earle comes up close to her.

He doesn't kiss her at once, but she is waiting. She is alarmed, she
hasn't yet made up her mind, but she is waiting, and he waits too. Her
raised hands appear in CAMERA and OUT, and she offers her face,
closing her eyes, murmuring.

HELEN
Just this once.

He kisses her.

INT. BURKE'S APARTMENT - NIGHT

He is in his shirtsleeves, vibrant, excited, his balding head sweating
with excitement and his voice pitched low, not to carry, yet dramatic,
acting it all out.

BURKE
He comes out of the drugstore . . .

And Burke moves away from the wall, from the photographs of his
life, carrying in his hands [a magazine meant to simulate the] boxes of
sandwiches and coffee.

BURKE
(continuing)
And he crosses over with the light. Then he goes
down the sidestreet to the side door of the bank.

The CAMERA PANS to now include Ingram who sits back on the hind
legs of a chair, teetering slowly, and watching the performance.

BURKE
(continuing)
It's a regular sized door, like this, no different,
except that in the top half there is a small glass
panel for observation. The guard opens the door.
This is the heart of it, Johnny . . . That door is on a
chain.

Ingram listens without expression.

BURKE
It holds the door open about so much.

[He opens the door about eight inches.]

BURKE
And the waiter hands the guard the sandwiches . . .

He [attempts to demonstrate passing] the imaginary boxes through the
opening.

The door is suddenly pushed open, and Slater appears. He stands
there, gazing past Burke to Ingram.

SLATER
Hello, Burke.

BURKE
Come in. Come in.

Slater sees Ingram teetering on his chair, natty, somehow very clear
and handsome, as if newly minted, in contrast with the roughness of
Slater and the general sloppiness of Burke. The chair stops, balanced
on its hind legs.

BURKE
Earle, I want you to meet Johnny Ingram. This is
Earle Slater.

The chair comes down and Ingram is just about to rise, as Slater nods
carelessly to Ingram and doesn't approach, but turns to Burke.

SLATER
Sorry I'm a little late, but I had girly trouble.

He slouches over to chair, away from Ingram, shedding his coat as he
goes which he flings to the couch, and sits down facing Burke.

SLATER
Where were you, Dave?

Slater is playing his role very big, being tough, easy, professional.

Burke's eyes narrowing as he looks at Slater and then a slow turn to
Ingram, who slowly leans back and begins to teeter again, almost
rocking on his chair. In the b.g, is Burke and to one side Slater.

BURKE
(after a hesitation)
I was telling him about the chain. Then the guard
locks the door again without ever unhooking the
chain and the waiter leaves.

Slater speaks somehow without addressing Ingram.

SLATER
That's right. The chippie is the chain.

BURKE
We got to figure out an answer on the chain.

SLATER
Maybe you can have him put a gun on the guard and
just barrel through the door.

The stillness in Ingram is not peace. It is negative, negative to the
project and negative to Slater.

                    BURKE
        What do you think, Johnny?

                    INGRAM
        I don't know.

He rises from the chair and goes to the window. He stands there and
gazes out on the night and the river and the wind.

A kind of contemptuous arrogance invades Slater's face. Ingram is what
he expected.

                    SLATER
        Tell about the car.

                    BURKE
        I got a beauty. Hopped-up motor with double
        carburetion in a beat-up station wagon body. I
        bought two stolen plates and the car can't be traced.
        It's a remade job that was used in smuggling.

Ingram moves to pour himself a drink from the bottles on the end table.
Slater and Burke watch him for a reaction, and there is none. Each
moment makes Burke more nervous, Slater more superior.

                    SLATER
        We have four police specials that have no history
        and a couple of shotguns.

                    INGRAM
        I thought this was an easy job. It sounds like
        D-Day.
                    SLATER
                (oozing superiority)
        Now don't you give those guns a thought. I'll take
        care of them.

                    INGRAM
                (hesitantly)
        I'm not thinking about the guns. I'm thinking about
        the chain.

Slater questions Burke with a glance of doubt, and his drawl gets heavier, his voice patronizing.

> SLATER
> Don't worry about it, boy, we'll be right there with you. All you got to do is carry the sandwiches. In a white monkey jacket. And give a big smile. And say yessir. You don't have to worry and you don't have to think. We'll take care of you.

Ingram's face is suffused with rage.

> INGRAM
> Then you'll have to start right now.

> BURKE
> (fiercely)
> Don't beat out that Civil War jazz here, Slater.

SLATER is surprised, taken aback by this attack.

> BURKE (CON'T)
> We're all in this together, each man equal and we're taking care of each other. It's one big play, a one and only chance to grab stakes forever, and I don't want to hear what your grandpappy thought on the old farm in Oklahoma. You got it?

Ingram has moved into the clear background, his face closed down, set, tight, waiting, Slater, is a little overwhelmed by this, by Burke's authority and his own need. He manages an uneasy smile.

> SLATER
> Well, I'm with you, Dave. Like you say, it's just one roll of the dice. Doesn't matter what color they are, so's they come up seven.

Burke darts a look at Ingram, who hesitates, then takes a deep breath.

Ingram's voice is calm and passionless.

INGRAM
It's all right, Dave. I got an idea about the chain.[18]

Ingram demonstrates with his hands as he explains. His voice is deliberate, without inflection. He is so obviously using his intelligence in this project and completely withdrawing his will.

INGRAM (CON'T)
Let's say the chain on the door is eight inches.
Make it ten for good measure. Now, if the box with
the sandwiches and coffee is big enough, the guard
just naturally has to unlatch that door.

He measures the distance between his hands to a foot.

INGRAM (CON'T)
Now, he can't expect me to turn it sideways because
of the coffee, right? So the box we use just got to be
big enough.

BURKE
(with immense admiration)
And he just naturally has to open that chain. You
got it, Johnny, you got it. It'll work. I know it'll
work.

He throws his arms around Ingram and gives him a bear hug. Ingram is watching Slater, who suddenly seems to be alone in the room, isolated again. Camera moves past the others to Slater, who slowly turns away from them.

INT. SLATER'S APARTMENT HOUSE - NIGHT

Slater rounding the banisters in hall.[19]

The hesitation and uneasiness so often present on his face when he is alone are particularly obvious now. The darkness, the emptiness emphasize his aloneness.

Approaching his own apartment door, his shadow looms and falls out.

INT. HOUSE

Slater opens the door into a dark apartment. He stands for a moment listening and then [walks forward].

At the threshold of the bedroom he pauses again. [His hand moves to the light switch.]

> LORRY
> Don't put on the light. I've been crying.

At first Slater is relieved, and then immense guilt floods in as fear goes and anguish replaces it.

Lorry is sitting up against the headboard of the bed, smoking, but now she puts the cigarette down and suddenly bursts into tears again, abandoning herself to the relief that he has returned. Slater sits on the bed, taking her into his arms. They cling to each other. Her face is swollen with many hours of weeping, regret and self-punishment.

> LORRY
> Earle, I'm like all the rest of them. I keep telling you how to live and not letting you be what you are.

> SLATER
> Never mind about me.

He kisses her, and then slowly, relaxing, she lies back against the headboard while he sits there in his coat and hat, feeling the comfort and security of this apartment, this woman, enfolding him, protecting him. He looks around in the darkness with a kind of wonder.

> SLATER (CON'T)
> I spoil everything. I can't help it. I just have to spoil it.

> LORRY
> Not for me, darling. Not for me.

She [caresses his hair].

LORRY (CON'T)
You know, I just kept waiting here and I thought
that if you would just come home, nothing would
ever spoil it for us. I thought of how I won't let
myself see the way you feel about the money, how
it has to be your own, or we just can't last, and you're
right. That's the way it is. Only don't leave me,
Earle. Please, darling, don't leave me.

Suddenly she embraces him, holding him tightly to herself.

SLATER
Lorry. Lorry. I'm never going to leave you. I been
leaving all my life. It's when I can first remember,
when the wind blew us off the land in Oklahoma.
We left. After that I never stayed, not in the army,
not in Detroit, not any place.

He gets up with a certain nervous tension, his inner life opening to him,
seeing it all.

He walks around the room, still in his hat and coat.

SLATER
I'd start something and it didn't work, right away
I'd blow it. And there was always something, a
lousy captain, a Polack foreman in the auto works.
Or it'd be too slow. Well, I'm getting too old to take
things slow. If I don't make it now, I never will.
And I mean with you, too. It's now or never.

Lorry watching him, her eyes still wet, her face naked.

LORRY
Aren't things ever easy for you, Earle?

Earle turns to her.

EARLE[20]
Only when I get mad. Then they get too easy. I
think that's why I get mad. To make it easy.

He returns to her, standing over her.

                    EARLE (CON'T)
          But I got something now, and I'm going to stick with
          it.

                                   [SHOCK CUT TO:]

EXT. HIGHWAY

Sign on front of Greyhound bus that reads: MELTON.[21]

[Bus on the highway.]

INT. BUS - DAY

Having sorted out the random faces of men, women and children, the
camera holds on Ingram, sitting alone on the right side, gazing out the
window with half-closed eyes. Hypnotized by the speeding
landscapes, there is bleakness in his eyes, nothing, the end of the road.

EXT. FARMLANDS - DAY

Hilly with stubbled fields, patches of wood, and mountains in the
distance.

An old station wagon carefully threads its way along a dirt road up to
CAMERA.

INT. STATION WAGON

Slater wears hunting clothes. He brings the car to a stop.

The dirt road opens into a paved highway. A sign there reads:
MELTON—23 MILES, THRUWAY—41 MILES.

The station wagon makes the turn and heads down the highway.

INT. STATION WAGON

First checking carefully in both directions, Slater guns the car, giving it a final test.

EXT. HIGHWAY

Car winding up and hurtling at CAMERA with a roar. The speedometer reads 112 mph.

INT. STATION WAGON

Slater's face is almost exultant, enjoying the sense of power he gets from the speed, the roar of the supercharged motor and the rush of wind against the car. Then he sets his face again, taps at the brake harder and harder until he brings the car down to a conservative speed and settles back for a nice safe ride.

EXT. AN OLD PAVED ROAD - DAY

A sedan makes its way slowly along the rutted, pot-holed road into CAMERA.

On both sides of the road are stone walls, rocky fields and tight copses of woods. Here and there along the shoulder are parked cars. We hear two BLASTS of a shotgun and the BARKING of a dog. The sedan parks some distance from the other cars.

Burke, in hunting clothes, carrying a Remington automatic shotgun and a knapsack gets out of the car. He locks it and starts off, just another hunter out for a day of sport. Two hunters and their dog go by in b.g.

[EXT. HIGHWAY - DAY

Greyhound bus moving forcefully toward CAMERA.

INT. BUS

Ingram, with some apprehension, looks at his watch.]

INT. STATION WAGON

Ted, a gas station attendant, in greasy overalls, a company cap jauntily on his head, is smiling in [directly at the CAMERA, in extreme close up. The word "Okay" from Ted's line has played over the last portion of the previous shot of Ingram.]

                    TED
        Okay. What'll it be, mister?

[Ted is looking through the driver-side window at Slater behind the wheel.]

                    SLATER
        Just gas. Fill her up.

He gets out and cautiously moves away, the CAMERA PANNING WITH HIM to the front of the station wagon.

He stops and studies the map in privacy as we hear the pump motor and bell. [There is the SOUND of the hood of the engine being opened.] He turns back to the car.

Ted is gazing at the power plant with admiration.

There is a spasm of alarm and anger on Slater's face as he rushes to the car.

                    TED
               (awed; whistles)
        Can you do 150 on a straightaway?

                    SLATER
               (savagely slamming down the
               hood)
        I said just gas.

                    TED
               (making a hands off gesture)
        Sorry, Mister.

Ted backs away and returns to nozzle.

TED
She's strictly sixty-five on the outside.

SLATER
(now covering up)
I'm a nut on motors.

He pulls up his collar and turns away, trying to keep out of direct view.

EXT. HIGHWAY- DAY

Burke is sitting on a small post, glancing at his watch. He knocks out his pipe, looks past CAMERA, jumps from his seat and takes several quick steps to the side of the road.

The station wagon draws up, Burke pulls open the door, slides in beside Slater, and closes the door as the station wagon is on its way again.

INT. STATION WAGON

Burke turns from setting the shotgun on the back seat.

SLATER
All set?

BURKE
(exuding confidence)
Gasses up, parked, and ready for the switch.

SLATER
(muttering)
If we get to it.

Burke glances curiously at Slater whose tension has been steadily mounting . . . not fear, but a kind of wild urge toward action which we glimpsed when he let out the station wagon.

BURKE
(continuing cautiously)
How you doing, Earle?

                    SLATER
          (playing it with some bravado)
     Just waiting for the whistle.

                    BURKE
          (glancing at his watch)
     Remember, I'm the one who blows it.

                                        [SHOCK CUT TO:]

EXT. HIGHWAY - DAY

The bus slams [down the highway with a loud blowing HORN. A half-second of the horn SOUND played over the tail of the previous shot.]

INT. BUS

Ingram, his face blank, stares out the window. The BEEPING of the bus's horn continues as it pulls out to pass a car.

Right under Ingram's window, the station wagon slowly appears. The face of Slater looks up and floats behind as in a drunken dream. [A solemn look is on Ingram's face.] He glances around. He looks at his watch.

INT. STATION WAGON

It is pulling back into the right hand lane and moving away. [There is a MATCH CUT to Burke making the same gesture with his watch as Ingram.]

                    BURKE
          (looking at his watch)
     Right on the nose.
          (as Slater increases speed)
     Take it easy. We've got to give him time.

There is the old uneasiness on Slater's face and a note of scorn in his voice.

                                        Odds Against Tomorrow   101

SLATER
Sure hope he doesn't screw it up.

BURKE
Did you go over the roads?

SLATER
Twice.

Burke looks at Slater's hands which are covered with gloves, as are his own.

BURKE
You kept your gloves on all the time?

SLATER
Quit mothering me, Dave.

BURKE
(smiling uneasily)
Doing all right.

SLATER
(irritably)
Look, Dave, I don't mind the action, it's the waiting. I wasn't made to wait and I been waiting all my life.

BURKE
(in a soothing voice)
It won't be long now.

SLATER
(grimly)
The sooner the better. When I gassed up, that dumb kid in the station opened the hood and saw the motor.

BURKE
What of it ?

SLATER
He surely admired it—and me.

BURKE
You worried about it?

SLATER
Not yet, but I'm working on it.

BURKE
(shrugging it off)
I hope that business with the chain works.

SLATER
The hell with the chain.

A concerned look from Burke.

BURKE
(glancing out the window again)
No fireworks.

SLATER
Sure.

BURKE
(seriously)
Just get this in your head, Earle. Ingram isn't a
powder puff.

SLATER
Look, I know you were a tough cop, Dave, but a
sudden noise in the night is like to frighten Brother
Bones.

BURKE
Johnny was in the same war as you.

SLATER
Sure, and he had the big white massa to hold his
hand. He better not crap out.

BURKE
He won't.

                            SLATER
                         (violently)
                   If he does, I'll hold his hand.

Another wary glance from Burke and they lapse into silence. Burke
puts his empty pipe in his mouth and sucks at it.

EXT. BUS STATION - DAY

The bus station is located on the busy town square. The bus is just turning
in here. [The first "Attention!" in the loudspeaker's address is played
over the image of Burke at the tail of the previous shot.]

                         LOUDSPEAKER
                   Attention! Attention, please! Bus 120 now arriving
                   from New York, will depart for Albany in five
                   minutes. Bus 120 will depart for Albany in five
                   minutes. Thank you.

EXT. TOWN SQUARE

The bus stops and a few passengers descend, among them Ingram. He
wears a new snap-brim hat and now has on dark glasses. He walks
toward the corner of Warren Street, where a signal light piles up the
usual Friday traffic.

Ingram joins several others waiting for the light. At the precise
moment the traffic moves, a car swerves out to hasten ahead, and right
in front of Ingram two fenders crumple. The drivers jump out while
across the street a cruising Melton police car pauses and two policemen
emerge .

Ingram takes one wary look, and then turns alertly to hurry off. As he
fades away behind the others who have seen the accident a VOICE
SOUNDS OFF CAMERA.

                         CHIEF'S VOICE
                   Hey there. You! You with the cap!

The head and shoulders of a very tall and fat man loom into f.g. In b.g., Ingram glances in the direction of the voice and stops dead. The man wears the cap and uniform of the Melton Police Chief and now he extends a hand toward Ingram and beckons.

> CHIEF
> Just a minute.

It is a critical moment, a turning point. Ingram forces himself to return, unconcerned, ambling back at a leisurely pace. The chief questions Ingram.

> CHIEF
> You see the accident?

> INGRAM
> (a friendly smile)
> No, I just heard the crash and there it was.

INT. CAR

In the station wagon, a few cars behind the accident, Slater [is intently watching].

> SLATER
> (his voice jumping with excitement
> and anger)
> You see him?
> BURKE
> (worried)
> I see him.

The drivers of the two cars which have locked fenders are arguing hotly, drowned out by a din of honking horns.

INGRAM AND CHIEF

The Chief is talking to Ingram who has his wallet out and seems to be showing him something, perhaps his driver's license. The second policeman is now directing traffic around the locked cars, trying to unsnarl the jam.

INT. CAR

Slater and Burke are trying to see what Ingram is doing.

> SLATER
> (choked with fury)
> What's that clown trying to do?

> BURKE
> (disturbed)
> Keep your shirt on.

EXT. CORNER

Ingram retrieves his wallet and strolls away while the Chief turns to a woman who saw the accident.

The station wagon passes the accident and policeman who is urging the traffic on, and turns down Warren Street.

Slater and Burke slowly pass Ingram who walks along easily, looking into shop windows as if nothing had happened.

The station wagon cruises along to the intersection at the bank where it turns left and drives down the side street.

Ingram lets his worried eyes follow the station wagon and then looks diagonally across the street.

He sees the front entrance to the bank and the old fashioned clock on the cast iron pole. It points to four-forty. Then CAMERA PANS with his eyes down the side street, taking in a mail box, and then ZOOMS to HOLD on the side door.

EXT. BRIDGE OVER RAILROAD TRACKS - DAY

A switching engine is proceeding under it and the station wagon is pausing over the top.

EXT. RIVERFRONT

The station wagon turns off the bridge and onto an area between an abandoned slaughter house and some old broken down shacks at the water's edge. In b.g. on the other side of the road is a complex of some kind of gas or chemical storage tanks. The car stops and the two men get out. They wait and look around anxiously. A moment later Ingram appears around the corner of the slaughter house, takes a quick look around, and then hurries toward them at the river.

The men come together. The movement ends in a repressed explosion from Slater who is blowing with tension.

> SLATER
> (his voice jumping at Ingram)
> You crazy?

> BURKE
> Shut up, Earle, what did the cop want?

> INGRAM
> (agitated, but ignoring Slater)
> How do you like that for luck? He asked me if I saw the accident.

> SLATER
> So you gave him your fingerprints.

> BURKE
> Did he see your license?

> SLATER
> How stupid can you get.

Ingram waits as if to count before replying, and then speaks to Burke again.

INGRAM

I got nothing in my wallet but a bus ticket and
fifteen bucks.

Burke breathes with relief.

BURKE

That's all?

INGRAM

That's all.
(beat)
But he got a good look at me, right up close.

He says this tentatively as if throwing it out for Burke's inspection.

BURKE
(just as casually)
You were wearing the glasses.

INGRAM

We were face to face.

BURKE

Your own mother wouldn't know you in those dark
glasses.

INGRAM

She would if I held up a bank.

SLATER
(violently)
Get wise to yourself, Ingram. You're just another
black spot on Main Street.

BURKE

Shut that ugly mouth of yours, Earle. Get in the
car.

INGRAM
(wheeling on Slater)
Some day I'm gonna snap off your poisoned head.

Burke steps between them, shoving Slater back. Burke is sweating, trying to hold his team together against the wildness, the violence loose in it.

BURKE

(turning to Ingram pleadingly)

Listen to me, Johnny. That cop wouldn't recognize you in a hundred years. We have to take *some* chances. You're a gambling man. Gamble.

Burke is clutching him, clutching at the last hope of his life which is slipping away. Ingram hesitates, still undecided, moistening his dry lips.

INGRAM

Depends on the odds.

Slater, beside himself, grabs Burke by the arm.

SLATER

Back up, Burke. The odds will never be right. I know how to handle him. I've been handling them all my life. He's no different because he's got him a pair of twenty dollar shoes.

INGRAM

All right, Slater, handle me.

Ingram goes into a half-crouch in front of Slater, ready, alert. Burke bellows in despair.

BURKE

Johnny!

And then his voice is lost in a greater overwhelming howl. All three turn toward the direction from which it comes.

A train is charging down the track, whistle hooting, rampaging along, shaking the earth under it as the cars slam by. Ingram is the last to take his eyes from it and finds Burke and Slater watching him.

BURKE
(simply)
It's now or never, Johnny. We're right up to the
line. We'll be done and away by 6:15.

INGRAM
You're sure you want to go through with this ?

BURKE
It's going to let us live again.

Ingram's face is a blank mystery.

INGRAM
(softly)
All right.

Slater smiles contemptuously. Burke beams and slaps Ingram's back.

BURKE
Good boy. We keep apart until six. Everything
like we planned. Let's move.

Slater, as he starts away from Ingram' s side.

SLATER
Next time you call me, I'm going to see you.

INGRAM
I'll be waiting.

Ingram slips on the dark glasses.

INGRAM (CON'T)
You aren't just another white spot to me.

Slater gets into the station wagon and drives off as Burke slaps Ingram
on the shoulder.

BURKE
Take it easy, pal. Don't worry about Slater. He's a
hard-nose but he's dependable in the clutch.
(with a confident wink)
It's gonna work.

Burke walks away from the river and Ingram goes toward it. The
UNDERSCORING RISES, bringing with it a mood of anxiety and
loneliness, as each man waits out on his own the crawling minutes
before zero hour.[22]

Ingram picks his way along the river's edge to an old wharf that sags
into the water.

He tests a rotten piling and sits on it. He stares at the water, the slow
turn and fill of the ride washing between the rotting piles, wooden
boxes tippling in the water, dead branches, a whiskey bottle. He
slowly takes off his glasses, dipping down his hand and cooling his
face with the water. Then he just sits there and waits.

EXT. PARADE HILL - DAY

Burke strolling into the little park above the river. He strolls over to
the statue, reading the inscription:

WHATSOEVER THY HAND
FINDETH TO DO
DO IT
WITH THY MIGHT

Then he goes to the railing and looks down. Ingram is sitting on the
wharf by the water's edge and the expanse of river in front of him.

EXT. RIVER'S EDGE - DAY

Camera pans with the current to Ingram watching the river, then
scanning the panorama.

The current pushes a mass of boards intertwined with old rags and rope into the pilings of the wharf. Bobbing along with it, caught in the loose cordage, is a small figure. There is a red dress, dark hair plastered across a pink face, yet all obscure, recognizable and shapeless at the same time.

Ingram's drifting gaze suddenly fastens and widens in horror.
The figure is being dragged along, and then snagged behind a piling.

We see Ingram's shock as he stares. And then, abruptly, as he starts to lunge forward, his face relaxes and breaks out in an expression of relief.

The mass is drifting in toward him now, closer, and has turned to reveal an old rag doll caught in it.

Ingram stares, his mind far away, the doll reminding him of his own little girl.

EXT. PARADE HILL PARK - DAY

A slow ZOOM up to Burke watching Ingram's incomprehensible actions below.

EXT. A FIELD - DAY

Close shot on the breech of a shotgun as it is snapped open.

Slater is standing by the open door to the station wagon, loading the shotgun. He pours a handful of shells into his jacket pocket, and then ties a surgical mask under his chin. With the car door still open he sits on the front seat.

Across the field is a broken stone wall. Slater glances at his watch. As he looks up again a rabbit hops out from some bushes by the wall. Slater sees it and freezes. It sniffs the air with twitching nose, takes a few more slow hops and stops again.

Slater is intent, his face suddenly boyish and completely absorbed in the sight. The rabbit sits motionless, then takes a few more hops.

Slater takes the shotgun from the car seat and slowly stands up. The rabbit is slowly hopping along. Suddenly it freezes dead still.

Slater aims along the shotgun on this easy target. He waits. The rabbit never moves.

Slater holds the gun on the rabbit, then slowly lowers it. The rabbit takes off, a blur of brown across the fields.

Slater out a step, snapping the gun to his shoulder, swinging on the rabbit and firing. With the blast of the shotgun, cut to:

EXT. PARADE HILL PARK - DUSK

Burke is idly tossing pebbles around a beer can on the ground, then he brushes off his hands, and looks off screen to the river.

The river is calm with hardly a ripple on it . . . the hazy far shore, the peace and tranquillity of this lovely moment at the end of the day.

Burke is staring, lost in thought. Now he turns briskly and looks up the length of Warren Street.

As dusk falls the activity of the night is beginning on the street. Here and there lights wink on. A neon sign starts to blink. The headlights of a car sweep a corner. Two more cars appear without lights yet. [A slow ZOOM into this scene.] The music cuts off abruptly—a moment of dead SILENCE—and then a deep, reverberating note.

EXT. BANK - NIGHT

The illuminated clock is pointing to the hour of six.

[Wider shot of bank.] CAMERA PANS slightly and we're looking down Warren Street, now really lit up, shop windows aglow, neon signs blinking, traffic moving. The offstage courthouse clock echoes a second stroke.

EXT. ANOTHER PART OF WARREN STREET - NIGHT

Burke has his cap on and his collar up. He comes up the street with a certain intangible urgency about him. [He walks forcefully up to the CAMERA, which begins to track with him at the exact moment that he reaches it, and continues to move with him on the sidewalk for four seconds.] And the clock strikes a third time.

EXT. TOWN SQUARE RAILROAD CROSSING - NIGHT

A freight train is going through, blocking traffic. Among the cars waiting is the station wagon.

We hear the clock strike, reverberating for the fourth time.

INT. STATION WAGON

Slater is behind the wheel, angry and frustrated at this delay.

[The clock strikes the fifth time.]

EXT. BACK STREET - NIGHT

Ingram is waiting for the station wagon on a quiet back street.

And the clock tolls for the sixth time.

EXT. BANK - NIGHT

The last customer comes out , and the front door is locked.

EXT. DRUG STORE ON WARREN STREET - NIGHT

Burke comes strolling past the drug store, stops to window shop for a minute.

INT. DRUG STORE

A waiter is preparing the order for the bank, the coffee containers out, the sandwiches being wrapped, the carton to one side.

A gaggle of teenagers, boys and girls, dominate the fountain while at the far end a couple of hunters are drinking coffee.

Ted strolls over to the fountain from the magazine rack.

> CHARLIE (THE WAITER)
> You know, I don't know which is worse, the Atom
> Bomb or you kids and your do-it-yourself cars.

> TED
> (addressing waiter)
> You should've seen the job I gassed up this
> afternoon, Charlie. Just an old beat-up station
> wagon—but the motor inside, mm, mm!

EXT. BACK STREET

Ingram in f.g. with the station wagon approaching from the end of the street. It slows down, hardly stops for Ingram to pull open the door and slide into the front seat.

INT. STATION WAGON

Slater drives. Ingram immediately starts pulling on the white linen clothes he finds on the seat, jacket, trousers, and apron.

> INGRAM
> The carton?

Slater indicates the back seat with his thumb. Ingram turns.

A dozen coffee containers and some sandwiches lie in a carton on the back seat.

EXT. BANK - NIGHT 23

[Medium shot] of the bank with draperies drawn and a little light spilling around them, the illuminated clock pointing to 6:04. [Zooming back reveals] the side street [and the side entrance to the bank].

EXT. DRUG STORE - NIGHT

Burke [has been taking in all of the above], almost choking with tension.

Burke, standing to one side of the entrance, glances inside.

A woman with shopping bundles and accompanied by two ten-year-old boys stops [at the entrance of the drug store]. The boys are playing with water pistols.

                              WOMAN
                    (to boys)
          Wait here and no nonsense with those guns.
                    (cuffing boy)
          You hear me?

She enters the drug store and the boys simultaneously squirt the pistols at each other, laugh and dodge around.

[EXT. BANK - NIGHT

Front entrance to bank and the illuminated clock reading 6:05.]

EXT. ALLEY BEHIND BANK

The station wagon comes cautiously down the alley with lights out and parks in front of another car, maybe ten yards from the entrance to the alley.

INT. STATION WAGON

Ingram, now all in white like the waiter, [puts on his surgical mask under his collar. Slater inserts a money sack under his coat. Ingram reaches to the back seat for the carton of sandwiches and coffee containers.] Slater pulls the key from the ignition, opens the door, and slides out.

                    INGRAM
      Let's have the key.

Slater closes the door.

EXT. CAR

Slater walks past CAMERA as Ingram leans out the window.

                    INGRAM
      The key!

Slater, either deliberately or not having heard Ingram, keeps going and turns the corner.

EXT. DRUG STORE

Burke watches for Slater and sees him.

EXT. SIDE STREET

Slater comes up to the mail box from where he can see Burke at his station in front of the drug store. Slater takes out some letters and stands there applying stamps to them.

INT. STATION WAGON

Ingram waiting and watching tensely.

EXT. DRUG STORE

Burke now keeps his eyes glued to the entrance of the store. The kids are ducking around Burke trying to shoot each other, laughing. Two hunters come out, their jackets open, their checked shirts bright. They are smoking cigars. They nod to Burke.

> 1ST HUNTER
> Get anything?

> BURKE
> Not a shot.

> 2ND HUNTER
> We jumped a couple of rabbits.

> BURKE
> Good. Good.

They wave and stroll down the street. One of the boys aims his gun at them and squirts without effect.

Burke watches as the girls come chattering out, letting the door swing back on the waiter just behind them, carrying the carton in both hands. One of the girls notices this and holds the door for him.

One of the boys takes aim on the waiter as he circles the girls and heads for the corner. Burke is moving from behind the girls to approach him just as the boy squirts his gun.

The waiter turns sharply into CAMERA as he is squirted by the water pistol.

Burke slips up behind the waiter who is looking in annoyance at the kids as they continue their play undeterred. Burke bumps him hard and the carton flips from the waiter's hand, spilling coffee and sandwiches.

At the mailbox, we see Slater's hands as he mails the letters.

[The bank clock reads 6:06.]

The waiter scrambles after the spilt carton with Burke hurrying to his side.

                              BURKE
            Brats!

                              WAITER
                          (disgustedly)
            Yeah!

The kids hustle up and start to help the waiter pick up the sandwiches and coffee. Burke drifts away.

                              1ST KID
            We're sorry. We'll help you.

Burke crosses the street to the opposite corner with several others as the light changes.

Slater now crosses unhurriedly to a point where he can look into the alley. Slater tugs at his hat in the direction of the station wagon.

INT. STATION WAGON

Ingram receives the signal. Across his face the cloud of the fatal moment, this last chance not to do it and yet the hesitation is illusory rather than real, for he moves, opens the door.

Ingram slides from the front seat, holding the carton, closes the door and then goes the distance to the corner quickly.

EXT. SIDE STREET

Slater crosses the street to the bank side, his eyes narrow, looking all around.

Burke walks down the bank side glancing once, casually, over his shoulder.

Angle on a side door as Ingram passes it by a few feet, then turns back so that his approach is from the right direction. Head down, averting his face, he knocks. And waits.

Burke in f.g. stands by the parked car fumbling for his keys as though he were about to get in. Ingram, in the middle distance, waits at the bank door, his white uniform shining back at him from the dark glass panel. Slater, in the b.g., bends to his shoe, pretending to tie the lace.

This is the waiting, the frozen moment, that never seems to end.

Ingram raises his hand and knocks again. As he does a hand appears, pulling back the shade a bit, and the face of the guard can be seen. Eyes smiling behind his glasses, he lets the shade fall back. Now there is the wait again.

Ingram's head is down, sweating it out.

The door opens on the chain, revealing the guard.

> GUARD
> Kinda late, Charlie.

His hand comes out while Ingram holds up the carton.

Ingram pushes it against the door, open about eight inches, and the guard's hand tugs the carton gently from the other side.

> GUARD'S VOICE
> They must be using bigger boxes.
> (closing door a little)
> Just a second.

We hear him fumbling with the chain on the inside.

> GUARD'S VOICE
> (annoyed)
> Darn chain . . . there.

And then, abruptly, the door swings open. The guard holds up his hands for the carton which Ingram transfers. In that instant, Slater springs behind Ingram, shoves him violently through the doorway against the guard, who staggers back, dropping the package. Slater goes charging in, heavy and fast, pushing Ingram in front of him. Burke, with his mask already up, lunges after him, closing the door behind them.

[The bank clock reads 6:09.]

INT. BANK CORRIDOR - NIGHT

Slater is pushing the guard through the open cage door at the end of the corridor. It is this gate that admits to the work area from the rear. Ingram has twisted the guard's gun out of its holster and holds it. Burke takes the knapsack from Ingram's hand. All three now have their masks up.

INT. BANK - NIGHT

There's lots of working space behind the teller stations. Three women and two men are working at a long table on which money is neatly stacked. The manager, just lighting a cigarette, works over some papers on a smaller table with the assistant manager and a secretary. Slater comes barreling into the room, herding the guard in front of him, the others close behind.

                    SLATER
               (hoarsely)
          Don't move.

We pan the stunned faces of the men and women working at the long table, ending with the ghostly face of the manager, the match still burning in his hand.

                    MANAGER
               (staring at guard)
     Joe.

The guard is in front of the three men. He turns toward the manager. Slater slams the guard into a corner.

The manager drops his match and begins to back away.

MANAGER
(in a strangled voice)
Don't shoot.

Slater is up behind him and slugs him with the gun butt, and he
collapses on the table. The secretary beside him moans.

SLATER
Shut up!

Instantly she is quiet. Now the women are frozen, absolutely
motionless. The manager leans on the table, holding his head,
whimpering.

Burke sets the knapsack on the table.

BURKE
(soothingly)
Just sit still everyone and behave.

Ingram gathers the money from the table, [putting it all in a large
pocket in Burke's coat], working as fast as he can, coolly, efficiently,
yet with a terrible urgency to get out and away. [Burke is
simultaneously filling a separate bag.]

Slater stands tensely over the situation, dominating the room, an
immense flood of violence seeming to flow from him. There isn't a
person in the room who doesn't know it will take very little to make
him shoot.

EXT. WARREN STREET - NIGHT

[The bank clock reads 6:13.]

The waiter, carrying a new carton, comes out of the drug store, heads for
the corner, and continues walking across the street. A Melton Police car
passes behind him. A policeman calls to him out the right window.

POLICEMAN
(kidding)
Hi, Charlie, got an extra?

WAITER
(humorously as he starts across)
Man, I got a dozen. All over the sidewalk back
there.

CAMERA PANS him across the street.

INT. BANK

Burke continues to fill the knapsack with bills. Ingram is stuffing more
into the game pockets of Burke's coat. Slater stands by the gate, his gun
up, his eyes continually prowling the room for signs of trouble.

EXT. SIDE STREET

[Only the shadow of the waiter against the wall of the bank is seen, as
he walks down the street along the side of the bank. The shadow is
absorbed as the actual figure of the man enters the shot. He knocks on
the side door of the bank.]

A KNOCK ON THE DOOR sounds startlingly loud against the taut
silence of the room.

[The sound freezes the robbers,] but Burke responds as though he had
expected it all along.

BURKE
The waiter.

Slater goes down the short corridor. He pulls open the door, grabs the
waiter by the coat front, hauls him inside and kicks the door closed all
in one continuous motion. The waiter starts to cry out in surprise and
Slater slugs him with the pistol butt.

The waiter falls as Ingram comes down the corridor and Burke, holding
the knapsack, stands at the end of the corridor where he can still
control the workers with his gun.

Ingram kneels by the waiter and raises his head which is gashed across
the forehead.

                    INGRAM
              (to Burke)
        Let's cut out before he kills somebody.

Ingram stands.

                    INGRAM (CON'T)
              (to Slater)
        Gimme the keys.

                    SLATER
        Dave, you get the car.

                    BURKE
              (surprised)
        But Johnny's supposed to get the car . . .

                    SLATER
              (handing Burke the keys)
        We got it made. C'mon . . .

                    INGRAM
        Gimme the keys.

Ingram reacts but Slater turns to face him with his gun up.

                    SLATER
        C'mon. . . . C'mon.

For an instant there is indecision on Burke's face, but he knows there
isn't time to reason, argue or hesitate. He has to go along with it.

                    BURKE
              (stepping forward)
        Keep the room covered.

EXT. BANK CORNER

The postman walks to the corner as the police car comes cruising back up
Warren Street.

POSTMAN
Oh, Pete. . . . Pete, can I see you a minute?

The police car stops and a policeman looks out the window.

POLICEMAN
Sure thing.

POSTMAN
(coming to car window)
I need another book of raffle tickets.

POLICEMAN
Well, I should . . .
(glancing off)
Hey . . .
(puzzled)
That's funny.

The postman turns casually.

Burke is coming out of the door, carrying his knapsack, and turning right for the alley in the flood of light from the open door.

The policeman gets out of the car, curious but not yet alarmed or excited.

POLICEMAN
Hold it, mister,
(louder, as he strides forward)
You there, the hunter!

[There is a ZOOM from the Policeman's perspective to Burke.] Burke turns around.

[INT. BANK CORRIDOR

Ingram and Slater both react to the voices outside.]

[EXT. SIDE STREET

Burke is stopped in his tracks, looking at the policeman. The policeman starts to walk toward Burke.

Burke begins to walk toward the policeman.] Burke's face is formed into a pleasant, friendly smile.

INT. BANK CORRIDOR

Ingram is frozen, listening with dread against the door. Slater wheels from his position at the end of the corridor and charges down it.

> INGRAM
> (intensely, [trying to prevent Slater
> from opening the door])
Stay there.

EXT. SIDE STREET

The policeman is coming one way and Burke the other. But at this moment the bank door opens again, flooding light into the street and Slater darts a look out.

The bank alarm goes off with a shattering din.

We see Burke's look of sudden despair.

We see the policeman's look of sudden alarm.

Slater fires at the policeman from the doorway.

The policeman dodges behind the car, pulling his gun.

> POLICEMAN
> (yelling)
Stick-up.

He points his gun right into CAMERA and FIRES. CAMERA EXPLODES.

Burke is hit. He stumbles sideways and pitches off his feet.

The second policeman fires from the window of the police car. The postman has vanished.

Slater and Ingram come out the door, running behind Burke for the alley. A shot erupts against the building.

Slater and Ingram round the corner full tilt. Ingram stops but Slater keeps going toward the station wagon.

> SLATER
> (yelling to Ingram)
> Into the car.

> INGRAM
> (yelling back)
> He's got the key.

Slater is at the station wagon, facing around, his eyes wild over the mask. He rips the mask off, opens the car door, grabs the shotgun and runs back to Ingram.

Ingram ducks around the corner, yelling.

> INGRAM
> To the car, Dave. The car.

Burke struggles up and takes a lurching stop toward the alley.

The policeman rises up behind the car, firing. Burke spins around and crashes to the sidewalk.

[The police are attempting to prevent people from rushing to the scene.]

Slater is at the corner, firing the shotgun. The sound is immense.

The policeman crouches behind the car. The buck shot at close range rips up the car, shattering the windows. The policeman is frantically reloading his gun.

A small crowd is milling toward the corner of Warren Street, some trying to push forward to see, and others, having seen, are scurrying back. A small man stands in the forefront, staring aghast.

SMALL MAN
My God, my car!

A policeman breaks to the forefront and frantically shoves back the little man and others.

Slater holds the shotgun ready, Ingram takes out a gun for the first time. A siren wails off-screen.

INGRAM
Cover me. I'll get Dave.

Ingram starts crawling around the corner as Slater pops out and blasts away with the shotgun. A State Police car, siren screaming, comes roaring in and skids to a stop across the intersection. Three troopers leap out. Two start firing even before they take cover.

Ingram scrambles back to the alley. A stray bullet shatters a window.

SLATER
(yelling)
Throw the keys, Burke.

Burke's face is drawn with pain and streaked with blood. He begins to crawl.

[POLICEMEN'S VOICES
(off-screen)
Give up. . . . You don't have a chance. . . .

Burke is continuing his painful crawl.

SLATER'S VOICE
(off-screen)
The key, Burke. Burke, the key!

POLICEMAN'S VOICE
(off-screen)
You there, in the alley, come out with your hands
up.

SLATER'S VOICE
(off-screen)
Burke! Give us the key!]

He gets the keys out of his pocket and [extends his arm as if he were handing the keys to one right next to him].

A trooper who has joined the policeman behind the car fires.

Burke is hit again, screams out in agony, and pitches over on his side.

The keys fall a few inches from his outstretched hand which claws the sidewalk of this no-man's land.

Ingram and Slater [observe this with despair].

INGRAM
(violently)
There are your keys. Have you still got it made?

Burke raises his head and wrenches in pain.

BURKE
Run, Johnny.

There's a moment of intense realization in his dying mind.

BURKE
I'm sorry.

Slater is looking around for an avenue of escape. Ingram stands quietly, utterly without hope, but knowing it is not quite finished yet.

SLATER
(chucking down the shotgun and
pulling a revolver)
Let's clear out.

INGRAM
You can't leave Burke here.

Burke is lying on the sidewalk. In b.g. are the two police cars, state and local, and the men crouched behind them.

Burke stirs and reaches for the gun.

The policeman [reacts to this gesture. The trooper] ducks down behind the car.

POLICEMAN
(yelling)
Look out! Drop that gun!

But Burke pulls the gun toward himself and holds it to his own head.

Ingram and Slater see Burke's terrible end [as the shot is heard off-screen]. On Ingram's face there is a flicker of the storm raging inside him.

SLATER
What do y'know. He sure ain't going to talk now.

Ingram wrenches around. [He grabs Slater by his jacket at the throat and begins slamming him against the side of the building.] He breathes words of loathing and hate into Slater's face.

INGRAM
[You bastard!24 You couldn't trust me, and you killed him.]

[The sound of a dog barking obscures the word "bastard."]

Slater turns and runs for it. Ingram fires. Slater is winged, staggers, but [fires back at Ingram] and makes the turn-off from the alley. Ingram goes tearing after him.

Burke is at last dead, his arms flung out, the body vacant and bloody. Behind him in b.g., the State Police car backs up and goes screeching off. The Chief and a third policeman are slowly moving toward the body, ready to move at any unlikely sign of life. The second policeman now comes out from behind the shot-up car.

EXT. GAS TANK COMPLEX - NIGHT[25]

The area here is filled with the shapes of tanks, pump houses, assorted equipment and their shadow patterns. In b.g. we can make out a glint of water and hear the lap and wash of the river. Some light comes from occasional floodlights on the cyclone fence. The wail of a siren blows in from the distance and starts to swell.

Slater's dark figure comes running in, soon followed by Ingram, all in white, gliding swiftly forward out of the thick darkness behind the lights, an easy target.

Slater is hunted, savage, desperate. He holds his gun hand to his shoulder where he has been nicked, turns to fire once behind him. In b.g. we hear the Police Car careening down the road, siren screaming.

Ingram darts behind a stack of oil drums, his gun up and ready for a clear shot at Slater.

The police car screeches to a stop, the occupants having heard the shot. Slater is running, once blocked from CAMERA by a lift-loader, looking around wildly. He sees the shadow pattern of steel steps against the side of a tank. The network of girders beneath the underbelly of a smaller oblong tank, making it look like some monster.

The steel steps, bathed in a blinding flood light, rise precipitously to the top of a tank. CAMERA is between the steps and tank. Slater comes charging up the steps and disappears into the top of the FRAME.

Ingram runs to the foot of the steps and starts up them. Slater has vanished into a void over the rim of the tank. As Ingram goes he is hit by a spotlight that stays on him.

EXT. ROAD OUTSIDE GAS TANK COMPLEX - NIGHT

The State Police car is drawn up here. The searchlight above it is beamed on Ingram. The troopers are behind their cars or any other cover available.

A young trooper is behind car. He is bringing a tommy gun to his shoulder. Instantly a seasoned trooper [warns him against firing].

SEASONED TROOPER
No! Hold it!

Ingram is running up the steps of the tank to disappear over the rim of the tank.

EXT. TANK TOPS - NIGHT

Wooden walks are laid out along the tops of five tanks here, connecting them by little ramps. The fifth tank is larger then the others, both in height and circumference and the ramp to it slants up at a steep angle. The other ramps are level. Slater and Ingram running after him, across these giant stepping stones at the bottom of the night, look almost like figures on the moon.

Ingram's face is blank, his waiter's uniform stained. He holds his gun up, ready to fire, but Slater, not in a white uniform, presents a difficult moving target.

Slater is all concentrated violence and hatred.

Slater whirls and runs on to the ramp to the big tank, stops near the end of it and makes his stand.

Ingram slows down at the foot of the ramp and then advances, one careful, deliberate step after another.

Slater is panting with tension and fury, motionless.

Ingram is now also motionless, rigid, transformed into something other than flesh and blood.[26]

The sickness staring from Slater's eyes.

Ingram's face is already a death mask with no humanity in it at all.

Both men are utterly engulfed in the immensity of their hatred. Every movement, every breath, every awareness of their being becomes enormously magnified as though the CAMERA were a microscope through which we watch this last moment of life.

They fire simultaneously. There is a blinding white flash accompanied by a tremendous explosion. And then even the white nothing burns away as though the SCREEN itself were being consumed in fire.

With the sound of several more detonations we go to a series of impressionistic cuts: a burning object sailing through the air, metal turning bright and melting, a belch of black smoke with a core of fire, a Niagara of gorgeous sparks cascading into the night.[27]

EXT. CYCLONE FENCE - DAY

Four figures are walking along the fence—the chief, a State Trooper captain, and two ambulance attendants. The fence running behind them [on which is seen a STOP - DEAD END sign], buckled here and there, charred, distorted, its regular pattern all out of kilter, with strange angular piles of smoking metal stacked behind it, evokes a shattered, not quite real world. A man in an asbestos suit passes by on the inside of the fence.

And there is WIND there, driving and howling as in the beginning long ago on Riverside Drive.[28]

The group enters the area where the dead have been laid out under blankets. They stop before two covered lumps on stretchers separated from the rest.

CHIEF
(pointing at the bodies)
Well, these are the two that did it.[29]

An attendant reaches down and pulls a blanket up into FRAME. [A jagged, uprooted telephone pole is a reminder of the destruction in the background.] With his other hand he pulls up the second blanket and stares down from one body to the other.

ATTENDANT
(expressionlessly)
Which is which?

The chief shrugs slowly.

CHIEF
Take your pick.

They pick up the stretcher and start carrying it along the fence in the opposite direction from which they came, CAMERA PANNING with them, until they turn off-screen. There is a sign on the fence [which had been foreshadowed earlier in the scene]. The swelling MUSIC accents our theme, underscoring the spent violence and exhausted emotion of tragedy played out, the useless destructive aftermath of HATE.

In close up we read the sign on the fence:

STOP
DEAD END[30]

CAMERA HOLDS for a long moment, then PANS DOWN TO a black puddle of water at foot of frame, riled by the breeze, a chiaroscuro of light and dark reflections. [This *final* image of black puddled water replicates the *first* image of the film—water and debris in a gutter—completing a pictorial symmetry of the modern wasteland.

Two central motifs of the wasteland theme—the MUSIC and the WIND—continue.]

After a pause the END CREDITS slowly roll up.

Ingram	HARRY BELAFONTE
Slater	ROBERT RYAN
Lorry	SHELLEY WINTERS
Burke	ED BEGLEY
Helen	GLORIA GRAHAME
Bacco	WILL KULUVA
Ruth	KIM HAMILTON
Annie	MAE BARNES
Coco	RICHARD BRIGHT
Kitty	CARMEN DE LAVALLADE
Moriarity	LEW GALLO
Eadie	LOIS THORNE
Soldier in Bar	WAYNE ROGERS
Girl in Bar	ZOHRA LAMPERT
Police Chief	ALLEN NOURSE

[Additional cast members not listed in the end credits:

Cannoy	FRED J. SCOLLAY
Bartender	WILLIAM ZUCKERT
George in Bar	BURTT HARRIS
Hotel Clerk	ED PREBLE
Elevator Operator	MIL STEWART
Ambulance Attendant	MARC MAY
Garry	PAUL HOFFMAN
Fra	CICELY TYSON
Guard at Door — Cannoy's Club	ROBERT JONES
Bank Guard	WILLIAM ADAMS]

Produced at
Gold Medal Studios
The Bronx, New York

THE END

Film Noir Caper: "The Morally Oriented Gangster Film."

"Between the desire
And the spasm
Between the potency
And the existence
Between the essence
And the descent
Falls the Shadow"
　　—T.S. Eliot, "The Hollow Men"

ANNOTATIONS TO THE SCREENPLAY
by John Schultheiss

1. The Fronts: John O. Killens.

ROBERT WISE: Harry Belafonte came to Los Angeles because his company, HarBel Productions, owned the property, and he thought that I might be interested in it. He got the script to me; I liked it very much and was keen to do it. It had the name John Killens on it. Harry said that he was a black novelist, and this was his first screenplay. It seemed logical to me that he would have a particular appreciation for this subject matter, so I accepted that as being the case. The deal was worked out for me to go back to New York—it was all going to be shot back there. When I got settled in, I got a call from Harry saying that he'd like to bring the writer over for me to meet. So at 11 o'clock the next day the doorbell rang, and I opened the door expecting to see Harry and the black writer. But it was Abe Polonsky. That was the first time I met Abe, and I found out he was blacklisted and couldn't get credit in his own name. So Killens had allowed Harry to use his name as a kind of ghost writer up front. He never wrote anything at all of the screenplay; he just gave his name to HarBel to use as a front for Abe.

The Fronts: Nelson Gidding.

ROBERT WISE: When we were getting toward the end of shooting, we needed to make a few little doctors in the script. I can't remember what they were, just a few little changes, and Abe was out of town someplace and was not available. I happened to have another writer named Nelson Gidding in New York working for me on another project. And so I just asked Nelson if he would step in; I told him what we needed, and he wrote a few lines—just very, very minor details. But as long as he had done some work on it—not really enough to justify showing a credit on the screenplay—the company and I felt that it might be just as well to put his name on it to help substantiate the fact that it was all legitimate, to keep Abe's cover going. But it was minor stuff, not enough to justify getting his name on it.

(Interview with Author, 11 February 1998.)

2. Poetry of the City.

"Only a newspaper struggled in the air
like a kite with a broken spine."
—Nathanael West, *Miss Lonelyhearts*.

This opening sequence of *Odds Against Tomorrow* was a particular favorite of the French director Jean-Pierre Melville (*Le Doulos, Le Samourai*: see Note 34, critical commentary), who loved educating his friends about the aesthetics of cinema. "Melville was a teacher through and through, which was especially obvious when he showed movies in his own screening room to staff and friends. The movies were, by the way, always the same: *The Best Years of Our Lives*, by Wyler, and most often, Robert Wise's *Odds Against Tomorrow*. It was the simple craftsmanship in the latter movie that Melville wanted to bring to our attention: the fluttering newspaper pages in the establishing shot, the surprise cut to the front of a speeding [bus]. These and many other shots he would always anticipate before they actually appeared on the screen." (Volker Schlondorff, "A Parisian-American in Paris," *The Village Voice*, 6 July 1982.)

An urban setting and atmosphere exist in the physical facts of the landscape (actual streets, structures, topography) and in its symbolism. James T. Farrell (who was proficient in evoking the palpable rhythms of the city in his novels, such as *Young Lonigan, a Boyhood in the Chicago Streets*, 1932) writes that "authors do not pick their images out of a grab bag, but rather they grow out of their own background and changing experiences. Many of the symbols they use are products of urban life. In their immediate sensory experiences they have been most affected by the sights, sounds, odors, and objects of an industrial city." ["In Search of an Image," *The League of Frightened Philistines* (New York: Vanguard Press, 1945), p. 156.)]

An indescribable city—huge, roaring, dirty, noisy, raw, stark, brutal; a city of extremes: torrid summers and sub-zero winters, white people and black people, the English language and strange tongues, foreign born and native born, scabby poverty and gaudy luxury, high idealism and hard cynicism! A city so young that, in thinking of its short history, one's mind, as it travels backward in time, is stopped abruptly by the barren stretches of wind-swept prairie! But a city old enough to have caught within the homes of its long, straight streets the symbols and images of man's age-old destiny, of truths as old as the mountains and seas, of dramas as abiding as the soul of man itself! A city which has become the pivot of the Eastern, Western, Northern, and Southern poles of the nation. But a city whose black smoke clouds shut out the sunshine for seven months of the year; a city in which, on a fine balmy May morning, one can sniff the stench of the stockyards; a city where people have grown so used to gangs and murders and graft that they have honestly forgotten that government can have a pretense of decency!

(Richard Wright, "How 'Bigger' Was Born.")

Twentieth-century life has thrust upon the modern artist certain obsessive concerns—a concern over man's aloneness and alienation; a concern over the collapse of community and the breakdown of tradition; a concern over the ineffectuality of love, language, and religion; the impact of mechanization; the materialism of modern life. These are the **themes** of modern art; they are also the themes of city fiction. To make these themes concrete, urban symbolism often equates physical elements in the setting with social or psychological characteristics of the city protagonists. The symbols not only suggest an interpretation of urban society but they usually contain implicit moral judgments. (See the critical commentary for discussions—in the context of modern poetry, specifically "The Waste Land" paradigm of T. S. Eliot—of the possible symbolic uses in *Odds* of the wind, birds, music, waterfront debris, fire, etc.)

[See Blanche Housman Gelfant, *The American City Novel* (Norman: University of Oklahoma Press, 1970), pp. 3-24.]

"**Welcome to Dark City**: Observe the mighty beast, mankind's riskiest experiment. A sprawling, soaring monster with a steel skeleton and a concrete overcoat. Some brilliant Frankensteins learned how to pump electricity through its arteries; now it lurches and crackles and spews non-stop. On its daylight streets you'll witness the most courageous of human endeavors: the will to co-exist. But when the curtain of night falls, you'd better head for home. Or learn first-hand about our truly ingrained trait: the desire to devour."

[Eddie Muller, *Dark City: The Lost World of Film Noir* (New York: St. Martin's Press, 1998), p. 14.]

The importance of **city imagery** to film noir is focused on in the "Film Noir" episode of *American Cinema* (1994), a documentary film series produced by the Corporation for Public Broadcasting and the

New York Center for Visual History. The episode's choices of descriptive language and film extracts to illustrate this noir aspect are relevant to the orientation taken towards *Odds Against Tomorrow* in this volume. The following is a summary of the significant passages from this segment:

PAUL ARTHUR [Scholar, Montclair State College]: A large portion of the Hollywood technical community had learned documentary technique working . . . for the various branches of the armed forces. So they were just more schooled in how to shoot in a more raw, less studio-bound, less stylized fashion. I also think that the experience of the American public with documentaries during the war led to a greater acceptance of semi-documentary or realist techniques in fiction films.

ANDRE DE TOTH [Director of noir films *Pitfall* and *Crime Wave*]: Shooting on location is a must for a film noir, because film noir is reality.

[The film images used by the documentary to illustrate these points are taken from Abraham Polonsky's *Force of Evil* (1948)—Joe Morse's (John Garfield) descent down the great stone stairway of the New York viaduct to the river shore to find his dead brother's body. "It was like going down to the bottom of the world . . . to find my brother. I found my brother's body at the bottom there, where they had thrown it away on the rocks by the river, like an old dirty rag nobody wants. He was dead."]

MARTIN SCORSESE [Director, *Mean Streets, Taxi Driver*]: It's incredible **city poetry** . . . the body there . . . lying there. I came from an area where sometimes you would see a body in the street that way.

PAUL ARTHUR: It was important for film noir to represent *real* cities, not these vague constructions on the studio backlot, to use the look of the city as a part of its stylistic web. The number of underground locations that we see in film noir is quite phenomenal . . . underground garages and subways and sewer systems. It's a manifestation of the underworld, of the secret world, a kind of labyrinth where criminals can hide in shadows . . . an image, a representation of a modern hell.

PAUL SCHRADER [Critic, screenwriter, director; *American Gigolo, Hard Core*]: When you are dealing in a doomed world, you go for **visual correlatives**. It's kind of hard to do a story of doom on a pleasant, sunny day.

SCORSESE: The image of Richard Widmark running in the streets in *Night and the City* [shown] is a seminal image of film noir. You can't think of [noir] without thinking of that image of the man running in the street at night.

The correlations to *Odds Against Tomorrow* are explicit: Joseph Brun's cinematographic treatment (See Annotation #11) of realistic landscapes, the creation of visual correlatives for psychological states, Abraham Polonsky's poetry of the city conveying a sense of inevitable doom.

3. *Music Annotation:* Introductory shot is accompanied by a jazz fugue between guitar, horns, and wind machine evoking a sense of coldness on the city streets. [Martin C. Myrick] (See separate essays on the composer John Lewis and the film score for *Odds Against Tomorrow* in this volume, pp. 299-313.)

Movie Music Overview: "Movie music today comes in two principal forms (three if you count the soundtrack pop songs marketed on CD). First, there is the score, written specially for the film, consisting of numerous cues composed for specific scenes. [E.g., Max Steiner, *Dark Victory*.]

"Second, there is source music, that is, music coming from a visible source on screen: a song is played on a jukebox, for instance. [E.g., Hitchcock's *The Man Who Knew Too Much* (both versions)] . . . Over time, inevitably, source music began to do without a (visible) source, as in *Easy Rider*, in which songs were played over scenes even though neither of the bikers had a radio.

"If there's any general rule that I've discovered in my years as a passionate collector and advocate of film music, it is that great directors—Federico Fellini, Max Ophüls, Jean Renoir, Stanley Kubrick, Martin Scorsese, Akira Kurosawa, Jean-Luc Godard, David Lean and Hitchcock come to mind—have a fine ear for music. They get the best scores from the best composers, and they choose the best source music.

"In the jazz tradition, which began in the 1950s by mixing orchestral music with the freer sounds of modern jazz, there are many masters—Lalo Schifrin, Alex North, Elmer Bernstein and Quincy Jones.

The finest record by John Lewis of the Modern Jazz Quartet may be his symphonic composition for Robert Wise's *Odds Against Tomorrow* (1959)." [Nicolas Saada, "In the Mood," *Civilization*, February/March 1998, pp. 76, 78.]

4. *Music:* Tympani is introduced to build tension against horns in crescendo, climaxing with Slater pounding his fist on the desk. This motif is used as a tension builder throughout the film. [Myrick]

5. *Music:* Tympani and horns build tension in ascending pattern while vibes counter in descending line—which signals Slater and Burke's further descent into corruption. As Slater sits the music resolves to a jazz interlude between bass and tympani. [Myrick]

6. *Music:* Horns are overlaid upon tympani and bass in a tension-building crescendo which abruptly climaxes, leaving tympani and bass in a resolving fade. [Myrick]

7. *Music:* Vibes and flute enter in an upbeat swing with the quartet, yet still create tension in ascending counterpoint which climaxes as Ingram and Slater cross paths outside the hotel. [Myrick]

8. **What's My Line?**

ABRAHAM POLONSKY: Ingram's argument is based on the notion of professionalism: we're not in that line of work. He's not resisting on moral grounds because he thinks it's evil. You got to know how to hold up banks properly. If you are holding up a bank and somebody resists, you have to shoot them. You got to be willing to shoot and kill. That's not for people like us. We're people; we don't hold up banks and shoot people. They're just petty people. So here are three people who have nothing to do with bank holdups—including the cop. The cop conceives a great setup—exploiting the fact that the waiter bringing food and coffee to the bank happens to be an African American—and the setup is what sells the caper to the others. But the setup is also what defeats them.
(Interview with Author, 25 July 1997.)

9. **Bird Imagery.**

Birds are used in this scene as a forceful component in a sudden and unexpected transition to the next shot, which forecloses the anticipated dialogue between the two men. Because of its striking visual presentation, this is the kind of moment that would be routinely attributed to the director—but this visceral element is in Polonsky's original shooting script. Polonsky: "To me a serious moment is coming up. It communicates expectancy, serious expectancy." (Interview with Author, 25 July 1997.)

Bird imagery is used symbolically in the opening scene of the film as well (as discussed in the critical commentary), prompting an allusion to the films of Carl Dreyer, who uses birds emblematically throughout his work. At the risk of producing what David Bordwell describes as "overwrought annotation," it is tempting to appropriate for use here Bordwell's poignant comment on Dreyer's intercutting of shots of birds in flight with close-ups of Jeanne at the stake: [human] "actions send sympathetic reverberations through nature." In *Odds*, the bird imagery is laced with ambiguity, connoting simultaneously hope and fatalism.

[See *Filmguide to La Passion de Jeanne d'Arc* (Bloomington: Indiana University Press, 1973), p. 56.]

10. **Censorship.**

The *Odds Against Tomorrow* shooting script was reviewed by Geoffrey Shurlock, of the Motion Picture Association of America, for its acceptability under the provisions of the censorship Production Code. Certain elements in the submitted screenplay were indeed perceived to be violations of the Code, which, according to Shurlock in his 23 February 1959 letter to HarBel Productions, "would have to be corrected before a picture based on this material could be approved by us." An examination of a few of the elements that the Production Code committee found objectionable might be revealing of the nature of the censorship process of that period. Some of the requested changes or deletions were made, but others were not.

Many of the objections or concerns dealt with language. The lyrics of all songs to be used in the production had to be submitted for approval. The following dialogue was deemed unacceptable: Kitty's "but send back the key" [not changed]; "crap," "faggot," "pansy" [all deleted], "rape" [not changed]. There was an admonition against the use of "nigger" [not changed].

The character of Coco "seems quite obviously to be that of a fairy. Any such impression in the finished picture would be unacceptable under the Code and could not be approved [not changed]. We call your attention specifically to some of his apparently effeminate mannerism such as giving Ingram's cheek 'a friendly pinch' [deleted] and the manner in which he flies back 'scratching and slapping' [deleted]. Please also be advised that the kneeing in the groin is unacceptable under the Code [deleted]."

Lorry's line in the screenplay, "Come here, you big clown," initiates this annotation on censorship, because the following segment in the shooting script provided the censors with a more dramatic basis for concern. This is what Polonsky wrote as a follow-up to Lorry's line:

CLOSE SHOT - ON EARLE

He begins to smile. His eyes crinkle and his mouth is soft and friendly. As he starts to bend over to Lorry, the ANGLE WIDENS. Without touching her, he puts his face to hers, kissing her. As he starts to straighten up, Lorry whirls the covers away with one hand, embraces him with the other and pulls him toward herself. She embraces him with a kind of absolute longing, more than sexual, as if against despair. It is a long kiss and finally he breaks her hold, firmly yet like a man who has to, not a man who wants to, and she is left sitting up in the bed, staring up at him while he walks away.

The committee's worry was "that the sequence contains very intimate lovemaking connected with the bed with Lorry clad only in a nightgown. If these intimacies are overly passionate or overly intimate (particularly considering Lorry's scant covering) it may not be possible to approve them under the Code. We earnestly suggest in addition to recommending the entire sequence to your taste and discretion that Lorry at some appropriate point put on a bathrobe or a bed jacket if this seems at all feasible." [The entire action was deleted.] Also of concern was the description, "She stands against the greater light in the next room so that we see her fullness, her body," as this, according to the censors, "seems to suggest a silhouette of her nudity." [Lorry pulls a blanket around her.]

A significant action that remains unchanged in the final film is Burke's suicide. In spite of this being considered "an outright Code violation and cannot be approved if it were to appear in the finished picture," the filmmakers made no alteration. Robert Wise: "It just seemed to be the right finish for him. He was seriously wounded and he didn't like the prospect of getting back into prison for umpteen years. We decided we were not going to change it—and we got away with it." (Interview with Author, 11 February 1998.)

11. **The Geometry of Traffic.**

If there is a single moment in *Odds Against Tomorrow* which synthesizes the fascination that the film might hold for those appreciative of the look and feel of post-WWII European art cinema, it is this modernistic high-angle perspective of the interchanges and bridges of the beltline (together with the extraordinary musical underscoring). Those familiar with the 1950s/1960s sterile landscapes of Fellini and Antonioni would recognize kindred imagery.

ROBERT WISE: That's the origin of *West Side Story*. Here's what happened . . . While we were in production on *Odds*, we were headquartered in Gold Medal Studios out in the Bronx and we used to travel up the eastside to 125th Street, fascinated with those ramps going over the bridges. So I began wondering what that would look like from above; it might be an interesting pattern. So we got permission to go on top one of those apartment houses right by East River Drive, saw this marvelous angle, and I shot clear across going up the Hudson.

When I needed an opening for *West Side Story*, I remembered this shot from *Odds*. I said we have to open *West Side* in the daytime. I got to wondering how to give the audience a view of New York City they've never seen, how the city looks like straight down. So I took one of those old New York Airways helicopters out on the west side, and there it was, my opening. It's a little abstract, but I think it helped put the audience in the frame of mind to accept these kids dancing in the street just down the way. That's what I was reaching for—to make that compatible. But it started from that 3/4 angle on *Odds*.

Cinematography for *Odds Against Tomorrow*.

WISE: I wanted it to have some edges to it. If there were a little extra gray in there it would be fine with me. I wanted this not necessarily to be a documentary, but very realistic. It's that kind of a story, and so I talked to Joe [Brun] about that. He had done enough pictures in New York that we had enough confidence that he'd be the man to do the film. He was actually European, but he was an established cameraman in New York. Since the picture was all being shot back there, it just seemed to be the thing to do to use a local cameraman. So when I told him of these ideas, he was very receptive, very contributing.

Joseph Brun. Cinematography credits of Brun's include: *The Whistle at Eaton Falls* (1951), *Walk East on Beacon* 1952), *The Joe Louis Story* (1953), *Martin Luther* (1953, for which he was nominated for an Academy Award), *Edge of the City* (1957), *Middle of the Night* (1959), *Hatari!* (1962).

Brun wrote a short piece for *American Cinematographer* (August 1959) on photographing *Odds Against Tomorrow*. His respect for Robert Wise dominates the narrative:

[Robert Wise] always means every word he says, and when the word does not come, a simple gesture expressing power and determination completes the sentence. This man breathes, lives, thinks in film terms; his heart beats at film speed. There is greatness in his simplicity and deep knowledge in his modesty. In brief, sheer enjoyment and inspiration for the director of photography.

Thus, when Robert Wise said to me: "I want an atmosphere of increasing menace and a climax of catastrophe; we shall ignore the rules and regulations of conventional visualization," I knew these words were not just another pre-production speech.

We used wide-angle lenses exclusively throughout the picture: 30mm, 25mm, 18mm, and quite often the 14mm made by Angenieux of France. Most close-ups were shot with the 30mm or 25mm, and occasionally with the 18mm. Foreshortening was used as a dramatic element. The 14mm was used for its truly amazing characteristics: not merely for its great depth of field and extremely wide angle, but especially for its presence and participation, and its wonderful rendition of architectural perspective. We used the zoom lens quite often, not as an instrument to obtain magnification or to approximate traveling shots, but as an editorial medium corresponding to a progressive fast or slow switch of image format, or as a rhythmic element in combination with sound and dialogue.

One-third of the picture was shot on location in the streets of a small town (Hudson, New York) by bitter, cold night. All studio shots as well as interior locations included apparent ceilings, thus multiplying the lighting difficulties. (p. 478)

12. *Music:* Tympani, snare drum, and tambourine engage in medium jazz march-shuffle in assistance to Burke's explanation of the plan. [Myrick]

13. **Editing.**

Kenneth Macgowan's *Behind the Screen: The History and Techniques of the Motion Picture* (Dell, 1965) was one of the standard film history and aesthetics texts during that burgeoning era of film scholarship. In his chapter "The Cutter—Right Arm of the Director," Macgowan cites *Odds Against Tomorrow* as being in the vanguard of 1950s editorial experimentation in international cinema. Under the heading "New Editorial Experiments," he writes: "In the 1950s there came attempts to drop the dissolve as an introduction to the past. . . . [Also] some of our more enterprising cutters started to experiment in another direction. They took pot shots at the dissolve that moves a story forward. They didn't throw it out the window, but in certain special cases they substituted straight cuts. . . . Robert Wise in *Odds Against Tomorrow* (1959) added a further excitement in cutting across time and space by keying the moves to a startling line. Here is an example: A criminal is explaining to a new acquaintance a plan for a bank robbery in which they will have a partner. The first man doesn't realize (as the audience does) that the other has a violent, almost maniacal, obsession with white supremacy. When the planner of the robbery casually [indicates] that the third partner is colored, the racist shouts, ["You didn't say nothing about the third man being a nigger."] and the film cuts immediately to the man they are talking about, a man the audience has come to like." (pp. 419-420)

This transition is one of the most powerful in the film, and represents probably the single most significant departure from the shooting script. In the original version, the next shot immediately following that provocative line (also on a direct cut) would have been that of Ruth Ingram opening the door to admit Johnny for his weekly visitation with Eadie. While this editorial approach would have also provided the white/black contrast to dramatize Slater's prejudice, it would not have made as much narrative sense, because it is not Ruth who will be interacting with Earle. A shock cut to Johnny is clearly more logical.

In the original shooting script the transition to Johnny in the club would have followed (also quite forcefully, it is assumed) the reference to Johnny by Bacco in the park: "Sure, a very entertaining boy at Cannoy's." And it is assumed that the transition would have worked well enough. Indeed, the approaches of both shooting script and continuity script that are based on direct cuts to Johnny at the club seem inherently capable of achieving substantial emotional impact—and are both lucid illustrations of the technique that Macgowan described as "cutting across time and space by keying the moves to a startling line." However, it could certainly be argued that a set-up line including Slater's racial epithet is more startling than Bacco's "entertaining boy" allusion. As previously mentioned, the Bacco/Johnny transition would then necessitate the weaker Slater/Ruth progression. And, perhaps most decisively, the Slater/Johnny juxtaposition benefits from the marvelous force of the jazz music of Johnny's performance to heighten the visceral effect of Slater's hateful words.

Every sequence of the film is brilliantly edited. It is axiomatic to invoke Robert Wise's background as an editor, including his two remarkable credits on Orson Welles's *Citizen Kane* (1941) and *The Magnificent Ambersons* (1942). Wise directed *Odds Against Tomorrow* with the editing clearly in mind, but he hired Dede Allen to be the credited editor. According to Cecile Starr, "Allen says Wise urged her to experiment with her own ideas. Her 'seamlessly crisp editing' has been singled out as one of the film's outstanding qualities."

Dede Allen. "When Robert Rossen asked her to edit *The Hustler* [1961], Allen began to acquire a cult following of her own. Credit for some of her stylistic innovations were sometimes attributed to Rossen, but she feels she influenced him a bit. She adds that since film is a collaborative effort, it's often difficult to sort out who is responsible for what.

"With *Bonnie and Clyde* [1967], Allen became an international film personality in her own right. The film has been called 'possibly the most stylistically audacious and thematically provocative American film of the 1960s," and its editing is said to have influenced virtually every American action film since then. Allen developed what Andrew Sarris has called [as an evolutionary phase in an editorial aesthetic noted by Macgowan in his discussion of *Odds*] 'shock cutting . . . wild contrasts from one shot to the next, which give the film a jagged, menacing quality and create a sort of syncopated rhythm.'

"Director Arthur Penn signed up Allen for so many subsequent films [*Alice's Restaurant* (1969), *Little Big Man* (1970), *Night Moves* (1975), *The Missouri Breaks* (1976)] that she sometimes was referred to as 'Penn's editor,' but during the late 1960s and 1970s she worked almost as often for George Roy Hill (*Slaughterhouse Five* [1972], *Slap Shot* [1977]) and Sidney Lumet (*Dog Day Afternoon* [1975, British Academy Award], *The Wiz* [1978])."

Famous actors have relied on her strong editing sense for films they directed: Paul Newman (*Rachel, Rachel*, 1968), Warren Beatty (*Reds*, 1981), Robert Redford (*The Milagro Beanfield War*, 1988). [See Cecile Starr, "Dede Allen," *The International Dictionary of Films and Filmmakers: Volume IV. Writers and Production Artists*. Edited by James Vinson (Chicago: St. James Press, 1987), pp. 9-10.]

14. *Music:* Orchestra and calliope engage in counterpoint. [Myrick]

15. *Music:* Vibes enter in ascending pattern against sustained horns, building tension through crescendo. [Myrick]

16. *Music:* Quartet enters joining guitar in a blues shuffle. [Myrick]

17. *Music:* Orchestral horns are overlaid on quartet. Horns and orchestra intensify in crescendo as quartet slows tempo. [Myrick]

18. *Music:* Horns in a descending fanfare signal Ingram's acquiescence and descent into corruption and hopelessness. [Myrick]

19. **Interiors.**

ROBERT WISE: "We based our operations out of the Gold Medal Studios in the Bronx, an old studio whose origins were D.W. Griffith and Pickford. Somebody had it resuscitated; it had a couple stages that were workable, and this is where we shot some of the interiors." (Interview with Author, 11 February 1998.)

Slater's return home, coming up the stairs, and entering his apartment is representative of the studio interior shooting.

JOSEPH BRUN: All studio shots as well as interior locations included apparent ceilings, thus multiplying the lighting difficulties. In one interior scene the camera was on the studio floor. Sol Midwell, my operative cameraman, had to follow Robert Ryan as he moves along a narrow corridor, through [an entrance hall], then to a bedroom. Walls and ceilings so enclosed the sets there was literally no room for any lights on the floor or on the catwalks. To overcome this problem, I decided to use a mobile microphone boom, temporarily inactive, to mount and move my lights in concert with the action and panning of the camera. Small spotlights were mounted on the mike booms which were extended out into the set. As the camera was panned, electricians moved the boom-mounted lights out of camera range but without altering their effectiveness as the source of illumination. It was an amusing and new kind of show in the studio.

(*American Cinematographer*, August 1959, pp. 478-479.)

20. **Earle Slater.**

This deep into the screenplay, various aspects of the character's behavior and attitudes having been revealed, it seems appropriate to attempt an analytical profile of Earle Slater. Note Earle's words about anger making things easy. They have a ring of familiarity:

> Sometimes, in his room or on the sidewalk, the world seemed to him a strange labyrinth even when the streets were straight and the walls were square; a chaos which made him feel that something in him should be able to understand it, divide it, focus it. But only under the stress of **hate** was the conflict resolved. He had been so conditioned in a cramped environment that hard words or kicks alone knocked him upright and made him capable of action—action that was futile because the world was too much for him. It was then that he closed his eyes and struck out blindly, hitting what or whom he could, not looking or caring what or who hit back.

The words are familiar because Richard Wright used them to describe Bigger Thomas in *Native Son* (p. 278; see discussion of this novel in the critical commentary, pp. 203-207), but they are presciently accurate for Slater's personality profile as well. Wright wrote in "How 'Bigger' Was Born": "What made Bigger's social consciousness most complex was the fact that he was hovering between two worlds—between powerful America and his own stunted place in life—and I took upon myself the task of trying to make the reader feel this No Man's Land. The most that I could say of Bigger was that he felt the *need* for a whole life and *acted* out of that need." It is marvelous irony that these insights about the black protagonist of Wright's novel apply with equal fidelity to Earle Slater, a character whose racism is obsessed with rejecting any suggestion of likeness or mutuality between him and a black person.

Throughout *Native Son* there is but one point of view: Bigger's. Wright "wanted the reader to feel that there was nothing between him and Bigger; that the story was a special *première* given in his own private theater." But in *Odds Against Tomorrow* there is dual attention paid to both Slater and Ingram. Both are portrayed sympathetically and negatively.

> BELAFONTE: Slater is more than just a racist. He is a working class guy in America who get trapped by the system—who does not know how to work his way out of the system—and has bought the story that it is race that is causing him to fail. He doesn't have a job, he's looking for a way out. *He's in exactly the same stuff Ingram's in.*
> (Interview with Author, 2 September 1998.)

In a certain perverse way, Slater is Ingram's double: in their desperation ("They're not going to junk me like an old car."); in their peculiar kind of incoherence and lack of logic ("Can't lose forever."); in their determination to take *some* action ("I got something now, and I'm going to stick with it."); and in their surrender to racial hatred that destroys them both.

> As for the Americans, it was not their cruelty or pessimism which moved us. We recognized in them men who had been swamped, lost in too large a continent, as we were in history, and who tried, without traditions, with the means available, to render their stupor and forlornness in the midst of incomprehensible events.
> (Jean-Paul Sartre, *What Is Literature?*)

What is fascinating is the similarity of the emotional tensions of the Slaters and the Ingrams and all the Bigger Thomases of the world. There is a universality in their situation. All of these personalities feel tense, afraid, nervous, hysterical, and restless. They are all "living in a world whose fundamental assumptions could no longer be taken for granted: a world ridden with national and class strife; a world whose metaphysical meanings had vanished; a world in which

God no longer existed as a daily focal point of men's lives; a world in which men could no longer retain their faith in an ultimate hereafter. It was a highly geared world whose nature was conflict and action, a world whose limited area and vision imperiously urged men to satisfy their organisms, a world that existed on a plane of animal sensation alone." (Wright, "How 'Bigger' Was Born.")

Wright emphasizes throughout *Native Son* that "there were two Biggers," one trapped by environmental determinants and the other aspiring to a better life and a more fully realized self. Likewise, there are two Slaters who comprise a radically divided nature: an unstable personality capable of sudden eruptions of violence (the soldier in the bar, the pistol whipping of the bank manager, the racial virulence toward Ingram)—and the other who is seen in intimately caring moments with the woman he loves, aspiring to a better life.

Robert Ryan.

ROBERT WISE: Bob was a marvelous, marvelous man. The character of Slater was so far from what Bob was himself, just the opposite of the kind of person he himself lived. Very liberal man, no racial feeling at all, one of the nicest actors that I ever worked with. (Interview with Author, 11 Feb 98.)

HARRY BELAFONTE: The person I most admire in that film is really Robert Ryan. Knowing him, his heart and soul, his commitment to truth and justice—he played the villainy of this character with such strength and conviction and with such humanity. And here's a guy who in his gut worked every day against the Slaters of the world. He made his portrayal very believable. (Interview with Author, 2 Sep 98.)

According to Robert Ryan, the role of Earle Slater originally caused him more mental torture and soul searching than any part he had ever done in movies. In a remarkable article in *Ebony* (November 1959, pp. 68-72), "I Didn't Want to Play a Bigot," Ryan explains:

I didn't want to play a bigot in another film for the simple reason that in real life I deeply detest racism of any kind and have opposed its expression and manifestations all my life. From the very outset of negotiations leading to my accepting the role of Slater I had strong misgivings about playing the part of a man who uses such offensive words as "nigger."

However, the more I looked into the script and studied the character of Slater the more I began to feel that he is not a Negro hater exclusively but a man who hates the whole human race.

Psychologically Slater is an interesting type. His resentment of Ingram (Harry Belafonte) was conditioned not alone by his background but peculiarly provoked by the kind of Negro he finds himself involved with. It just so happens that this young Negro is better looking, better dressed, more intelligent; is, in fact, everything that Slater would like to be but isn't. All this helps to intensify Slater's racial feeling.

I changed my mind about playing Slater after re-reading the script and appreciating its excellent qualities. The script shows that the character Ingram, generally considered to belong to a so-called "inferior" racial group in our society, emerges as the most dignified, intelligent and superior person in the drama.

Odds Against Tomorrow says something of real significance and says it well, dramatically, without preaching. The script was balanced, perceptive and provocative. For one thing it doesn't claim that racial feeling is all on one side. The character played by Belafonte has deep feelings of antagonism toward white people. Such feelings do exist among many Negroes and are perfectly normal, natural reactions to the way they have been and are treated by many whites.

21. The Melville-Wise Connection.
"The surprise cut to the front of a speeding bus" was another particularly gratifying moment in *Odds* for the French director Jean-Pierre Melville (see Annotation #2).

ROBERT WISE: The concern is always with the way you deliver things. I like it whenever we can shake the audience up a little bit—a shock cut—move it along, give it a goose. And this transition is one of them. [See Annotation #13 for a discussion of another example of shock editing.]

QUESTION: This kind of editing evidently is part of the reason why the film enjoys such a high reputation in Europe. Were you aware of the praise from Jean-Pierre Melville?

WISE: Oh, he was a big fan, I know. Matter of fact I met him once when I was in Europe. An actor friend of mine, Richard Crenna, was doing a film for him [*Un Flic* (1972), Melville's last film], and he told me that Melville's such a fan of mine, and so I went out to the studio with him one day and met Melville. With great pride he took me into the projection room to show me part of a reel he had shot, a moment from one of his own movies. The interest was actually in the sound itself, some kind of a door closing, I think. This was a sound that he had taken from one of my pictures and had used in one of his. It might not have been in this last picture he did, but he was very proud of the fact that he had taken the sound effect out of one of my pictures. (Interview with Author, 11 February 1998.)

22. A Cinematographic Challenge.

"The most challenging part of the assignment, perhaps, was an important exterior sequence which, in the story, was to start at 4:30 p.m. in full daylight and continue into full night, with continuous action on the part of the three principal actors. Director Wise, who rarely uses dissolves for editorial transitions [see Annotation #13], wanted continuous photographic progression over the whole sequence without resorting to dissolves. Extremely careful planning and a long streak of bad weather enabled us to achieve this interesting sequence. As a result audiences will actually witness the end of a day and the birth of a night in its full progression." (Joseph Brun, "*Odds Against Tomorrow*," *American Cinematographer*, August 1959, p. 479.)

23. *Music:* Guitar and strings imitate ticking clock as trombones and trumpets build tension, matched with shots of the bank's clock. [Myrick]

24. Language.

Ingram's line in the shooting script at this point is: "You dirty stinking white." This was changed on the set to "You bastard." Robert Wise: "There's a thing that happened that I find so interesting, in view of the freedom we have for language on the screen. Belafonte is at Ryan's throat, pushing him against the wall, and says, "You bastard." But they didn't like that, so I put a dog's barking over it so you couldn't really hear it cleanly. He says it but it's like he's mouthing it. [Once alerted to this moment, one can easily discern the word.] I got away with it." (Interview with Author, 11 February 1998.)

25. *Music:* Typani and jazz cymbals counter in tense rhythm with snare drum sounding march rolls underneath. [Myrick]

26. *Music:* Cymbal crescendo builds tension to climax. [Myrick]

27. The Ending: Modern Myth or Anti-Myth.

"From the eve of war to the society of consumption, the tone has changed. A savage lyricism hurls us into a world in complete decomposition, ruled by debauchery and brutality; to the intrigues of these wild beasts and spectres, [the filmmakers] bring the most radical of solutions: nuclear apocalypse."
—Raymond Borde and Eugene Chaumeton,
Panorama du Film Noir Américain

This analysis of the ending of *Kiss Me Deadly* can extend relevantly to the analogous endings of *White Heat* and *Odds Against Tomorrow*.

White Heat (1949, directed by Raoul Walsh, screenplay by Ivan Goff and Ben Roberts) ends with Cody Jarrett, "one of film noir's most crippled and maladjusted protagonists," shooting it out with police from the top of a huge tank of explosive gas. Consistent with the film's perceived strategy of audaciously encouraging the post-WWII audience to accept a psychotic protagonist, "a tragic grandeur . . . is achieved . . . in Cody's delirious and explosive *self-immolation* atop a metallic pyre." (Blake Lucas, *Film Noir*, p. 312.)

Kiss Me Deadly (1955, directed by Robert Aldrich, screenplay by A.I. Bezzerides) moves film noir from the personal, self-imposed, suicidal madness of Cody Jarrett into the political implications of a nuclear-age Pandora's box of technology gone wrong. Lily Carver opens the box, and the radioactive material sets her on fire and begins a chain reaction which, in Alain Silver's words, "becomes the purifying fire that reduces the nether world of *Kiss Me Deadly* to radioactive ash."

Odds Against Tomorrow emphatically continues the relentless movement toward "complete decomposition." From an authorial perspective, it reflects the vision of Abraham Polonsky found in *Force of Evil*, which rejects a "reformist framework" in favor of a process of revenge. Polonsky puts his existential spin on a Marxist set-up: "Like corporate liberals, the left looked to the environment for the causes of crime, but to them, these causes were part and parcel of the system, not accidents of poor social engineering. Describing the experience of watching Walsh's *White Heat* in prison, where he was serving a one-year sentence for contempt of Congress, unfriendly witness John Howard Lawson wrote [in *Film in the Battle of Ideas*] that many of his fellow inmates 'recognize that the forces which drove them to vice or crime are inherent in our present social system.' *Force of Evil* does the same. . . . According to Polonsky, he wanted to finish up on a pessimistic note, with Joe's recognition of his own moral disintegration. Polonsky rejected the implication . . . that one man can save the system. . . . The concept of social control is essentially irrelevant to Polonsky, because it implies a society worth salvaging. Despite its jaundiced view of capitalism, however, *Force of Evil* doesn't revert to the rather simpleminded environmentalism of late-thirties films like *You Only Live Once* (1937). The system may corrupt Joe, but it doesn't excuse him." [Peter Biskind, *Seeing is Believing: How Hollywood Taught Us to Stop Worrying and Love the Fifties* (New York: Pantheon Books, 1983), p. 196.]

In *Odds Against Tomorrow* the combat is not projected on the field of internal madness or political ideology, but on the platform of personal hatred. This pits Polonsky's vision against the rapprochement that William McGivern contrived for the source novel, and it preserves a toughness that even Richard Wright's *Native Son* (an ongoing benchmark reference in the critical commentary) fails to sustain.

Note that murderer Bigger Thomas, at the end of *Native Son* (discussed in the critical commentary, pp. 203-207), is able to experience a vision of human solidarity in which all people "touch" one another:

> Slowly he lifted his hands in darkness and held them in mid-air, the fingers spread weakly open. If he reached out with his hands, and if his hands were electric wires, and if his heart were a battery giving life and fire to those hands, and if he reached out with his hands and touched other people, reached out through those stone walls and felt other hands connected with other hearts—if he did that, would there be a reply, a shock? . . . And in that touch, response of recognition, there would be union, identity; there would be a supporting oneness, a wholeness which had been denied him all his life. (Wright, *Native Son*, pp. 419-420.)

As a result of his momentary wholeness, Bigger can tentatively reach out to the world in love rather than violence:

Another impulse rose in him, born of desperate need, and his mind clothed it in an image of a strong blinding sun sending hot rays down and he was standing in the midst of a vast crowd of men, white men and black men and all men, and the sun's rays melted away the differences, the colors, the clothes, and drew what was common and good upward toward the sun. . . .

Had he killed Mary and Bessie and brought sorrow to his mother and sister and put himself in the shadow of the electric chair only to find this out? Had he been blind all along? (Wright, *Native Son*, p. 420.)

There is none of this in *Odds Against Tomorrow*. As in all Polonsky narratives, there is a chilly lack of sentimentality.

ROBERT WISE: We were too close on the heels of *The Defiant Ones* [1958], where the two came together at the end. I didn't think we could make a film about the same racial problem, and have the same resolution where they get together. I wasn't comfortable with that. I didn't like that. It seemed to be too pat somehow. But we could get the same message over by doing the reverse, by having them both get lost in the holocaust at the end there. And by doing that say "hate destroys." This is what happens when you have this kind of hatred. Nobody wins. (Interview with Author, 11 February 1998.)
[See Sergio Leeman, *Robert Wise On His Films: From Editing Chair to Director's Chair* (Los Angeles: Silman-James Press, 1995).]

The *White Heat/Kiss Me Deadly/Odds* trinity has produced a rather large pile of collective rubble with their holocaustal endings. But with Ingram and Slater performing their final dissolute and cruel ballet, and by the film resolutely avoiding the *deus ex machina* of "brotherhood-of-man" contrivance, *Odds* sits atop the apocalyptic wreckage with distinction.

28. No Exit.
"Strange angular piles of smoking metal . . . a shattered, not quite real world . . . and there is WIND . . . as in the beginning . . . "

Existentialism was despairingly humanist rather than perversely anarchic, and it had a different attitude toward violence; thus if the surrealists saw the Hollywood thriller as a theater of cruelty, the existentialists saw it as an absurdist novel. For critics who were influenced by existentialism, film noir was especially attractive because it depicted **a world of obsessive return, dark corners,** and *huis clos.*

(James Naremore, "American Film Noir," p. 20.)

All the dystopian markers are there in the post-explosion scene: dark corners and dead ends; apocalyptic rubble with no exits; and the obsessive, oppressive presence of the wind—a recurring motif symbolizing wasteland desiccation, sterility, and (through its identification with Slater) racial hatred.

29. *Music:* Tension is resolved with counterpoint between flute, vibes, horns, and guitar. [Myrick]

30. **End of the Line.**
Music: Wind machine and guitar return to opening counterpoint motif, then slide into a quartet shuffle during closing credits. [Myrick]

The following is another segment from the "Film Noir" episode of *American Cinema* (1994):

ALBERT BEZZERIDES [Screenwriter, *Kiss Me Deadly*]: I think our world is heading for chaos, and not very many people seem to be shivering about it. We should be all shivering in our boots right now. I was so tired of gangster pictures by then, I'd seen them all, that I thought a new feeling should be put into [*Kiss Me Deadly*]—and I made it more political. I think that writers shouldn't separate themselves from their reality; they should bring the reality into what they are doing. At that time in the '50s the nuclear stuff was new, and it was kind of frightening what was going on.

[Bezzerides's comments play over visuals from *Kiss Me Deadly*: Pat Murphy (Wesley Addy) intoning nuclear age buzz words—"Manhattan Project," "Los Alamos," "Trinity."]

I was affected strongly by what I read in the newspapers, the comments I heard on the radio and television, and these somehow got into the story. And I think a story of this kind should have that kind of feeling, because we're living in a world, we're not living in a movie. The motion picture should reflect the world in some way, and I tried to do that.

[Extract Shown: the ending of *Kiss Me Deadly* (1955)—the "cleansing" explosion. The following words by Paul Schrader apply just as accurately to *Odds Against Tomorrow* (1959).]

SCHRADER: *Kiss Me Deadly* obviously ends with the holocaust. The doomed character finally finds the bomb—and the world is over. . . . It's just a matter of these doomed characters: when are they finally going to explode . . . and take the world with them. It's the end of the line. You can't go much further.

Schrader here is reprising his analysis, from "Notes on Film Noir," of what he calls **third-phase noir films**, "which were painfully self-aware; they seemed to know they stood at the end of a long tradition based on despair and disintegration and did not shy away from the fact. . . . The third phase is rife with end-of-the-line noir heroes." [*Film Noir Reader*, pp. 59-61.]

The DEAD END icon—the last image of *Odds Against Tomorrow*, which is the last emblematic work of the classic film noir phase—literally signifies (linguistically, philosophically, generically) the end of the line.

Unholy Alliance. "*Odds Against Tomorrow* is a seedy, unpleasant take on life in America in the late 1950s. The French like this one, what with racial hatred, hair-trigger violence, tramp wives, bleak highways, lonesome landscape, wet, dark streets. The U.S.A. at its best. There is a great deal of truth in this one, though, and, as usual, that's hard to take."

—Barry Gifford, *The Devil Thumbs A Ride*.

Noir Motivation. Bacco (Will Kuluva, right) strikes Ingram (Harry Belafonte) with a string of pearls, which leaves its mark while the pearls "cannonade around everywhere, falling like glittering hail all over the room." In William McGivern's source novel, *Odds Against Tomorrow* (Dodd, Mead, 1957), Johnny Ingram "had a terror of being beaten; it was an old fear; it had been with him all his life." In Abraham Polonsky's screenplay, Ingram's motivation for involvement in the caper becomes extra-personal and more significant. Bacco to Ingram: "Have that dough at my place tomorrow night or I'll collect it from you or that ex-wife of yours or your kid."

Music and Utopia. "John Lewis [of the Modern Jazz Quartet] wrote the excellent music score performed by a large orchestra which includes Milt Jackson, *vibs*; Percy Heath, *bass*; Connie Kay, *drs*; Bill Evans, *pno*; and Jim Hall, *gtr*." (See David Meeker, *Jazz in the Movies*.)

It is often the function of musical numbers to express the utopian desire that the characters cannot fulfill in their lives. There is a psychological appeal of jazz improvisation. "Can we *talk* our way out of a tight spot, dance away from trouble? A fetish figure, the *Janus Dog*, received urgent requests from Kongolese petitioners hammering nails into it in the form of one nail per wish." Here, in the wake of Bacco's violent threats, Ingram bangs frenziedly on the vibraharp— seeking therapeutic release in his cacophony, "playing off the big blow-up in him which is tearing him apart." (See Alfred Appel, *The Art of Celebration: Twentieth-Century Painting, Literature, Sculpture, Photography, and Jazz.*)

The integration of **multiple and parallel sets of characters and family relationships** is a structural signature of Abraham Polonsky screenplays. "One of the key elements or discoveries in the modern aesthetic is the unfinished work. There's a whole bunch of unfinished stories going on with plenty of push behind them because of what's hanging on the characters. And never any attempt to tie anything up, ever. Things just kind of go on, and bounce off one another, and suddenly the film is over." (Abraham Polonsky)

Helen Svenson & Esmarelda Villalobos. Helen (Gloria Grahame), with "a pervy-erotic fascination with murder," says to Earle Slater: "How did it feel when you killed that man?" This is an often-cited Polonsky scene by critics, perhaps second only to his "Everybody dies" (*Body and Soul*), and is quoted (purloined?) years later by Quentin Tarantino in *Pulp Fiction* (1994), when taxi driver Esmarelda says to Butch: "You are the first person I ever met who has killed somebody. So, what was it like to kill a man?"

[Polonsky's films have been a reservoir of inspiration for others in a variety of contexts: *Body and Soul*—for Tarantino again in *Pulp Fiction*, as the stimulus for the moment when Butch in the dressing room comes out of the flashback; *Force of Evil*—for Francis Ford Coppola in *The Godfather* films (1972, 1974: "It's only business"), and for Oliver Stone in *Wall Street* (1987, pervasive narrative allusions (snaffling?), which extend also to a *Body and Soul* appropriation: "It's all bucks, kid. The rest is conversation.").]

CRITICAL COMMENTARY

Odds Against Tomorrow:
Film Noir Without Linguistic Irony

by John Schultheiss

"Don't beat out that Civil War jazz, Slater. We're all in this together, each man equal and we're taking care of each other. It's one big play, a one and only chance to grab stakes forever, and I don't want to hear what your grandpappy thought on the old farm in Oklahoma. You got it?"

"Well, I'm with you, Dave. Like you say, it's just one roll of the dice. Doesn't matter what color they are, so's they come up seven."

[*Odds Against Tomorrow*, 93]

In 1959, Harry Belafonte's own company, HarBel Productions, in association with Max Youngstein, a young producer at United Artists who was attracted to politically challenging independent films, released *Odds Against Tomorrow*, a crime story with socially conscious overtones, which historians of the genre have concluded is the last significant work of the classic black and white film noir period.[1] The theme is integration—or else. Belafonte found the source novel by William P. McGivern,[2] and saw it as a cautionary tale about the racism that might "rip apart our destiny together."[3]

A significant group of talents had to be organized for this project, and in his efforts as producer—the only African American in this capacity at the time—Harry Belafonte would successfully circumvent the Hollywood timidity that had weakened earlier black material, including his own few films. Belafonte would select director Robert Wise, whose earlier works, such as *The Curse of the Cat People*, *The Set-Up*, *Born to Kill*, and *The Captive City*, demonstrated his facility with somber themes in both expressionistic and realistic idioms. John Oliver Killens, a black novelist and friend of Belafonte's, was engaged to act as a front for Abraham Polonsky, who would write the screenplay. Polonsky, whose previous recognized credit was *I Can*

Get It for You Wholesale (1951), was blacklisted, and received no further official feature film credit until *Madigan* (1968). His fronted screenplay (Nelson Gidding's name also would eventually be included in the cover writing credits) fused a social conscience with crime melodrama. Indeed, as a realistic genre film with social significance, *Odds Against Tomorrow*, in Belafonte's proud memory, "changed the face of Hollywood forever."[4]

Analytical Summary

Here is a narrative synopsis of *Odds Against Tomorrow* which forgathers, as an outline for the critical discussion (**key concepts in bold**), issues of theme and genre, elements of style, concepts of hero, and continuities of literary and film tradition that will be addressed more extensively at appropriate points below:

Dave Burke, Earle Slater, and Johnny Ingram are **existentially challenged**. Each in his own circumstances of relentless futility, like Sisyphus at the foot of the mountain, has continually managed to "find his burden." They, like other dramatis personae of the **roman noir** and **film noir**—functioning here stylistically within a **Third Stream musical (jazz)** ambiance and a visual landscape akin to **modernist poetry**— will conclude that the only relief from their burden will be found in **crime**. The film is a grim foray into the disjointed lives of this trio of losers, and in the criminal perspectives of these **noir protagonists**, especially those of Ingram and Slater, resides the central dramatic momentum of the narrative.

BURKE (Ed Begley), the organizer of the bank robbery caper, is an ex-policeman who had been on the force 30 years, who had his own squad and knew everybody. In a "session with the State Crime Committee I got a year for contempt . . . because I wouldn't talk. Everybody was my friend until they needed a patsy." [22]

(Polonsky's choices here of the words "Committee" and "contempt" are redolent of the lexicon of the **blacklisting** era; the refusal to talk and the reference to "patsy" are indicative of the Hollywood sell-out ritual, the process which Polonsky himself was currently experiencing, the process which necessitated the fronting of his screenplay by Killens and

Gidding. These details are consistent with the evocative blacklisting motifs that are a continuing thread in Polonsky's novels, feature scripts, and teleplays.[5])

Burke was a fall-guy, and now he lives in a cheap hotel near Riverside Drive with a police dog for a partner. "I got to get out of this trap. They've kicked my head in." [33] [These bracketed numbers in the text are references to the pages of the *Odds Against Tomorrow* screenplay in this volume.]

SLATER (Robert Ryan) is a dour, hard-bitten ex-convict and racist. But his **racism** is merely one facet of a sociopathic personality prone to impulsive acts of violence and fits of self-doubt and despondency. Blown off the land in Oklahoma during the Depression, he has been running all of his life. When something was started, "right away I'd blow it." And somebody was always victimizing him—"a lousy captain, a Polack foreman in the auto works." It seems as if the world is constantly trying to "junk [Slater] like an old car." The only time things get easy are "when I get mad. Then they get too easy. I think that's why I get mad. To make it easy." [96] But he is getting old, and if he does not make it now, he never will. Burke is offering him a (criminal) opportunity, and this time he is going to stick with it. Slater's "convoluted reasoning is both pathetic and ironic."[6]

INGRAM (Harry Belafonte), in a major departure from the way the character was conceived in the **source novel by William McGivern**, is a musician, a nightclub entertainer. He is described by Polonsky as wearing "fine, conservative, and expensive clothes. His face is delicate, calm, the face of someone who has learned to live within his weakness and strength, one who no longer tries. There is nothing restless or urgent about him. His elegance is part of his character." [25-26]

But he is also an **African American noir protagonist** who is free-wheeling and too fast with a buck, a self-destructive gambler, deeply in debt to a vicious gangland loan shark—"way past the liferopes and praying for a miracle." [31] Ingram is a charismatic presence, less of a criminal than the others, but exuding **film noir ambiguity**. He very much loves his young daughter and his estranged wife, but his gambling has so polluted the quality of family life that his wife has rejected him for the sake of the daughter.

Ingram's warm instincts for his family consistently emerge, but, like Slater, he is capable of expressing racial hatred toward his wife's "ofay" (a derogatory term for whites) friends. A noir narrative begins to touch the edges of a **social-problem text ["protest" literature or cinema]**[7] as the black protagonist explodes cynically: "You and your big white brothers. Drink enough tea with 'em and stay out of the watermelon patch and maybe our little colored girl will grow up to be Miss America, is that it?" In a man of such dignity and strength, this emerges disturbingly as a touch of self-pity or self-hatred: "Why don't you wise up. It's their world and we're just living in it." [83]

Ingram had initially rejected Burke's caper idea for what appeared to be both practical and moral reasons: "It's not your line, Dave. That's the firing squad. That's for junkies and joy boys. We're people." [32] But he is susceptible to the criminal enterprise as the result of coercion by the gangster Bacco, who threatens both his wife and daughter: "Have that dough at my place tomorrow night or I'll kill you and everything you own." [55]

Thus, these characters have been drawn to each other more by the commonality of bitterness and failure than by the holiness of their cause.

In the **"morally oriented gangster film"** (Colin McArthur's phrase), the careful planning and execution of a large-scale robbery remains secondary to the examination of character and obsession and the evocation of mood. "It became the prototype of a series of films throughout the 1950s in which a group of men from various backgrounds, some criminal, some nearly so, some respectable, but all with special skills, come together for the purpose of the robbery, the rewards of which they are kept from enjoying by internal tensions and, sometimes, a malicious fate."[8] This defines exactly the milieu in *Odds Against Tomorrow*, where the tension that finally wrecks the group's cohesion and purpose is the irresolvable racial conflict between Slater and Ingram.

Slater has no desire to cooperate with Ingram on equal terms, and Ingram has no intention of working in a subservient position. So the men are at a stand-off, each asserting his individual sense of pride and social attitudes with equal force. Having unwittingly created this potent racial situation, Burke must now act as the restraining force—making it clear to both that he has no time for racial prejudice, because such antipathies will only jeopardize the success of the whole operation.[9]

Indeed, because of Slater's selfish cowardice and thoughtless action, the robbery is reduced to chaos, with Burke, seriously wounded, committing suicide. In what is both the climax of the wrecked mission itself and the climactic moment of racial confrontation, Ingram (motivated by revengeful anger) and Slater (by fear) turn on each other. Given both men's experiences and temperaments, neither can survive the outcome. Slater and Ingram, white and black, face each other in classic duel position with revolvers on top of gas-storage tanks—and together explode themselves out of existence. The indistinguishability of the charred corpses in the final shot comprises both racial irony and moral coda: "the useless destructive aftermath of hate." [134][10]

That the conflict can only be resolved in violence reflects both the tendency of the genre as well as the specific racial context. "At this narrative level, the film is effective and radical, in that the conventional liberal-racial theme is an organic part of the genre's workings. In other words, it is not simply a racial movie operating separately from popular genre conventions (which clearly previous racial presentations and most subsequent ones are); *Odds Against Tomorrow* is outstanding, equally in terms of the gangster motif and in terms of the evolutionary racial motif. The film's use of rounded characterization gives texture to the principal characters' racial as well as non-racial motivations. This represents a significant deviation from the usual racial depictions of the 1950s and 1960s."[11]

Film and Poetry

Unreal City,
Under the brown fog of a winter dawn,
A crowd flowed . . . , so many,
I had not thought death had undone so many.
—T.S. Eliot, "The Waste Land"[12]

The wind floods with immense force. . . .
Underscoring music accompanies. It is in a modern,
moody, sometimes progressive jazz vein, carrying
an overtone of premonition, of tragedy—of people
in trouble and doomed.
[*Odds Against Tomorrow*, 14]

Wind. Music. The dark poetry of the city.

These textured elements are established from the beginning as part of the tight embroidery of Abraham Polonsky's screenplay of *Odds Against Tomorrow*. They become objective correlatives awakening subjective emotion throughout the narrative. They are motifs reflecting the inevitability of the film's title for the destinies of the troubled and doomed protagonists.

Music. Wind.

"The music will be a continuing and highly expressive voice in the story," Polonsky writes, in that same first scene—essential for the modernistic interstices of concept and emotion. "Often guitar and vibes, or piano and guitar, will counter each other, while at other times the quartet will engage in a swing shuffle, with orchestral brass, strings, and tympani sounding dissonant progressions in opposition, at times resulting in a manic crescendo of despair." Composer John Lewis, of the Modern Jazz Quartet, creates a moody counterpoint between wind machine and a harp-like guitar, reflecting the film's "build up of desperate tension, resulting in futility and hopelessness." [See Martin Myrick's separate essay on the film score in this volume, the source of these quotations.]

Indeed the screenplay text and the produced film do objectify, in Polonsky's poetic and premonitory phrase, "an arena in which the wind can drive and shake the howl."

> The gray sky looked as if it had been rubbed with
> a soiled eraser. It held no angels, flaming crosses,
> olive-bearing doves, wheels within wheels.
> Only a newspaper struggled in the air like a kite
> with a broken spine.
> —Nathanael West, *Miss Lonelyhearts*[13]

The cinematic, dream-like poetry begins with the credits— abstract expressionistic patterns, kaleidoscopic graphics. Then the jarring and sensuous opening images of the film: the buildings, trash cans, water in a gutter shimmering in the sun, newspapers and piping gulls riding the wind. The visual and the aural orchestration "pitches characters and settings into mysterious emotional geometries," so as to make us realize that a crime film is, when authored as astutely as this one, "a species of pure cinema in the same way that the motion picture camera is especially well suited to rituals of alienation."[14]

As in the musical counterpoint, there is a richly elaborated opposition between the realistic backgrounds of New York and the stylized treatment they receive. This is the stuff of modern poetry, "the poetry of the commonplace." When William Carlos Williams wrote:

> *so much depends*
> *upon*
> a red wheel
> barrow
>
> glazed with rain
> water
>
> beside the white
> chickens.[15]

or when Vladimir Nabokov wrote:

> "We sit down and I start telling my friend about utility
> pipes, streetcars, and *other important matters*."[16]

they are alerting us to the importance of quotidian beauty; for so much *does* depend on our ability and our willingness to see the world around us, to be aware of tone, of contrast, of unpretentious things, to appreciate the difference between design and accident.

Quotidian beauty is essayed in *Odds Against Tomorrow* by bestowing an aura of the marvelous upon ordinary urban decor. Louis Aragon has written that American crime films "speak of daily life and manage to raise to a dramatic level a banknote on which our attention is riveted, a table with a revolver on it, a bottle that on occasion becomes a weapon, a handkerchief that reveals a crime, a typewriter that's the horizon of a desk."[17]

In *Odds Against Tomorrow*, Aragon would have appreciated the visceral prominence of a chain on a bank door. (Slater: "That's right. The chippie is the chain." [91]) This object is the dramatic centerpiece of the robbery caper itself, and is a talisman of Ingram's intelligence and creativity. With no counterpart in the McGivern novel this is Polonsky's invention, a salient ingredient in the transformation of the book's Ingram character, a marvelous elevation of the ordinary to the dramatically significant.

Aragon, who was writing a piece of surrealist film criticism "On Decor," would have also celebrated a man whose face is "splotched with a wine-colored birthmark," [16] "the geometry of traffic" [42; see annotation #11]; a string of pearls striking Ingram across the face, cannonading, "falling like glittering hail all over the room" [54]; a slow, spectral zoom into the town of Melton, the activity of night beginning on the street, the music cutting off abruptly—a moment of dead silence—and then a deep, reverberating note: Burke walking forcefully up to the camera, which begins to track with him at the exact moment that he reaches it. A clock tolls. [113-114]

To the extent that Polonsky's screenplay resonates this poetry of the commonplace, it puts into practice his "Utopian Experiment," a theory of screenwriting, a direction "toward compression, density, structure, elegance, metaphor, synthesis, magnitude, and variety, all held within a unified verbal structure. I am, of course, speaking of poetry, and the literary form I have in mind for the screenplay is the poem. . . . which would guide the attention through concrete images (as in metaphor); which instead of stage directing the action would express it; which instead of summarizing character and motive would actually present them as data."[18]

Director Robert Wise's involvement in reciprocating Polonsky's poetic approach to the screenplay is evident from the opening shots of the film, in which some infrared photography helps establish the "overtone of premonition, of tragedy, of people in trouble and doomed." [14] Wise: "Infrared film tends to turn blue skies kind of blackish and white clouds very unreal. It's a very moody feeling, and I used it in a few of those shots in the beginning. I wanted to stamp the picture visually from the very beginning, when we had the wind going, with a deep, heavy mood. . . . And then I used it again, outside of Hudson later in the picture, when they were sitting around waiting to do the bank job. It could be effective at shooting somebody's back, while they were waiting in the dark, the clock. It just heightens a dramatic mood somehow more than regular black and white film. I didn't want the look to be polished, braced up and glossy."[19]

The sky explodes with light . . . the sky in which piping gulls ride the wind. Now suddenly, a little black boy appears, five or six years old. He is holding his outstretched arms like bat wings, and he is running before the sweep of the wind, letting it carry him along so that he seems to himself to fly. . . . There is the wind, and along the side a line of black and white children, one after another swooping along in the wind, their coats open like wings. Their voices pipe high like gull cries. The last flyer is a black girl. . . . She seems to jump aloft, so lightly do her giant flying steps take her, and she tumbles into Earle. Tight two shot of Earle and the girl, with her in his arms.

SLATER
You lil pickaninny, you goin' to kill yourself
flyin' like that, yes you are.
[*Odds Against Tomorrow*, 15]

Polonsky now layers the opening with bird imagery. "Created, as related in Genesis, on the fifth day, the bird with its gift of flight symbolizes all human hopes for physical, emotional, psychological, and spiritual transport—for ecstasy and transcendence."[20] Slater's hopes have been raised (by Burke's summons), and his expression "is now alive with pleasure in the wind." [14-15]   But what a dark foreshadowing of the destructive end for all of them is contained in the collision between Slater and the little black girl, who is arrested in her flight.   Slater smiles and "his face is naked, soft, yet touched with willfulness"—and he compresses all their destinies into a single, tragic, prophetic conceit: the attempts to fly will end in death.   He will stop Ingram's hopes just as he impedes the little girl—his first words shape a presentiment for the consequences of a virulent racism.

For Ingram, the possibility for transcendence and the premonition of tragedy are also symbolized by birds.   This striking moment occurs at roughly the end of the first act, and its visceral effect and dramatic significance are, like most of these ineffable details, impossible to paraphrase. Burke has joined Bacco in the park to discuss Ingram.   Bacco is standing in a dark coat and hat "like St. Francis among the beasts feeding a flock of pigeons."   The two men begin to discuss the subject of Johnny Ingram.   Fatalistically, Burke's intervention on Johnny's behalf portends conjunctively financial salvation and physical destruction for both of them.   These complex implications are contained in Polonsky's remarkable closure to the scene. With no further words spoken, this:

"Burke moves closer to Bacco with a sudden seriousness, while around the birds shatter the air with wings."
DISSOLVE [37]

A powerful, poetic metaphor: Burke's sudden movement gives flight to hope; the same movement seals their fates. There is an oneiric logic and impact to the transition—elliptical and shocking—the augmented fluttering of the wings terminates further conversation, blurring into the light of the next shot, "pale, a little blue, shimmering with dust and haze." [37] Polonsky designed this in the script, but the Wise rendering of it obviously exceeds verbal description.

Patterns of images like these, embedded in the text, not symptomatic of usual linear storytelling, cut the symbols loose from their moorings. Symbolism, at its most successful, contrives to communicate emotions by images whose connection with the subject and whose relevance to one another we may not always understand. According to critic Edmund Wilson, "instead of disentangling a complex emotion into a series of varying moods," this method of symbolism "telescopes the whole thing by a few stenographic strokes. . . . Instead of attempting to reduce an unearthly elusive sensation to the lucidity of simple language—invents for it a vocabulary and a syntax as unfamiliar as the sensation itself."[21]

Perhaps not of the same degree of poetic subtlety as these more recessive motifs, there are other poetic images in the film more conventionally conveyed, which nevertheless offer character insight and are contemplative of deeper figurative meanings.

There is an especially rich montage episode before the robbery sequence, somberly established by Polonsky: "The underscoring rises, bringing with it a mood of anxiety and loneliness, as each man waits out on his own the crawling minutes before zero hour." Ingram's introspection—Polonsky's description, Wise's visualization, Lewis's music—evokes, of course in more contracted fashion, *Paterson* by William Carlos Williams[22] and the wasteland imagery of T.S. Eliot:

"He stares at the water, the slow turn and fill of the ride
washing between the rotting piles, wooden boxes tippling in the
water, dead branches, a whiskey bottle. . . . The current pushes
a mass of boards intertwined with old rags and rope into the
pilings of the wharf. Bobbing along with it, caught in the loose
cordage, is a small figure. There is a red dress, dark hair
plastered across a pink face, yet all obscure, recognizable and
shapeless at the same time."   [111-112][23]

When asked about the approach of finding poetic possibilities in everyday, banal experience, Polonsky replies: "There is no such thing as 'everyday' in life. It all has possibilities for profound communication. While this sequence does not advance the narrative in a linear fashion, it does advance the story in the sense that it deepens the characters; it shows the realms of being in the characters. This is an opportunity to explore their existential and philosophical existence, working on both an intellectual and an aesthetic level. The aesthetics of a work of art plays the same role as the mathematics which are basic to the scientific description of the nature of events. And the aesthetic function gets rid of the unimportant things, and introduces elements which are *apparently* unimportant but very significant. This is what poets do. That's why they write poetry instead of equations."[24]

In the same montage episode, the physical landscape—an inscription on a statue in a park—seems to summarize Burke's internal resolve:

WHATSOEVER THY HAND
FINDETH TO DO
DO IT
WITH THY MIGHT [111]

And, as the montage builds, the next scene in the field, conveyed exclusively through images, provides an additional confirmation of, indeed crystallizes, Slater's mental instability [112-113].

What is so extraordinary is that with this sequence the film is prepared to commit three long minutes of screen time—a remarkable poetic tapestry, devoid of dialogue—to making palpable the psychic minutiae of these three desperate men.

The Waste Land Paradigm. "The Waste Land" (1922) by T.S. Eliot, widely and variously imitated by other poets, copiously analyzed, is undoubtedly the most famous and influential poem written in English during the first half of the 20th century. This work, along with other Eliot poems like "The Hollow Men" (1925) and "The Love Song of J. Alfred Prufrock" (1917), is seen as a study of sterility as a state of being.[25] It compels an analogy between two central images: a modern city and a desert. In the natural landscape the land is unfruitful. The soil is sandy and easily dispersed by the wind. Desolation is reflected in scenes of dry grass and cracked earth. With the two images (linked together by the symbol of the Fisher King), the poem might be said to be about a king whose city has become, or is becoming, a desert. The key to reading the poem is getting at the implications of the desert metaphor by means of an analysis of the *kinds of lives led by the city-dwellers.*

It is *Odds Against Tomorrow*'s concern with sterility in this social order, in the landscape, and in the destructive relationships of the men that prompts discussion of the wasteland conceit. The film, produced almost a half-century after Eliot's early poems, is a cinematic dramatization of the symptoms and causes of the modern temper in literature and art: anxiety, insecurity, radical doubts about human freedom and human dignity, a sense of incompleteness, impermanence and incoherence, the lack of a spiritual center, compass, or equilibrium, the inability to communicate with one another.

The desert image frames the poem by its appearances in the first and last sections. The same structure for the film: from the first shot to the final shot, the wind is a relentless, desiccating presence—symbolically shriveling the possibilities for racial harmony. It began laying waste to Slater's soul, "when I can first remember, when the wind blew us off the land in Oklahoma" [96], and he seems to bring this withering wind with him into the hotel and into the elevator with the African American operator, who comments on the wind howling in the shaft. Polonsky writes, "The car rattles and the wind screams," and Wise tracks the camera more closely to Earle—as if to provide sensory indexing of his desiccant character. [18] Slater's impact is to dry up the positive spiritual essence of every environment he's in. And his (and Ingram's) monument is to be found in the literal desert at the end: a fence is buckled, "charred, distorted, its regular pattern all out of kilter, with strange angular piles of smoking metal stacked behind it, evoking a shattered, not quite real world."

And there is WIND there, driving and howling as in the
beginning long ago on Riverside Drive. [133]

The first section of "The Waste Land," entitled "The Burial of the Dead," also the title of the Anglican burial service, sets the tone of the poem as a recitation of grief and lamentation. Various characters and scenes are introduced which are allusively symptomatic of the living death of the 20th-century wasteland. The inability of the inhabitants to communicate with one another results in "tedious argument/Of insidious intent" ("Prufrock," lines 8-9). People do not talk to one another. They recite monologues for which there are no answers. They are unable to love. Sexual relationships are a combination of lust and boredom.

In *Odds Against Tomorrow*, it's not just the horses who have their noses bobbed [47]; most attempts at communication are ineffectual, frustrated, truncated:

Bacco to Ingram: "You're saying what to me?" [53]
Ruth to Ingram: "I won't listen when you talk like that." [83]
Kitty to Ingram: "It was better when you wanted it." [49]
Lorry to Slater: "I'm just like the rest of them. I keep telling you how
   to live and not letting you be what you are." [95]
Helen to Slater: "How did it feel when you killed that man?" [87]
Slater to Ted: "I said just gas." [99]
Burke to Slater: "But Johnny's supposed to get the car . . ." [124]
Slater (regarding) Burke: "He sure ain't going to talk now." [130]
Ingram to Slater: "You bastard!" [130]

   The title of section II of "The Waste Land"—"A Game of
Chess"—is suggested by a play by Thomas Middleton, which was an
expression of the anti-Catholic, anti-Spanish sentiment prevalent in
England in 1624. This "protest" play is designed as a chess game, in
which the Protestant, English faction is symbolized by white; the
Catholic, Spanish faction by black. The color symbolism of the racial
conflict in *Odds Against Tomorrow* is self-evident. (See more extended
discussion of color symbolism and linguistic ironies below, pp. 213-219.)
   Eliot (III: "The Fire Sermon") is a firm believer that in order to
live profitably in the present, a person must be aware of the lessons of
the past, to be able to see elements of the past in the present. But while
Eliot is trying to recognize the wisdom of the past, the film forcefully
asserts that the racial attitudes of the past must be discarded. Burke to
Slater: "I don't want to hear what your grandpappy thought on the old
farm in Oklahoma. You got it?" [93] Of course, Slater does not get it,
and his failure to learn from Burke's history lesson means death.
   Jazz inspired many "serious" composers and painters of the
1920s, though in "The Waste Land" Eliot evokes jazz and cabaret music
as two more coarsening or trivializing aspects of modern life.

               Is there nothing in your head?"
                        But
        O O O O that Shakespeherian Rag—
        It's so elegant
                  So intelligent[26]

   Where Eliot evoked the art of the past to make the present
appear worse, Matisse, Lachaise, and Picasso, among others, did
exactly the opposite. The joyful energy in their sculpture and dance and
beach paintings projects perfectly the idea and pulse of the willed
"primitivism" of sophisticated modern artists.

We can contemplate the psychological appeal of jazz improvisation. Can we at least *talk* our way out of a tight spot, dance away from trouble? How many nails did a Congolese villager have to hammer into a fetish figure such as the *Janus Dog* before any wish was answered? [This figure, made c. 1900 by villagers of the Western Kongo (of wood, cloth, resin, animal teeth, shell, and iron nails), received urgent requests from petitioners in the form of one nail per wish.] What was the percentage of success over the long run? If you ran out of nails, could you just knock on wood? *Thump! Thump! Thump!* It's the sound made by the dancers' feet; an NBA player taking the ball downcourt; Molly Bloom's heartbeat as she thinks about the sea; Babe Ruth tapping home plate before he cocks his bat; Brancusi's mallet and chisel as he pounds into being one of his exalted birds in space or pseudo-African totem poles.[27]

Music in film, as with poetry and art, is intuitive, instinctive, and extremely emotional. As Richard Dyer has argued, in "Entertainment and Utopia," it is often the function of musical numbers (enabled precisely by the breach with realism and all pretense of verisimilitude) to express the utopian desire the characters cannot fulfill in their lives.[28]

In *Odds Against Tomorrow*, jazz music imbues two dramatic set pieces, as Ingram (Belafonte with the Modern Jazz Quartet) attempts to gain some kind of existential control over his chaotic world through his singing and playing (each percussion on the vibraharp a wish for deliverance). In his first number, "My Baby's Not Around," he laments that he "just can't make that jungle outside my front door. . . . You got to come and hold me before the morning sun." [46-47] It is a cry of anguish, but there is a sense of a melancholy ordering of details.

By the second number, in the wake of Bacco's violent threats, Ingram's musical control has descended into gibberish. Even after Annie has finished her song, Ingram continues to bang frenziedly on the vibraharp. In the spirit of the petitioners to the *Janus Dog*, who pound nails of hope, Ingram is seeking therapeutic release in his cacophony, "playing off the big blow-up in him which is tearing him apart." [56-57][29]

Section IV of "The Waste Land" is entitled "Death by Water." Water and Fire frequently have ambivalent meanings in Eliot's poetry. Water could function as a destructive element in which one may drown, but also as a fertile and saving element that a sterile land needs. Fire could be employed as the ceaseless agitation of desire to which life in time is subject—and as the purging fire of suffering that purifies us.

> Phlebas the Phoenician, a fortnight dead,
> Forgot the cry of gulls, and the deep sea swell
> And the profit and loss.
>   A current under sea
> Picked his bones in whispers. As he rose and fell
> He passed the stages of his age and youth
> Entering the whirlpool.
>   Gentile or Jew
> O you who turn the wheel and look to windward,
> Consider Phlebas, who was once handsome and tall as you.[30]

To understand death by water in the literal sense, Phlebas was a man who drowned, whose body has been decomposed by the sea, and who has no hope of another chance at life. His death by water was real and final.[31]

Eliot speaks to problems which are of great concern today to everybody: air pollution, water pollution, illicit sex, lack of communication between people, meaninglessness in life. Our problems result from the same malaise which affects the Waste Land. Ours is the state of mind which is out of touch, and a state of being which brings about sterility in every walk of life. We must reconsider our situation and our choices or we will share the fate of Phlebas the Phoenician.

The fate of Slater and Ingram in *Odds Against Tomorrow* is "Death by Fire." Unlike the poem's last section, "What the Thunder Said," which advances specific cures for the meaningless life of the inhabitants of the Waste Land,[32] the film offers only purgation and fear. The explosions at the end expunge the racial hatred and the superficial physical differences of the two men, but tendentiousness is limited to a warning sign on the fence: STOP. DEAD END. [134] We must reconsider or we will share the fate of Earle Slater and Johnny Ingram.

The symbolic structures of these works stimulate an emotional response before our minds have propounded the riddles. In both instances, we get the impression of something troublesome and rather sinister from which the poet is trying to escape. There is also a longing for peace, desire of an assuagement, if even by death, of some torturing thirst of the spirit.

The poetic dimensions of the film help explain its modernity, and underscore the importance of Robert Wise's direction in rendering the essence of Polonsky's text. *Odds Against Tomorrow* is a "caper" film, a modernist poetic work, "a criminal's version of a medieval quest"—which will "culminate in a vision of stark nihilism."[33]

The French Connection

I first met Jean-Pierre Melville[34] in 1959, after a screening of *Johnny Guitar* at the Filmclub Cinéquanon.   My classmate Bertrand Tavernier introduced us.   Melville thought Nick Ray's film was awful.   Standing in his hat and coat beneath the trees that lined the Boulevard des Gobelins, he begged us to turn our backs on what he considered to be misguided works like *Johnny Guitar* and to look instead to the American classics for inspiration.   Biased as he was, he contended that only two—at that time disdained—directors counted for anything at all: William Wyler and Robert Wise.

Melville was a teacher through and through, which was especially obvious when he showed movies in his own screening room to staff and friends.   The movies were, by the way, always the same: *The Best Years of Our Lives*, by Wyler, and most often, Robert Wise's *Odds Against Tomorrow*.   It was the simple craftsmanship in the latter movie that Melville wanted to bring to our attention: the fluttering newspaper pages in the establishing shot, the surprise cut to the front of a speeding [bus].   These and many other shots he would always anticipate before they actually appeared on the screen.

—Volker Schlondorff,
"A Parisian-American in Paris"[35]

Our immediate predilection tends to be for faces marked with the brand of vice and the neon lights of bars rather than the ones which glow with wholesome sentiments and prairie air.

—Eric Rohmer,
"Rediscovering America"[36]

Tragedy doesn't go at all well with dinner-jackets and frilly shirtfronts: it has come down in the world.   Tragedy is the immediacy of death that you get in the underworld, or at a particular time such as war. . . . There's still a bridge on the

River Kwai nestling somewhere in my heart. I like futility of
effort: the uphill road to failure is a very human thing. In his
progress from achievement to achievement, man comes
inevitably to his last, absolute defeat: death.
                                    —Jean-Pierre Melville[37]

Odds Against Tomorrow in 1959 was at the confluence of many
rich literary and cinematic textures, on the edge of so many modernistic
and postmodernistic currents of creative experimentation, at the apogee
of film noir as an idiom. The film reverberated with many cultural
forces, in the reciprocal between American and French artistic and
intellectual sensibilities. Indeed, as James Naremore elucidates, in his
invaluable "American Film Noir: The History of an Idea": "film noir
belongs to the history of ideas as much as to the history of cinema; it
has less to do with a group of artifacts than with a discourse—a loose,
evolving system of arguments and readings, helping to shape
commercial strategies and aesthetic ideologies. . . . Film noir is both an
important cinematic legacy and an idea we have projected onto the
past."[38]

American writers are above all rebels. Their revolt against
"all the lies that stifle us" (Dos Passos) have found an echo in
the various European literatures of the post-[WWI] years. It
was an identity of views which confirmed young American
writers in their tendencies and attitudes.
                                    —Philippe Soupault,
                                    Europe, 15 October 1934 [39]

       Specific citations from French and American cultural history
can serve as parallels or cross-references to the thematic or stylistic
implications of *Odds Against Tomorrow*. A big boom enjoyed by
American literature and film in France occurred in the years
immediately following World War II, but relevant cross-fertilization
begins much earlier.
       Vivid characters from American literature, such as Cooper's
Natty Bumppo, Melville's Ahab, and London's Wolf Larsen, are
physically hard and emotionally tough. All are supremely adept at
their crafts. All espouse objectives which frequently do not square with
conventional moral norms. All are pragmatists who employ
questionable means toward desirable ends. They are the splendid
ancestors and prototypes of the tough guy hero who emerged in the

popular fiction of the 1920s and 1930s and who is still very much with us in more ways than we can possibly discern.[40]

BURKE
Just what I said, fifty to seventy-five thousand, like that, all in small bills.

INGRAM
And you need Johnny Ingram? I'm just a bone picker in a four-man graveyard.

BURKE
It's a bank job.

INGRAM
Aren't we social climbing, David?

BURKE
What can I do?

INGRAM
Find a hobby, man, anything. They sure changed your color when they rehabilitated you at Sing Sing.

BURKE
Fifty grand can change it back.
[*Odds Against Tomorrow*, 31, 33]

The writer who more than any other transformed these characters into the tough guy, and thus fathered the hard-boiled heroes who populate the tough novels and films of the 1930s and after, was Ernest Hemingway. From Hemingway's novels and stories were derived the manner, the world view, and the qualities of character which defined the tough guy.[41]

M.E. Coindreau, in *Nouvelle Révue Francaise* (November 1932), reviewing Hemingway's *Death in the Afternoon*, wrote: "Mr. Hemingway cannot forget that he is a member of that band of *enfants terribles*, those post-war writers who, in order to react against the puritanism of their country, adopted the 'tough guy' type. Their influence was excellent and they have certainly contributed to rid American literature of the sentimental insipidities which rendered it anaemic."[42]

American literature made an impact on Europe through the tough novel. On Andre Malraux's recommendation, Andre Gide read

William Faulkner and Dashiell Hammett, with equal seriousness. "French critics," says Wallace Fowlie in *A Guide to Contemporary French Literature* (1957), "in many cases paid earlier and more sophisticated attention to contributions of American art than American critics."[43] In 1946, Horace McCoy was hailed in Paris as the first American existentialist and as the peer of Hemingway and John Steinbeck. If, as Camus suggests in "The Myth of Sisyphus," the human condition is one of eternal, ineffective motion, it is understandable that the French would admire a novel about an American dance-marathon: Horace McCoy's *They Shoot Horses, Don't They?* Critics have consistently noted Albert Camus' debt to James M. Cain, identifying parallels between Camus's *The Stranger* and Cain's *The Postman Always Rings* Twice, a novel, it should be noted, that was extremely popular in Paris in the late 1930s. In 1946, Marcel Duhamel (a publisher and editor who had translated, among others, a collection of Hemingway short stories) started *Série Noire* in Paris, bringing out three books a month (150 by 1955), which were hard-boiled American, or *style américain*, murder novels.[44]

What attracted some French readers to these works was the fact that they revealed an acute consciousness of the tragedy of the human condition in the modern world, an awareness made all the keener by the war and also by the excesses of an industrial civilization which had been pushed farther in the United States than in Europe. American writers, in a way, found themselves in a privileged position on account of the magnifying power of American civilization. French intellectuals sympathized with their revolt and appreciated the quality of their lucid pessimism.[45]

French critic Maurice Nadeau: "What gives American literature the glamour it has for us today is not that it is more talented than ours, but that it expresses more faithfully, more sincerely, and more brutally the despair of our time."[46] Fowlie sums up the tough guy's appeal to the French: "In a very special way, they have heeded the Hemingway myth of the man aggressively virile, opposed on all sides by society or fate."[47] Hemingway gave a striking picture of the crisis of man in a war-torn, over-industrialized world, and his French readers recognized their own predicament in that of his heroes.

EXT. SIDE STREET

We see Burke's look of sudden despair. He is hit. Burke's face is drawn with pain and streaked with blood. He begins to crawl. He gets the keys out of his pocket and extends his arm as if he were handing the keys to one right next to him. Burke is hit again, screams out in agony, and pitches over on his side. The keys fall a few inches from his outstretched hand which claws the sidewalk of this no-man's land. Ingram and Slater observe this with despair.

INGRAM
There are your keys. Have you still got it made?"

Slater is looking around for an avenue of escape. Ingram stands quietly, utterly without hope . . .

[*Odds Against Tomorrow*, 127-129]

With deep pessimism, the *film noir* and the *Série Noire* showed the European the futility of the wish-come-true in an absurd world. The crime narrative dealt with fundamental drives and reflexes. It was at this level during the Depression, World War II, and afterward that Europeans were living their lives. Europeans recognized the world of violence as their own, and the tough characters reflected facets of themselves. To deal with the world, they aspired to the tough-mindedness of the American hero as outsider. Tough writers seemed to deny the validity of established institutions and attitudes, and they refused to judge violent behavior in a world made absurd by individual and state violence.[48]

> Unlike most moviegoers my own age, I didn't identify with the heroes, but with the underdog and, in general, with any character who was in the wrong. That's why Alfred Hitchcock's movies, devoted to fear, won me over from the start.
> —François Truffaut[49]

> *Odds Against Tomorrow* has a European flavor. It has even been compared to *Rififi*,[50] but erroneously so. *Rififi* was a great fun picture. *Odds Against Tomorrow* is solemn from the first to the last scene, unrelieved by one iota of humor.
> —Wanda Hale[51]

Odds Against Tomorrow would seem to constitute a companionable text for French sensibilities.

"The film is a mixture of French style and American iconography—a work of vigorous cinematic intelligence devoted to outlaws, misfits, and passionate individuals, it sums up an existentially ambiguous combination of defiance and fatalism."

These phrases are extracted from the language used by Peter Hogue to analyze the work of Jean-Pierre Melville.[52]   But they are also incisively descriptive of *Odds*, and their mutual applicability to this American film and this French director perhaps helps clarify why Melville holds the Polonsky/Wise work in such high esteem.

François Truffaut manifestly admired the work of Robert Wise, whose *Born to Kill* (1947) he described as "Bressonian." (For Truffaut to conjoin Wise's work with that of French director Robert Bresson,[53] a great favorite of the *Cahiers du Cinéma* critics, is high praise indeed.) As concrete support for Truffaut's astute analysis, consider the following by P. Adams Sitney: "The intricate shot-countershot of Bresson's films reinforces his emphasis on seeing, as does his careful use of camera movement. Often he *reframes within a shot to bring together two different objects of attention.*"[54] [Emphasis added.]

There are three felicitous examples of this in Wise's direction of *Odds Against Tomorrow*. (1) In the elevator of the Juno Hotel at the beginning of the film, Wise reframes a wider angle to a slightly tighter perspective—as an early warning insight into Slater's racial antipathy [18]. (2) Later, in Burke's room, Slater is angrily about to depart, when Burke, smiling and with "comfortable confidence," tantalizes him with the possibility of picking up $50,000. Slater freezes at the door, "feeling the immense weight of the numbers." The phone rings . . . delaying Slater's decision. Burke, concluding the phone call, turns to Slater. "Well?" As an emotional heightening of the tension involved in the anticipation of Slater's decision, Wise again tracks in unostentatiously, but with an unerring dramatic astuteness, to underscore the significance of the moment. [23] This is a nuance of directorial instinct, surely a Bressonian quality admired by Truffaut, recessive yet decisive, that characterizes only the most stylistically appropriate and controlled *mise en scène*. (3) Toward the end of the film, when Burke enters Warren Street "with a certain intangible urgency about him," a shot analyzed above (p. 172) as a passage of quotidian poetry, Wise again employs a variation of reframing the images through a strong dynamic of static camera, moving camera, and moving object. Burke's strong forward walking movement coalesces with perfectly timed camera movement for a disturbing yet exciting assertion of his (criminal) determination. [114]

More of Sitney on Bresson: "A dominant theme of his cinema is dying with grace. In three of his films the protagonists commit suicide. In two films they give themselves up as murderers. Death, as he represents it, comes as the acceptance of one's fate. The three suicides emphasize the enigma of human will; they . . . are pure acts of accepting death."[55] In *Odds Against Tomorrow*, whether it is virtual suicide (Ingram and Slater unwisely but perhaps predeterminedly firing bullets at each other on those gas tanks)—foreshadowed by Ingram's prescient, "Wake up . . . we're committing suicide" [69]—or literal suicide (Dave Burke) [130], all three deaths are as enigmatic as racial evil and personal guilt. (Ten years later, Abraham Polonsky will end his *Tell Them Willie Boy Is Here*, 1969, by having Willie Boy commit symbolic suicide: by challenging Sheriff Cooper without bullets in his rifle, he thus ensures his own death.)[56]

Further supplementing his appreciation of Robert Wise, Truffaut's review of Wise's *Executive Suite* (1954) estimates Wise's talents as an *auteur* (making reference to *The Set Up*, 1949, and Wise's work with Orson Welles), and concludes that the triumph of Wise's filmmaking resides in his elevation of craft to the realm of art.[57]

The *Cahiers du Cinéma* Debate. A polemical tension developed during the 1950s in the ranks of the French film journal, *Cahiers du Cinéma*, and it is relevant here to an analysis of *Odds Against Tomorrow*, a work which could represent something of a test case for the contrasting positions. The critical opposition was basically between the commitment (by an Andre Bazin, for example) to a *mise en scène* at the service of liberal-humanist subject matter and treatment— and an opposing tendency (by a Luc Moullet, for example) interested not at all in liberal-humanist good intentions, but concerned only with *mise en scène* as the essence of cinema.[58]

Within another configuration, this is the same issue being addressed by Claude Chabrol in "Little Themes."

Anyone who wants to make a film on a theme of his own choosing has two solutions open to him. Depending on his aspirations the filmmaker can describe the French Revolution or a quarrel with the next-door neighbors, the apocalypse of our time or the barmaid who gets herself pregnant, the final hours of a hero of the Resistance or an inquiry into the murder of a prostitute. It is a question of personality: the important thing, surely, is that the film should be good, that it should be well directed and well constructed, that it should be good cinema. The only distinction one can make between the apocalypse and the prostitute, the revolution and the barmaid, the hero and the quarreling neighbors is on the level of the ambitiousness of the theme. For there *are*, of course, big and little themes. Anyone who doesn't agree should put up his hand.[59]

To illustrate, Chabrol cites, albeit not by title, *The World, The Flesh and the Devil* (1959—ironically another Henry Belafonte film)[60] as an example of a project based on the mistaken elevation of message over art: "Some people are gullible enough to be taken in: maybe the film is imperfect, but the subject is of such importance that everyone should be interested in it. . . . A big theme is no more valuable than a small one. It is a decoy which from time to time becomes a booby-trap."[61]

Perhaps, but among socially engaged filmmakers there is such an intense desire to eschew what they perceive to be Hollywood's "fog of escapism, meretricious violence, and the gimmick plot attitude of the usual movie that," writes Abraham Polonsky, "it becomes very clear that an artist who happens to bring even a tag of daily experience into the studio is making an immense contribution to the screen. The struggle for content, for social reality, no matter how limited the point of view, is a necessary atmosphere for growth in the American film."[62]

Thus, anticipating, perhaps precipitating, the *Cahiers* debate, Albert Maltz provoked a historic controversy in Marxist circles around this issue, with his "What Shall We Ask of Writers?" While acknowledging that important writing cannot be socially idle—"that it must be humane in content"—that works of art can be weapons in people's thinking and in the struggle of social classes, Maltz nevertheless believed that the concept that art must serve immediate political ends like a leaflet is an artistic straitjacket. "An artist can be a great artist without being an integrated or a logical or a progressive thinker on all matters. This is so because he presents, not a systematized philosophy, but the imaginative reconstruction of a *sector* of human experience. . . . Where art is a weapon, it is so only when it is art."[63]

Chabrol identifies "The Apocalypse of Our Time" (the atomic bomb) theme, a sub-division of his BIG HISTORICAL THEMES category, within which he discusses *The World, the Flesh and the Devil*. [See Chabrol's derisive summary in note.[64]] And Jim Pines, in *Blacks in Films*, does indeed refer to it as a "message" film, locating it within the pattern of liberal-humanist ideology: "Certainly more than any previous racial movie, it offers in precise terms that crucial question, 'What is the ultimate moral responsibility of human beings living in this racially configurated society?'"

But significantly more respectful of the film than Chabrol, Pines maintains: "It also reveals in no less striking a way the specific terms in which social-racial reality was perceived during the crest of the civil rights period. In this sense, *The World, the Flesh and the Devil* embodies the essence of 1950s liberal-humanist ideology and idealism, and is therefore one of the most important films of the period."[65]

Nevertheless, it is the "on the nose" liberal-humanist film that Chabrol is addressing, and thus he turns to another main heading in his essay called BIG HUMAN THEMES. Within this category he identifies "The Brotherhood of Man" theme, exemplified by *The Defiant Ones* (1958), another film concerned with racial tolerance.

There is no question that the presentation of a "liberal-humanist ideology" can be problematic. The stylistic tone and structural orientation toward the material are crucial.

> **Abraham Polonsky:** Unfortunately, in most social-problem fiction, the artist falls into the trap of trying to find local solutions in existence for the social conflicts, instead of solving them in feeling. This is, of course, the industry's demand for happy endings.[66] [In this regard, *Odds Against Tomorrow* seems exempt.]

Above all, writes Albert Maltz, the approach must present "all characters *from their own point of view*, allowing them their own full, human justification for their behavior and attitudes, yet allowing the [viewer] to judge their objective behavior. *This is the special wisdom art can offer us.*"[67]

It is not the theme that is decisive. The film must first work as an organic piece of art, in Chabrol's words, "well directed and well constructed . . . good cinema." He concludes: "There's no such thing as a big theme and a little theme, because the smaller the theme is, the more one can give it a big treatment. The truth is, truth is all that matters."[68]

Although Chabrol does not mention *Odds Against Tomorrow*, it would seem that implicitly the film could be accommodated by his "Brotherhood of Man" thematic sub-division. [*Odds Against Tomorrow* is discussed below within a film history pattern which includes these other films, pp. 228-236.] But *Odds* has a toughness and a resilience to liberal sanctimoniousness that the other two titles lack, and an inference is being made here that Chabrol would agree that *Odds* avoids the "booby-trap" of the "big theme film."

Odds Against Tomorrow is a film that indeed deals with an important topic, but, as an Abraham Polonsky film noir, it is shrouded by the toughness and honesty of the genre. The Claude Chabrol who blended these attributes in his own genre-bending *Les Bonnes Femmes* and *Une Affaire des Femmes* would approve.

Thomas Cripps outlines the social/political possibilities for this conceptual approach:

> Of all the genres, the most insistently political was film noir, with its despairing portrayal of America as John Kenneth Galbraith described it—a civilization marked by private excess and public squalor. Equal parts oldtime gangster movie and social problem movie, film noir sketched an America down at the heels, wheedlingly corrupt, despondent over the unexpectedly mixed results of victory after World War II, and, far from the New Deal optimism with which it had entered the war, consumed by a vague dread.

> Both the gangster film and the film noir lent themselves to the needs of the system, [but] in gangster movies, society learned to reform and thereby remedy the causes of crime, whereas in the film noir outcomes were more ominously ambiguous.[69]

What Claude Chabrol, Luc Moullet and others—like American Manny Farber (who dealt with this and related issues in his own irascible style, in such pieces as "The Gimp," "Hard-Sell Cinema," and "White Elephant Art vs. Termite Art"[70])—really objected to were the *excesses* of the social problem/message movie. Perhaps the message movie and film noir were two sides of the same political coin. But the former often, in exposing some social dysfunction, too stridently called attention to the need for reform. The latter, with its narrow, darkened focus and the unremitting despair at its core, insisted that the status quo, complete with crooked cops and fatcat criminals, was inevitable. Message movies called attention to the paltry gains that had been made toward war-borne hopes for "a better world." Film noir shrugged its shoulders and lived with what had been dealt. It had an easier time of formulating a politics of its art. Its moody style and its fatalism corresponded to the cool, deadpan manner of the increasing audience of self-consciously, even willfully, alienated youth. The themes of isolation, uncertainty, and ambiguity must have exerted a strong appeal to anyone who was wary of collective politics and inclined to treat social issues in terms of personal ethics.[71]

Many left-oriented screenwriters and directors were logically drawn to film noir. "In their hands, film noir approached a kind of Marxist *cinéma manqué*, a shrewdly oblique strategy for an otherwise subversive realism."[72]

> Noir is a stylistic safety blanket that lets us deal with crime and chaos without saying what's really on our minds. The linguistic irony of noir is that with a few exceptions (Chester Himes, Walter Mosely) it has always been a white style: that is to say, a style made by, for and about white people. What it rarely deals with is race.
>
> —David Ansen,
> "The Neo-Noir '90s"[73]

The *Film Noir* Paradigm. Because it challenged the facile narrative style of prewar Hollywood, film noir made possible a new politics of the movies. Certainly, Abraham Polonsky must have thought so when he wrote *Body and Soul* (1947) and *Force of Evil* (1948), dark movies in which the boxing arena and the numbers racket were used as allegories for the meanness of capitalism. Polonsky's "*Odds Against Tomorrow* combined the dark cityscape of film noir with the politics of the racial left that had carried over from the war. The evocative combination of realism and studio gloss eloquently sketched a once stable society turned on its end."[74]

The construction of film noir helps make the American-French liaison more comprehensible. Further illumination results by holding up *Odds Against Tomorrow* to the "film noir series" criteria which were formulated by the French authors of the seminal book on the subject. Raymond Borde and Etienne Chaumeton, in "Towards a Definition of Film Noir," from their *Panorama du Film Noir Américain*,[75] discern the following definitional elements:

✤ It is the presence of **crime** which gives film noir its most constant characteristic. Film noir examines crime and murder from within, from the **point of view of the criminal**. Film noir situates itself within the very criminal milieu and describes it, sometimes in broad strokes, sometimes in depth with correlative subtlety.

Odds Against Tomorrow: The entire narrative foregrounds the criminal perspective. Meticulous details are provided regarding the planning and execution of the heist. A key scene involves the discussion regarding the problem of the chain on the bank door, and Ingram's clever solution. [91-94] The Melton Hotel scene, where Burke describes the robbery scenario to Slater, is the most compellingly staged segment in the film: there is the ominous opening of the venetian blinds; the camera, representing the criminals' point of view to the street, follows from the front window of the hotel room to the side window the movements of the waiter as he makes his way from the drug store to the bank, accompanied by Burke's commentary outlining the relevant facts—the entire scene is a remarkable tapestry of suspenseful mood, an intense immersion in the criminal milieu. [43-46] The architectural and character facets are in Polonsky's screenplay, and Wise has never directed a more involving atmospheric sequence.

The Moral Irony Issue. Statement of the problem: "It may be ethically dubious to make a plea for racial tolerance by showing a criminal act being defeated by racism." Attempted resolution: "It is a fact, however, that audiences invariably wish to see bank robbers get away with it; so that, by rooting for the robbers, they ipso facto espouse the film's antiracism, a simple but shrewd maneuver."[76]

Another attempted resolution: "Because Ingram is the brunt of another character's overt racial prejudice, we tend to romanticize him and see him as more hero than criminal."[77]

Polonsky: "Audiences tend to root for the criminals, because criminals express revolt against the conventions that are destroying everybody. That's why Marxism is such a marvelous analysis illuminating the deep problems of the capitalist economic, and it's hopeless when it comes to inventing a society that will work. Because for that society to work, everybody has to be born in heaven. The solution to the problem depends on a society of idealists living in a utopia, and this will never work because of the nature of things. Evolution doesn't work because people are born with a heavy urge to get together. Evolution works because people are born with an urge to survive at any cost. *Odds Against Tomorrow* is based on a situation that can have no other conclusion except destruction." [Ingram has few illusions that Burke's idealized scheme will work; beginning with his first dialogue with Burke, his terse analyses catalogue a counter-current of reality and pragmatism: "That's the firing squad. That's for junkies and joy boys. . . . I did all my dreaming on my mother's knee." (32)]

Polonsky: "One of the virtues of film noir is that you're able to treat these difficult subjects within a natural context which is morally mixed, full of contradictions and randomness. The Greeks may have discovered it, but we live it. The moral point we are making occurs within an immoral milieu. It is a situation in which noble attitudes don't work. In order to survive you do all the kinds of things that you ordinarily might be opposed to.

"Ingram gives in to racism himself against Slater, but there is no contradiction in the premises of this story. It says that racism is no good no matter where it is. If it's the people committing crimes it will destroy them. If it's people trying not to be criminals, it will destroy them too. Because that's the nature of racism: it's an absolute evil like greed." (Interview with author, 7 July 1998.)

The Black-Character-as-Criminal Issue. The historical position of *Odds Against Tomorrow* as the first Hollywood feature with a black noir protagonist forces a consideration of racial implications that would simply not be relevant for the typical film noir. The very raising of the black image issue in an era of political correctness involves an inherent provocation to misinterpretation of motives. Indeed, white/European/Anglo-Saxon readers or viewers seldom seem to think this way about characters that are interpreted as "one of their own."

The White Perspective. Nevertheless, the noted African American writer Richard Wright, when he was conceiving of the black noir protagonist Bigger Thomas for his novel *Native Son*, felt that his portrayal of an African American as murderer was a matter of some creative circumspection and social sensitivity: "What will white people think if I draw the picture of such a Negro boy? Will they not at once say: 'See, didn't we tell you all along that niggers are like that? Now, look, one of their own kind has come along and drawn the picture for us!' I felt that if I drew the picture of Bigger truthfully, there would be many reactionary whites who would try to make of him something I did not intend. And yet, and this was what made it difficult, I knew that I could not write of Bigger convincingly if I did not depict him as he *was*: that is, resentful toward whites, sullen, angry, ignorant, emotionally unstable, depressed and unaccountably elated at times, and unable even, because of his own lack of inner organization which American oppression has fostered in him, to unite with the members of his own race. And would not whites misread Bigger and, doubting his authenticity, say: 'This man is preaching hate against the whole white race?'

"The more I thought of it the more I became convinced that if I did not write of Bigger as I saw and felt him, if I did not try to make him a living personality and at the same time a symbol of all the larger things I felt and saw in him, I'd be reacting as Bigger himself reacted: that is, I'd be acting out of *fear* if I let what I thought whites would say constrict and paralyze me." (Wright, "How 'Bigger' Was Born.")

The Black Perspective. There are further implications to Wright drawing such a picture of Bigger Thomas, from the perspective of the black middle and professional classes who, having escaped Bigger's pattern themselves, did not want people, especially *white* people, to think that their lives were so much touched by anything so dark and brutal as Bigger. A single paragraph sums up their attitude: "'But, Mr. Wright, there are so many of us who are *not* like Bigger. Why don't you portray in your fiction the *best* traits of our race, something that will show the white people what we have done in *spite* of oppression? Don't represent anger and bitterness. Smile when a white person comes to you. Never let him feel that you are so small that what he has done to crush you has made you hate him! Oh, above all, save your *pride!*'

"But Bigger won over all these claims; he won because I felt that I was hunting on the trail of more exciting and thrilling game. What Bigger meant had claimed me because I felt with all my being that he was more important than what any person, white or black, would say or try to make of him, more important than any political analysis designed to explain or deny him, more important, even, than my own sense of fear, shame, and diffidence." (Wright, "How 'Bigger' Was Born.")

It should be kept in mind that the American film has historically contained a preponderance of negative black images, and it is frankly disingenuous not to acknowledge that honorable black artists (like Harry Belafonte) and enlightened white intellectuals (like Abraham Polonsky) were availing themselves of their unique opportunity (at that particular crossroads in film history) to introduce a more accurate and less stereotyped picture of black people to the public than had previously been presented. The ambiguity of the Johnny Ingram character in *Odds*—a basically decent person, with a weakness for gambling, who loves his family and is, in true noir fashion, swallowed up by racial hatred and violence—makes an examination of the racial implications more complex. [There will be more discussion of the Polonsky and Belafonte conceptions of Johnny Ingram in the film history and film and literature sections below.]

Authorial Perspectives. In 1926, the editors of *The Crisis*, the journal of the National Association for the Advancement of Colored People (NAACP) sponsored a symposium which was called "The Negro in Art: How Shall He Be Portrayed." The editors of the publication solicited answers to questions about black characters from well-known writers of the day, such as Sherwood Anderson, H.L. Mencken, Langston Hughes, Sinclair Lewis, Countee Cullen, and Charles W. Chestnutt.

In 1989, *The Crisis* symposium was replicated by Frankie Y. Bailey for *Out of the Woodpile: Black Characters in Crime and Detective Fiction,* and, very significantly for our purposes here, this forum focused on the writing of *crime* literature. Writers of the genre were asked questions about the depiction of black characters. Particularly germane is the following: "Does the portrayal of sordid, foolish, and criminal black characters help to convince the reading public that this is how blacks 'really are'?"

The writers' responses were generally articulate and wise (see note)—the essence of which is fairly accurately distilled in the following by writer Susan Moody [*Penny Post,* 1985]: "If it is the mark of a good writer to reveal individual truths, it could be argued that the mark of the great writer is to show the universal truths that unite all men. It is this in the end that is going to persuade prejudiced readers that blacks are people like themselves. For a writer to deny that there are sordid, foolish, or criminal blacks would be as irresponsible as claiming that all whites are solid, churchgoing citizens or that all mothers-in-law are harridans. Writers who depend on the kind of emotive propaganda that panders to the prejudices of their readers should be working for the tabloids. Readers who are taken in by it deserve the writers they get."[78]

✦ Moral determinism. The narrative is manipulated so that at times the moviegoer sympathizes with the criminals. There are unstable alliances among individuals in the heart of the underworld. The criminal milieu is an ambiguous one, where a position of strength can be quickly eroded.

> *Odds Against Tomorrow*: This is a criterion which could have been developed with *Odds* in mind. The psychic chemistry of Burke, Ingram, and Slater formulates an impossible compound, and existential slipperiness will prevent a successful experiment. Here racial prejudice will prove to be an insuperable evil—and will defeat them all. So much attention is paid to these men that we do come to perhaps sympathize (Ingram) or empathize (Slater, Burke), but Ingram gets it right when he says: "I know I got

rid of a headache. Now I got cancer. Wake up, Dave, we're committing suicide . . . this is three o'clock in the morning." [69]

❋ The noir protagonist is ambiguous, often more mature, almost old, and not too handsome. He is often enough masochistic, even self-immolating, one who makes his own trouble.

Odds Against Tomorrow: Slater is the rancid, self-pitying racist, who is introduced by Polonsky as "rangy, powerful, a natural athlete in his forties, with an expression taught to be impassive and indifferent" [14-15], and as portrayed by Robert Ryan, who was actually 50 when the film was shot, there was "a brooding intensity that suggests coiled depths. Cut off from the world by the strength of his feelings, he seems to be in the grip of torrential forces."[79]   (See character profile above.) Ingram, as portrayed by Harry Belafonte, is young and handsome, but his obsessive gambling more than satisfies the "self-immolation" trait, and he and Slater turn it into something more than a character flaw at the end with their fiery self-destruction.

❋ There is ambiguity surrounding the woman. This new type of woman, manipulative and evasive, as hard bitten as her environment, ready to shake down or to trade shots with anyone, has put her mark on noir eroticism, which may be at times nothing more than violence eroticized.

Odds Against Tomorrow: This would be the character of Helen, portrayed by Gloria Grahame. She plays the fatal woman type "not as a victimizer, a cruel tyrant, but as a victim, whimpering and aching and even good-hearted. Grahame has a timorous, appealing, little girl quality; thin-lipped, squeaky-voiced, slit-eyed, pumpkin-faced, wrinkling up her nose and face like a mouse, she is found hiding in smoky tenement rooms waiting for her men. Abused and humiliated in her search for love, she is noir's pre-eminent masochist, the inevitable cast-off moll."[80] Here she is Slater's loopy neighbor. "When Slater reneges on a promise to babysit her child, she runs a considerable gamut spanning annoyance at Slater's no-show, concern for her temporarily unattended infant, flirtatiousness, and finally a pervy-erotic fascination with murder."[81] Speaking of violence eroticized:

INT. SLATER APARTMENT-NIGHT

Earle watches her as she ambles around the room. She is letting herself be seen, with no particular intention in mind, but she is conscious of his maleness and her femaleness at the moment. Now she makes her turn. Her face becomes curious, almost greedy with curiosity.

> HELEN
> I'd like to ask you something, but you must promise not to be angry.

> SLATER
> All right. I promise.

She pauses, seems to take a deep breath and asks then in a small and rather tentative voice.

> HELEN
> How did it feel when you killed that man? [87]

This scene may very well be second only to *Body and Soul*'s "What are you going to do, kill me? Everybody dies." as the most cited moment in Abraham Polonsky's work. It is also similar in its hint of perversity to the scene in Polonsky's *Force of Evil*, between Joe Morse and Doris Lowry in the back seat of his car, when Joe imputes a dark instinct to the woman: "You're a sweet child . . . and you squirm for me to do something wicked to you. Make a pass for you, bowl you over, sweep you up . . . take the childishness out of you and give you money and sin."

> SLATER
> (to Helen)
> You want me to make your flesh creep. [88]

✤ Film noir has renovated the theme of violence. A sporting chance has given way to settling scores, beatings, and cold-blooded murders. Twitching and stigmatized, an unknown breed of men rose up before us. Twisted killers, sweating in fear, suddenly boil over. As for the ceremony of execution itself, film noir has the widest array of examples.

> *Odds Against Tomorrow*: Slater, "frustrated, ugly in feeling," confronts a young soldier (Wayne Rogers) in a bar. "He knows he mustn't do anything: he knows it from his past, from everything that has ever happened to him," but he drives a crushing blow into the soldier's body. He is "like some crazy animal let out of his cage and ready for anything." [73, 76] Slater tends to boil over. The sudden spasm of violence in shooting the rabbit shows his hair-trigger nature. [113] He savagely beats the bank manager and the waiter: "an immense flood of violence seeming to flow from him. There isn't a person in the room who doesn't know it will take very little to make him shoot." [122]
>
> Even Ingram's forbearance has its limits, and Slater's cynical indifference to Burke's death provokes him to "breathe words of loathing and hate into Slater's face." [130] Ingram's violence toward Slater on the gas storage tanks is the culmination of a pattern of noir apocalyptic imagery. (Thematic implications of the ending are discussed below, pp. 258-259, and in annotations #'s 28 and 30.)

✤ Anxiety. There is something of the dream in this incoherent and brutal atmosphere, the atmosphere common to most noir films—expressed as an epigraph from Lautréamont: "The bloody channels through which one passes to the extremities of logic." The context of the narrative dilemma is such that the viewer expects confusion. In a true film noir, the bizarre is inseparable from what might be called the uncertainty of motivations. Does a fleeting figure in a nightclub indicate a possible ally or an enemy? Honor among thieves, an extortion network, unexplained motives, all this verges on madness. All yield the same result: disorienting the spectator, who can no longer find the familiar reference points. Good and evil go hand in hand to the point of being indistinguishable. Robbers become ordinary guys: they have kids, love young women, and just want to go home again. The primary reference point of earlier days, the moral center, is completely skewed.

Odds Against Tomorrow: Perhaps the nightmarish centerpiece of the film (other than the cataclysmic finale) is the delirious aftermath of Ingram's showdown with Bacco in Cannoy's club. Ingram, distraught and drinking because of the threats to his family, breaks into Annie's performance of "All Men Are Evil" on the bandstand. The episode becomes a phantasm for his anguished mental state. He sings louder, wilder. He begins to say any crazy thing that comes to mind. As Annie shouts out the real words, he "makes pirouettes of verbal frenzy around her."

> Well, it tells you in the good book
> And they teach the same in school
> That a man get his hands on you
> And he'll use you for a mule.
> My mama gave me warning
> And now I know it's true.
> She said, "All men are evil."
> And daddy that's you.

> ANNIE
> (observing it all sadly)
> That little boy is in big trouble.
> [*Odds Against Tomorrow*, 55-56]

This sequence has been discussed above (p. 178) as part of the film's poetic structure (Ingram musically aspiring his anguish), but it functions perfectly here as an eloquent manifestation of Borde and Chaumeton's noir benchmark of "anxiety."[82]

Polonsky's **creation of a domestic life** for both Slater and Ingram encourages the moral ambiguity which the French writers found so subversive of traditional narrative expectations. While Helen's baroque curiosity achieves legendary status in the pattern of noir eroticism, the involvement of the other two women enables the film to engage a more typical social reality. Lorry (Shelley Winters), Earle's live-in girlfriend, is loyal and devoted to him beyond any consideration of money. (It is he who remains gloomy, ashamed that she supports them both.) And Kim Hamilton gives a sensitive portrait as Ruth, Ingram's ex-wife who is trying to maintain a respectable home for her child. In this regard, note this oblique tribute to Abraham Polonsky: "*Killens* [Polonsky] provides a rare look at black middle-class life in the 1950s: when Belafonte visits his estranged wife, he finds her in the middle of a PTA meeting. It's a typical New York social scene, a mix of white liberals and bright young black professionals."[83] (Interest in these parallel relationships extends beyond their capacity to create moral ambivalence within this generic context. The integration of domestic, interstitial, often unfinished, character tableaux is very much a part of a Polonsky structuring aesthetic. Accordingly, this dimension of the screenplay will be discussed at greater length below, pp. 255-256.)

The moral ambivalence, the criminality, the complex contradictions in motives and events, all conspire to make the viewer co-experience anguish and insecurity. Borde and Chaumeton conclude: "All the films of this cycle create a similar emotional effect: *that state of tension instilled in the spectator when the psychological reference points are removed. The aim of film noir was to create a specific alienation.*" (Italics in original.)[84]

Pauline Kael once wrote, controversially, that *Citizen Kane* (1941) was the greatest and culminating effort in Hollywood's decade-long (1930s) fascination with the romantic or "screwball" comedies, especially those with newspaper backgrounds.[85] Analogously, *Odds Against Tomorrow* (1959), by its relentless saturation and consolidation of the narrative patterns and stylistic motifs of the film noir of the 1940s and 1950s, completes *its* decade as the "last and most fatalistic of the genre."[86]

The Black Protagonist of the *Roman Noir*:
The Literary Tradition

It is a thesis of this critical commentary that *Odds Against Tomorrow* is the first major studio production with an African American character manifesting these French-identified descriptive attributes of the noir protagonist. That is, *Odds*—with Harry Belafonte's Johnny Ingram as noir protagonist—is the first film noir without linguistic irony. (This is discussed below as such, as part of the film history pattern.)

However, while it enjoys a certain movie primacy, there were several noteworthy literary works with African American *roman noir* protagonists that pre-date the film. A brief survey of some of these pertinent novels and short stories might allow *Odds Against Tomorrow* to be perceived within a richer cultural context.[87]

Roman noir literally means "black novel," and is nomenclature associated with the French *Série Noire* line of American hard-boiled murder/thriller novels. It is a term that the French extended to the novels by, for example, Dashiell Hammett, Raymond Chandler, or Horace McCoy, but it is more precisely descriptive of the work by such writers as James M. Cain, Jim Thompson, Cornell Woolrich, and David Goodis. It is a label that in a pristine sense fulfills the French notion of both *noir* and *maudit*, the accursed and self-destructive.[88]

The criteria abstracted from Borde and Chaumeton to help shape a definition of *film noir* are useful here for the literary construct, especially the component which examines crime from the criminal perspective. This is the contribution to the writing of crime fiction which is usually attributed to James M. Cain. It is this technique derived from Cain's writing which makes possible an examination of motivation that is more convincing, precisely because it is internalized, than any character revelation written from the investigator's point of view. In Cain's novels, his noir characters are compelled by motivations with terror in them: "I think my stories have some quality of the opening of a forbidden box, and that it is this, rather than violence, sex, or any of the things usually cited by way of explanation, that gives them the drive so often noted. Their appeal is first to the mind, and the reader is carried along as much by his own realization that the characters cannot have this particular wish and survive, and his curiosity to see what happens to them, as by the effect on him of incident, dialogue, or character."[89]

This personal, criminal perspective is, therefore, essential and predominant in the primal films noirs and romans noirs. But another extra-personal attribute seems almost as inextricably involved. Note how a **political/social dimension** surfaces in the following separate analyses of two different writers of noir novels.

> James M. Cain: "Although he shows no direct interest in the political consequences of the Wall Street crash . . . the spectres of the crisis stalk around the edges of his fiction. . . . This historical period is an external fact which shapes the broad contours of the internal action of the text."[90]

> Jim Thompson: "Thompson remained a political writer. . . . He sees not only the violence of the murderer but the implicit violence of the social structures that shape him, the cannibalistic system of relationships within which he flounders, innocently bewildered. The horrors of the individual psyche are located within the organized horrors of state and church and family."[91]

According to Claude Chabrol: "No matter how much a scenarist or director may seek to distract, a thriller must be profound, because it speaks of life and death." According to Patricia Highsmith: "If a suspense writer is going to write about murderers and victims, he should be interested in justice or the absence of it in the world we live in; he should be interested in the morality, good and bad, that exists today; he should be interested in human cowardice or courage, and not merely as forces to push his plot this way and that."[92] Most of the literary works in the following discussion (including *Odds Against Tomorrow*) are layered with such social or political ramification.

Literary Noir Antecedents. The following is a brief review of selected short stories and novels, worthy of attention because of their literary quality, which antedate the film *Odds Against Tomorrow* in their portrayals of African American noir protagonists—works which, in theme and style, reflect previously identified noir-genre attributes. Because of their artistic implications and conceptual authenticity, the works of African American writers Richard Wright and Chester Himes will be addressed. And, because he seems to function as something of a cultural centerpiece via the intersection of the roman noir and jazz, white French writer Boris Vian ("Vernon Sullivan") receives consideration.

In the 1950s—the decade of blacklisting, McCarthyism, jazz-noir, and *Odds Against Tomorrow*—these men were all living in Paris. There was a colony of black American writers, artists, singers, actors, and journalists in the city, on the run from the everyday hardship of life in their own country. It was estimated that there were about five hundred American blacks in France, and that about half of them were living in the capital. In Paris, they felt able to breathe freely, perhaps for the first time.

Richard Wright hardly knew Boris Vian, but he would have recognized the tall young man who played jazz trumpet at Club du Tabou, who had translated one of Wright's stories for *Présence Africaine* in 1946, and who in the same year had written a novel under the pretense of being a black author. Wright might even have noticed that the theme of *J'irai cracher sur vos tombes* (*I Shall Spit on Your Graves*) has some compatibility with that of *Native Son*.

Richard Wright (1908-1960). In the Great Depression that followed the stockmarket crash of 1929, black Americans were among the hardest hit. As the decade of the 1930s ended, Richard Wright used a psychopathic killer to symbolize the condition of black urban America.[93] Bigger Thomas, the black "bad man" of *Native Son* (1940), is the prototype of the African American noir protagonist.

> The day *Native Son* appeared, American culture was changed forever. No matter how much qualifying the book might later need, it made impossible a repetition of the old lies. In all its crudeness, melodrama and claustrophobia of vision, Richard Wright's novel brought out into the open, as no one ever had before, the hatred, fear and violence that have crippled and may yet destroy our culture. . . .
>
> Wright told us the one thing even the most liberal whites preferred not to hear: that Negroes were far from patient or forgiving, that they were scarred by fear, that they hated every moment of their suppression even when seeming most acquiescent, and that often enough they hated *us*, the decent and cultivated white men who from complicity or neglect shared in the responsibility for their plight. Wright forced his readers to confront the disease of our culture, and to one of its most terrifying symptoms he gave the name of Bigger Thomas.[94]

Bigger Thomas is brought into the white Chicago home of the Daltons as their new chauffeur. He is awkward and ill at ease, confused by the naive gestures of kindness from the daughter, Mary Dalton, and her communist boyfriend Jan. When the intoxicated Mary passes out in the car as he is driving her home, Bigger decides he must get her into the house without waking her parents. He carries her to her bedroom. When her blind mother comes into the room, he presses a pillow over the girl's face to keep her quiet because he fears the consequences if he is found in the girl's room. He suffocates her. Still acting out of fear, Bigger decapitates the body, stuffs it into a blazing furnace, and returns home to sleep. But even though the death is an accident, Wright presents it as inevitable. It is something that Bigger Thomas has been moving toward all his life.

Bigger begins to rationalize that in killing Mary Dalton he has destroyed symbolically all the oppressive forces that have made his life miserable. He is proud, for "he had murdered and created a new life for himself."

As the investigation into Mary's disappearance begins, Bigger implicates both his mistress, Bessie and Jan. Mary's bones are eventually found in the furnace, a situation which makes it necessary for him and Bessie to flee. Deciding that Bessie will become a great liability, Bigger, partially out of fear, brutally murders her. He flees through abandoned buildings until he is finally captured on a rooftop.

There are an inquest and a trial, where Bigger is represented by Boris A. Max, his communist lawyer, who in his summation explores the causes and effects of fear and racism, arguing that society is partly to blame for Bigger's crimes. Despite Max's eloquence, Bigger is convicted and sentenced to die in the electric chair. An appeal to the governor fails.

In an essay, "How 'Bigger' Was Born," Wright acknowledges these noir potentialities: "There seems to hover somewhere in that dark part of all our lives, in some more than in others, an objectless, timeless, spaceless element of primal fear and dread . . . a fear and dread which exercises an impelling influence upon our lives all out of proportion to its obscurity."[95] James Baldwin writes that, "No American Negro exists who does not have his private Bigger Thomas living in his skull."[96]

Wright's great achievement, according to Margaret Walker in *Richard Wright, Daemonic Genius*, is his application of modern psychology and philosophy to black and white racial patterns and human personality, particularly the inner turmoil of black personality, and to the black male, who is seen as an outcast, criminal, or marginal man. According to Edward Margolies, "Wright at his best was master of a taut psychological suspense [noir] narrative. . . . He wove themes of human fear, alienation, guilt, and dread into the overall texture of his work."[97]

The essence of noir: given the precise circumstances, anybody could become a criminal. Note the continuity of darkness in Wright's 1946 short story, "The Man Who Killed a Shadow," opening paragraph:

> IT ALL BEGAN long ago when he was a tiny boy who was already used, in a fearful sort of way, to living with shadows. But what were the shadows that made him afraid? Surely they were not those beautiful silhouettes of objects cast upon the earth by the sun. Shadows of that kind are innocent and he loved trying to catch them as he ran along sunlit paths in summer. But there were subtler shadows which he saw and which others could not see: the shadows of his fears. And this boy had such shadows and he lived to kill one of them.[98]

Raymond Chandler described this world as a "wet emptiness" whose streets were dark with something more than night." The atmosphere is one in which the familiar is fraught with danger and the existential tonalities of "fear" and "trembling" are not out of place; there is also a sense of "dread" which is taken to mean a pervasive fear of something hauntingly indeterminate. For Bigger, "he knew that the moment he allowed what his life meant to enter fully into his consciousness, he would either kill himself or someone else."[99]

The noir protagonist in "The Man Who Killed a Shadow" is Saul Saunders, born black "into a world that was split in two, a white world and a black one, the white one being separated from the black by a million psychological miles." Saul is another version of Bigger. Both kill a white woman to silence her. ("He heard that if you were alone with a white woman and she screamed, it was as good as hearing your death sentence, for, though you had done nothing, you would be killed.") Both hide the body, and both continue their lives "as though nothing had happened." When Saul awakes the next day after the murder, he remembers the incident as if it were a movie: "When at last the conviction of what he had done was real in him, it came only in terms of flat memory, devoid of all emotion, as though he were looking when very tired and sleepy at a scene being flashed upon the screen of a movie house."[100]

It is interesting to note how these literary antecedents cross-reference the motion picture, as both Saul Saunders and Bigger Thomas perceive their own actions as if these exist through and in the language of mass culture. Ross Pudaloff has argued that much of Bigger's character is formed by the gangster movies he sees:

> [His origin is] in that popular figure of thirties melodrama, the tough guy. After Mary's body is discovered in the furnace, for example, Bigger reaches for his gun, thinking to himself "he would shoot before he would let them take him; it meant death either way, and he would die shooting every slug he had." Since this fantasy does not materialize, it prompts the reader to ask where the gratuitous lines come from and what function they serve in the novel. They obviously come from gangster movies and detective stories to shape Bigger's character; he has become what he has consumed. His attitudes about Bessie [his girlfriend] similarly mimic those of the hard-boiled school when he thinks to himself, "a woman was a dangerous burden when a man was running away."[101]

Most disastrously for Bessie, his decision to kill her comes as much from such American myths of sex, crime, and punishment as it does from any real danger she poses to him. Bigger knows that "some cold logic not his own, over which he had no control" demands her death.

Bigger's murder of Bessie is a controversial aspect of the text, for Bigger is under no immediate necessity to kill Bessie, whom, paradoxically, he has forced to accompany him. *Native Son* scholarship is troubled by this. Wright's literary friend Jane Newton objected strenuously to Bessie's murder as "both unnecessary for the development of the plot and insufficiently motivated."[102] Harold Bloom feels that Bessie's murder is "intended to make Bigger a figure beyond sympathy. What the slaughter of Bessie does is worse than that, since it calls in doubt the novel's apparent outcry against social injustice."[103]

Odds Against Tomorrow: Ingram's violent assault on Slater at the end, in a sense doubling or sharing his racial hatred is in its turn an unsettling aspect of the film text. This action by a generally sympathetic character, the locus of audience identification, demonstrates the screenplay's disinclination to solicit facile emotional response.

As to the controversy in *Native Son*, Michel Fabre offers an existential explanation: the murder exemplifies Bigger's "right to 'create' . . . by rejecting the accidental nature of the first murder with further proof of his power to destroy."[104]

In the same existential pattern, the noir protagonist of Wright's *The Outsider* (1953) is Cross Damon, who is not an ordinary man, but a thinking, questioning black man facing the complexities of 20th century life. This gripping tale is divided into five sections: "Dread," "Dream," "Descent," "Despair," "Decision;" with a sixth "D"—"Death"—permeating all sections. (*Native Son* is divided into "Fear," "Flight," and "Fate." The alliterative chapter titles of these novels—as well as those of another Wright roman noir, *Savage Holiday* (1954)—imply a kind of determinism which hint from the start, in an essential noir modality, the futility of the pursuit of freedom. Yet freedom is the central quest in all Wright's fiction.[105]) As the lexicon suggests, Damon, a murderous noir intellectual, faces a philosophical dilemma:

If he was to be loyal, to love, to show pity, mercy, forgiveness; if he was to abstain from cruelty, to be mindful of the rights of others, to live and let live, to believe in such resounding words as glory, culture, civilization, and progress, then let them demonstrate how it was to be done so that the carrying out of these duties and the practicing of these virtues in the modern world would not reduce a healthy, hungry man to a creature of nervous dread and paint that man's look of the world in the black hues of meaninglessness.[106]

Specifically, in the existential world, Cross Damon is unhappily married, menaced by a pregnant mistress, and deeply in debt. Caught in a subway accident, he plants his identification papers on a badly mangled corpse and, having chosen a new personality for himself, devotes the remainder of his life to concealing who he really is.[107] This involves a flight from Chicago to New York, joining the Communist party, and several murders.

Like Bigger Thomas, Damon moves from an accident to deliberate murder, and is plagued by a "spiritual malady," the dilemma of the *ethical criminal*: "the millions of men who lived in the tiny crevices of industrial society completely cut off from humanity, the teeming multitudes of little gods who ruled their own private worlds and acknowledge no outside authority." Paradoxically, even though he has murdered four men, he is supposedly (in his own eyes) innocent, because he can see to the core of a corrupt society, and can find no values in which to believe or act. He knew, therefore, "how close to crime men of his kind had by necessity to live."[108]

Jazz: Take Two. Because of the centrality of jazz to *Odds Against Tomorrow*—especially the way it provides a kind of emotional indexing of Johnny Ingram's desperate situation—it is pertinent to observe that Richard Wright similarly links Cross Damon's sense of homelessness to what he calls "demonical jazz music."

> The strains of blue and sensual notes were akin to him not only by virtue of their having been created by black men, but because they had come out of the hearts of men who had been rejected and yet who still lived and shared the lives of their rejectors. Those notes possessed the frightened ecstasy of the unrepentant and sent his feelings tumbling and coagulating in a mood of joyful abandonment.[109]

Damon was capable of experiencing a mood of joyful abandonment and a lack of repentance at this point in the narrative, but after murdering Joe Thomas, "he came to feel that this music was the rhythmic flauntings of guilty feelings." For the expression of these musical paradoxes, Wright brings together (as in "demonical jazz") some marvelous juxtapositions like "rebel art," the oxymoronic "woeful happiness" of the "innocently criminal," and the syncopated outpourings of "frightened joy" existing in guises forbidden and despised by others:

> He realized that this blue-jazz was a rebel art blooming seditiously under the condemnations of a Protestant ethic. . . . Blue-jazz was the scornful gesture of men turned ecstatic in their state of rejection; it was the musical language of the satisfiedly amoral, the boastings of the contentedly lawless, the recreations of the innocently criminal . . . Cross smiled with depressed joy as he paced about his room, his ears full of the woeful happiness of the blues and the orgiastic culpability of jazz.[110]

The juxtaposition of literature to music—rebellion to art—is, of course, a routine creative instinct for the Abraham Polonsky who wrote: "Welcome to that cocktail of sound and color, improvised, polyphonic, American jazz. Jazz is a liberation of music from the chains of convention and snobbery. It comes from the human heart, not from the academies. It is free. It is honest. It is art the way art should be. All the rest . . . is merely literature."[111]

Chester Himes (1909-1984).

In an essay published as "Dilemma of the Negro Novelist in the U.S.," Chester Himes wrote:

> The question the Negro writer must answer is: how does the fear he feels as a Negro in white American society affect his, the Negro personality?
>
> There can be no understanding of the sexual impulses, of Negro crime, of Negro marital relations, of our spiritual entreaties, our ambitions and our defeats, until this fear has been revealed at work behind the false fronted facades of our ghettoes; until others have experienced with us to the same extent the impact of fear upon our personalities.
>
> If this plumbing for the truth reveals within the Negro personality, homicidal mania, lust for white women, a pathetic sense of inferiority, paradoxical anti-Semitism, arrogance, Uncle Tomism, hate and fear and self-hate, this then is the effect of oppression on the human personality. These are the daily horrors, the daily realities, the daily experiences of an oppressed minority.
>
> And if it appears that the honest American Negro writer is trying to convince his audience that the whole Negro race in America, as a result of centuries of oppression, is sick at soul, the conclusion is unavoidable. It could not conceivably be otherwise.[112]

It is this conception of fear and its psychological corollary, rage, that links all Himes's fiction. (It will be remembered that the titles of the opening chapters of both of Richard Wright's noir novels establish this context of anxiety: FEAR—*Native Son* and DREAD— *The Outsider*.)[113]

Himes is primarily known for his so-called Harlem Domestic series of mystery and detective novels, featuring characters named Coffin Ed Johnson and Grave Digger Jones. But only one work in that series pre-dates *Odds Against Tomorrow*, the appropriately titled *A*

Rage in Harlem (originally published as *For Love of Imabelle*, 1957). This novel and three additional earlier works by Himes—*If He Hollers Let Him Go* (1945), *The End of a Primitive* (1955/1997), *A Case of Rape* (1956/1963)—possess the ambiance of the noir world and portray African American protagonists imbued with violence and fear.

"The most interesting transit across Los Angeles's literary scene in the 1940s was probably the brief appearance of Black *noir*. Los Angeles was a particularly cruel mirage for black writers," writes Mike Davis in *City of Quartz*.[114]

> CHESTER HIMES: Los Angeles hurt me racially as much as any city I have ever known. It was the lying hypocrisy that hurt me. Up to the age of thirty-one I had been hurt emotionally, spiritually, and physically as much as thirty-one years can bear, and still I was entire, complete, functional; my mind was sharp, my reflexes good, and I was not bitter. But under the mental corrosion of race prejudice in Los Angeles I had become bitter and saturated with hate.[115]

If He Hollers Let Him Go is Himes's portrait of Los Angeles as this racial hell. The story is narrated in a first person, hard-boiled style by noir protagonist Bob Jones, a young black man working in the defense industry during World War II. Written at a time when lynching was not uncommon, race intrudes upon Jones's every thought and action. During the highly compressed four-day period of this novel, Jones loses his job, his girl, and his army deferment; he is falsely accused of raping a white woman and that forces him to enlist to avoid jail.

The theme of fear pervades the novel. One main idea persists: the black man trapped in a racist society will be destroyed by its brutal psychological terrors. Bob Jones is an educated, articulate, and sensitive person, but he is afraid. This is from the first chapter of Chester Himes's first novel, but he never wrote a more powerful or shocking passage:

> I got so the only place I felt safe was in bed asleep.[116]

> I was even scared to tell anybody. If I'd gone to a psychiatrist he'd have had me put away. Living every day scared, walled in, locked up. . . . I had to fight hard enough each day just to keep on living. All I wanted was for the white folks to let me

alone; not say anything to me; not even look at me. They could take the goddamned world and go to hell with it.

Suddenly the baby started bawling in the next room and I heard the bed squeak as Ella Mae got up to feed him. . . . Then all I could hear was the sound of the baby sucking greedily, and I thought if they really wanted to give him a break they'd cut his throat and bury him in the back yard before he got old enough to know he was a nigger.[117]

An existential framework is useful here. Bob Jones's intelligence links him to Cross Damon. He is an idealist trapped in a world that negates idealism. He refuses to have his identity defined by society as a nigger; he strikes back and is progressively destroyed. He is driven compulsively to fantasies of violence—an act of self-assertion which is his only means to restore his sense of manhood. This is also his potential link to Bigger Thomas.

But Jones is psychologically incapable of carrying out his violent fantasies. He plots the murder of Johnny Stoddard, a white worker at the plant, and he stalks him. Although he cannot act out his violent desire, he derives a measure of satisfaction from it, because it is clear that Stoddard fears him. But a major difficulty rests in his unexplainable desire for Madge Perkins, a white coworker, one mingled with hatred and repulsion, and in his ambivalence toward his own race. His terror stems from his powerlessness, his inability to find an appropriate stance from which to fight. Bob is thus partly trapped by his own weakness.

His anger makes him a memorable character. Poised and generally self-confident, Bob willingly moves into battle; although the pressures are deadly, he remains resilient. He is framed on a trumped-up charge of rape by Madge, is severely beaten by white workers, and is jailed. He is forced to enlist in the Army. Although the American Dream excludes him, Bob Jones's final line of dialogue (reminiscent of an Abraham Polonsky existential assertion) affirms his strength: "I'm still here."[118]

The End of a Primitive is perhaps the darkest of Chester Himes's roman noirs.[119] The situation is deadly, as Himes admits: "I put a sexually-frustrated [white] American woman [Kriss Cummings] and a racially-frustrated black American male [Jesse Robinson] together for a weekend in a New York apartment, and allowed them to soak in American bourbon. I got the result I was looking for: a nightmare of drunkenness, unbridled sexuality, and in the end, tragedy."

HIMES: What I wanted to show is that American society has produced two radically new human types.   One is the black American male. Although powerless and small in numbers, he can serve as a political catalyst. The other type, the white American woman, has developed into something beyond our imagination.

MICHEL FABRE: Your novels very often deal with the black man-white woman relationship. Is this a personal obsession?

HIMES: I think this is related to one of Western culture's strongest themes. In our culture, the white male both places the white woman on a pedestal and victimizes her. Just the way the black man is victimized. This makes them natural allies. Their mutual attraction derives, in part, from a subconscious wish to break taboos. The black man also wants to possess the white woman sexually as a form of revenge against his white oppressor. In spite of this, the black man is capable of giving the white woman a kind of love she can find nowhere else. This is what I attempted to show in *A Case of Rape* and *The End of a Primitive*.

FABRE: *The End of a Primitive* is indeed one of the best depictions I know of sexual psychology.

HIMES: There's a lot of violence in this novel, and a frightening struggle between sexes and races, but I also incorporated tremendous compassion for the anguish these two characters suffer.

The novel shows a white woman's desperate quest for love among those she believes are primitives. She's looking for the kind of admiration that twentieth-century American culture denies her, but she fails to understand that the man she seeks it from is an extremely complex personality, which is why the affair ends so tragically.

FABRE: Yes. Jesse Robinson can't help gradually coming to hate her. What do you hate most yourself?

HIMES: Racism and what it has done to me. The paranoid delusion that I've been placed on earth simply to be the victim of humiliation.[120]

Racial rage is always steaming beneath the surface of Himes's noir protagonists. At the climax of this novel Himes has Jesse Robinson murder Kriss Cummings, in a violent actualization of the murderous impulses that for Bob Jones, in *If He Hollers Let Him Go*, remained only fantasies.

An Aside on Linguistic Irony

The context of Himes's novel is perhaps as appropriate a point as any to acknowledge the linguistic provocations that emerge, when the African American protagonist is the centerpiece of a critical analysis conducted within the framework of the *conventional* notions of roman and film noir. The linguistic ironies become extraordinary as the inextricable racial signification of the *black* hero becomes linked in the diegesis to the *noir* atmospherics and stylistics of the genres. As Robin Wood writes: "'White' and 'black' are peculiarly unfortunate, because of the way we automatically associate those terms with 'good' and 'evil.' Its basis, which appears to exist in all known cultures, and goes back through the centuries to the dawn of consciousness, is in the opposition of light and darkness, and has nothing properly to do with race whatever. . . . [There is, therefore, a] desirability of separating, once and for all, the word 'black' from any racial connotations."[121]
But if one were to feel that Wood puts the point too benignly, and that a more politically aggressive indictment of a "negative ideology of color" were justified, here's Gladstone L. Yearwood: "Hollywood's language of imagery [and] its star system all emanate from a series of primal ideological supports which have at their base the political subordination of blacks and women and the symbolic repression of these in social intercourse. In popular narrative realism, fear, suspense, chaos, savagery, for example are all signified within a matrix of darkness. In contrast to the use of darkness and blackness in films such as *The Black Hole* or *Star Wars*, its delineation in *Sweet Sweetback's Baadasssss Song* or even *Shaft* occurs within a different range of meanings. Any cinema which is built upon the notion of blackness as evil, as in *Star Wars*, functions as a primary vehicle for the continued subordination of blacks."[122]

The greatest sensitivity and concern arise where color tropes invoke political metaphor—what James Snead describes as *metaphorical chains*:

White	Black
Light	Darkness
Sun	Soil
Good	Evil
Purity	Pollution
Feeling	Thought

These chains have most often been used by whites against non-whites, and I believe that no effective political alignment can presume to ignore them. It is as useless to rely upon purely ethnic, anthropological, or sociological definitions as it is to insist upon an essentialist definition of skin color; white power has triumphed, after all, as a historical, economic, and finally a *conceptual* form of oppression and hence must be combated on these levels of its operation—and more.[123]

Linguistic Irony: Take Two. As part of Jesse Robinson's interior monologue in the last chapter of *The End of a Primitive*, Himes uses language that is very hip to its ironic potential. As a way of rationalizing his actions, Jesse's "mind became sealed within a sardonic, self-lacerating humor," resulting in some tricky manipulation of the words "primitive" and "human being."

"Your trouble, son," his thoughts continued without interruption. "You tried too hard to please. Showed right there you were a primitive. A human being never tries to please. Not restricted by conscience like a primitive. You're human now. Went in the back door of the Alchemy Company of America a primitive filled with all that crap called principles, integrity, honor, conscience, faith, love, hope, charity, and such, and came out the front door a human being, completely purged. End of a primitive; beginning of a human. . . . They'll know damn well you're human. Be in all the newspapers: BLACK MAN KILLS WHITE WOMAN. Not only natural, plausible, logical, inevitable, psychiatrically compulsive and sociologically conclusive behavior of a human being . . . but mathematically accurate and politically correct as well. Black son of a bitch has got to have some means of joining the human race. Old Shakespeare knew. Suppose he'd had Othello kiss the bitch and make up. Would have dehumanized the bastard.[124]

Additional Aside: This is the kind of linguistic trickery employed, in a further reversal of Himes's meanings, in *Little Big Man*,[125] where Indians are viewed as "human beings" and white people are portrayed as genocidal primitives.

Ultimately, however, Himes's roman noir deracinates the usual linguistic and color signification. As Robinson, the black noir protagonist, sees it: his descent and absorption into evil is a movement from black (primitive purity) to white (moral decay). Chester Himes is deconstructing the protocols of the noir idiom—the result is a postmodern roman noir *with* linguistic irony.[126]

For Johnny Ingram, the noir protagonist of *Odds Against Tomorrow*, there is a similar movement. From the moment which establishes perhaps his most stable (primitive) moral position—his turning down Burke's proposal, characterizing himself as "people" [32]—to his giving in to violent hatred at the end, his decline has been orchestrated by and he has come to share Slater's racial virulence. To employ Himes's linguistic construction, Ingram has become white.

Himes's *A Case of Rape* recounts the trial in Paris of four American black men (Caesar Gee, Sheldon Edward Russell, Theodore Elkins, Scott Hamilton) for the rape and murder of Elizabeth Hancock, and the efforts of another black expatriate, writer Roger Garrison, to exculpate them. This short novel is written in a dispassionate, almost journalistic style, but it ominously conveys the social implications of personal fear and guilt. Himes: "I was experimenting with form. I wanted to show that in cases where a black man is accused of rape—guilty or not—the whole affair is politicized. Just the idea of a black man being accused of rape in a white society is political."[127]

Four American Negro men had been caught in a room with a white woman who had died from the combined effects of an over-dose of an aphrodisiac and repeated sexual employment. In the minds of most of the people of this civilized world, they had been guilty since the banishment of Ham, the second son of Noah.

They were sentenced to life imprisonment.

Only the American Negro press raised doubts of the defendants' guilt. But this did not arise from the manner in which the trial had been conducted nor from lack of evidence to support the verdict. It was the natural reaction of American Negroes to suspect all justice rendered by whites.[128]

The objective style notwithstanding, this is not exclusively a political tract. Along the way, personal noir intimations emerge:

Scott Hamilton, one of the black defendants, is revealed to have "contracted all the forms of mental illness he had tried from the beginning to cure in [Elizabeth Hancock]. He suffered all the fears and frustrations and anxieties and paranoia she had first suffered. He reached a stage where he could bear it no longer. He was afraid he might kill her."[129]

Roger Garrison, the investigator seeking to help the convicted black men, "had hoped secretly he might discover them to be guilty," and "loved violence when committed upon the white race, and regretted such was not the case."[130]

And the chapter "The Strange Fruits of Fear" brings us full circle back to the motifs of fear and trembling that are so pervasive in the works of Richard Wright: "It was always best for any Negro to deny any charge lodged against him, to deny it totally and continuously, rather than try to explain the degree of his guilt. . . . Negroes have been so conditioned by the injustices of American courts that they will automatically plead innocent even in the fact of obvious guilt."[131]

Readers of this novel are influenced to consider whether the greater crime was rape or the conviction of innocent men for rape on racial preconceptions. Himes's percept is that all men of whatever race bear some measure of the guilt "for mankind's greatest crime, man's inhumanity to man." A disturbing narrative concludes with noir's greatest generality and perhaps its greatest truth: "We are all guilty."[132]

In 1957 Himes was invited by Marcel Duhamel, editor of the famous *Série Noire* of Gallimard Publishing, to write a crime novel in the American hard-boiled style which for so long had fascinated the French. The book, *For Love of Imabelle* (later titled *A Rage in Harlem*), was an instant success, was awarded a French literary prize, the "Grand Prix de Littérature Policière" in 1958, and Himes became the most popular among the French reading public of all the black writers who emigrated to Paris is the 1950s.

Violence as a noir experience is an artistic form in the novels of Chester Himes. Like Hemingway, Hammett, or Chandler he presents violence without emotional attachment, acting as a sort of camera eye, and in doing this Himes could rely on his own self-knowledge. In his autobiography, *The Quality of Hurt* (1972), he writes that one of the reasons he survived his seven-year sentence (for armed robbery) in the Ohio Penitentiary was because the other inmates feared his temper:

> I could never bear to be used against my will in any capacity. In comparison with most of the black convicts in the Ohio Penitentiary my five feet nine inches in height and one hundred-and-sixty-five pounds in weight made me practically a midget. But I had such violent seizures of rage that I made men twice my size quake with fright. In my fits of insensate fury I would have smashed the world, crushed it in my hands, kicked down the universe. I became blind, defenseless; many times I would have been killed except for the aura of violence surrounding me and the incredible distortion of my face.[133]

In depicting his novelistic violence, Himes adds the qualities of the grotesque and the absurd—and the stylistic flourishes of a kind of street poetry. Note how the inherent poetic essence of Himes's writing is able to sustain the reconfiguration of a *prose* passage from *A Rage in Harlem* into verse:

> *Looking eastward from the towers of Riverside Church,*
> *perched among the university buildings on the high banks of the*
> *Hudson River,*
> *in a valley far below,*
> *waves of gray rooftops distort the perspective like the surface of a sea.*
> *Below the surface, in the murky waters of fetid tenements,*
> *a city of black people who are convulsed in desperate living,*
> *like the voracious churning of millions of hungry cannibal fish.*
> *Blind mouths eating their own guts.*
> *Stick in a hand and draw back a nub.*
> *That is Harlem.*
> *The farther east it goes, the blacker it gets.*[134]

In this passage Himes focuses the noir style on black people themselves. For Borde and Chaumeton, film noir is black because the characters have lost the privilege of whiteness by pursuing lifestyles that are misogynistic, cowardly, duplicitous, that exhibit themselves in an eroticization of violence. Critic Manthia Diawara interprets this material as the text for a *roman sociologique*:

> Himes opposes that which is above—Riverside Church and the buildings of Columbia University—to that which is below—Harlem—to highlight less an aesthetic state of affairs than a way of life that has been imposed on black people through social injustice, and that needs to be exposed to the light. Himes's text is a protest novel which deploys the noir style to shed light on the desperate conditions of people who are forced to live below. [Continuous with the linguistic manipulations and paradoxes employed in *The End of a Primitive*,] *A Rage in Harlem* uses the conventions of the noir genre to subvert its main tenet: that blackness is a fall from whiteness. For Himes, black people are living in hell and white people in heaven not because the one color is morally inferior to the other, but because black people are held captive in the valley below the towers of Riverside Church.[135]

Diawara's reading of the text as a social-problem novel notwithstanding, *A Rage in Harlem* contains a plenitude of ingredients from the noir aesthetic.

The noir protagonist: Jackson is positioned as a noir character (as were so many others, in works based on the same concept) in these short sentences: "Jackson had never stolen any money in his life. He was an honest man. But there was no other way out of this hole." (p. 10) Soon: "He felt as though he had stumbled into quicksand. Every time he struggled to get out, he went in deeper." (p. 24)[136]

Noir anxiety with a racial twist: "Jackson felt as though he were at the bottom of the pit. He'd been clubbed, shot at, skinned up, chased, and humiliated. The knot on his head sent pain shooting down through his skull like John Henry driving steel, and his puffed, bruised lips throbbed like tom-toms. . . . Colored folks and trouble, Jackson thought, like two mules hitched to the same wagon." (p. 85)

Noir desperation: "Jackson had the feeling of sitting in the middle of a nightmare. He was sealed in panic and couldn't get out. He couldn't think. He didn't know where he was going, didn't know what he was doing. Just driving, that's all. He had forgotten why he was running. Just running. He felt like just sitting there behind the wheel and driving that hearse off the edge of the world." (p. 136)

Noir landscape: Harlem—the farther east it goes, the blacker it gets:

Up there in Harlem, Park Avenue is flanked by cold-water, dingy tenement buildings, brooding between junk yards, dingy warehouses, factories, garages, trash-dumps where smart young punks raise marihuana weed.

It is a truck-rutted street of violence and danger, known in the underworld as the Bucket-of-Blood. See a man lying in the gutter, leave him lay, he might be dead. . . .

These folks over here'll steal a blind man's eyes. (pp. 93-94)

However, the noir landscape of the final novel to be discussed, in this background survey of roman noirs with black protagonists, is the American South. Its author lives in Paris and is white.

Boris Vian (1920-1959).

If it were necessary to elect a single figure from among that circle to act as an emblem of the 1950s [when Paris was newly liberated and St.-Germain-des-Près was the center of the world], the choice would not be Camus, nor Sartre or de Beauvoir, but Boris Vian.
                    —James Campbell, *Exiled in Paris*[137]

The ambiguity of the myth of Vian partly results from the scandal surrounding the publication of his first book, *J'irai cracher sur vos tombes* (1946) [translated as *I Shall Spit on Your Graves* (1948); adapted for theater and performed in Paris (1948); adapted for film by Vian and Jacques Dopagne, directed by Michel Gast (1959)]. Jean d'Haullin, an editor and a friend of Vian, was searching for ways to improve business at his publishing house, Editions du Scorpion. He asked Vian to advise him as to which American author to publish, American literature being much in fashion. Vian responded that he would write a best-selling American-type potboiler himself. Within two weeks, he wrote *J'irai cracher sur vos tombes*. Published under a pseudonym, supposedly a translation by Vian of a work by an African American novelist named Vernon Sullivan, *J'irai cracher sur vos tombes* is one of Vian's four Vernon Sullivan novels and his only important success during his lifetime.[138]

The novel focuses on racial problems in America, an issue that Vian learned about from his friends, black jazz musicians. The protagonist-narrator is an African American, Lee Anderson, who can easily pass for a white person. Within the skein of black noir protagonists created by Richard Wright and Chester Himes, and anticipating the Polonsky reworking of the Johnny Ingram character in *Odds Against Tomorrow*, Vian cast Lee Anderson with the idea "that one can imagine and also meet Negroes just as 'tough' as white men."[139] To avenge his brother, lynched for having kept company with a white woman, Anderson sleeps with two sisters, both beautiful, rich, and white. He then reveals his true identity and brutally kills both. After a pursuit by the police he is caught and lynched.

The noir element of revenge, with a racial twist, is a central current in the novel: "As for its background, one must see a manifestation of a desire for revenge in a race still, whatever one may say, over-worked, badly treated, and terrorised, a sort of temptation of exorcism, against the domination of 'real whites.'" (Vian, "Preface.")

There is only one thing that matters, and that is to have revenge, full and complete revenge. . . . (p. 80)

I now felt that I had both of them hooked. I felt very good inside me and I'm sure my kid brother was happy in his grave. I stretched out my hand to him. It's nice to be able to shake your brother's hand. . . . (p. 143)

Until that minute I hadn't thought of all the complications my plan to kill both of the girls would bring about. But I had to do something for [my brother] and for my own sake too. I know some men more or less like me who try to forget their blood and who go over to the side of the whites for all purposes, not even having the decency to refrain from knocking the colored race when the occasion demands it. I could kill men like that with a lot of pleasure, but I had to do things in the proper order.

First the Asquith girls. [They] would be my first test-case. Then after I'd gotten that over with, I thought I'd go after something really big. Maybe a senator, or something like that. I'd have to have plenty to keep myself calm. But I had to think things over a little about how I'd get away with it, once I had those two dead females on my hands. . . .

When the whole business was over, I expected to let their parents in on it. They'd know that their darling daughter had got it from a "nigger." (pp. 157-158.)

Anderson murders the two women, is pursued by the police, and is finally captured in a barn—"several bullets struck him in his hip." (p. 199) Here, immediately following in (the complete) Chapter XXIV, are the final words of the novel: "In the near-by town, they strung him up anyhow, just because he was a 'nigger.' Through his torn pants seat his black-white bottom stuck out mockingly at the world." (p. 201)[140] James Baldwin maintains that perhaps the only reason the novel was considered obscene[141] is that it is concerned with the vindictive sexual aggression of one black man against white women. "What informs Vian's book is rage and pain: that rage and pain which Vian (almost alone) was able to hear in the black American musicians, in the bars, dives, and cellars, of the Paris of those years. . . . Vian would have known something of this from Faulkner, and from Richard Wright, and from Chester Himes, but he *heard* it in the music, and, indeed, he saw it in the streets."[142]

Jazz: Take Three

I insist, call me "racist" if you like, that white people will never be able to equal blacks when it comes to jazz; I'm sorry to repeat it so often.
—Boris Vian, *Jazz Hot*, 1948.

There are only two things: love, all sorts of love, with pretty girls, and the music of New Orleans or Duke Ellington. Everything else ought to go, because everything else is ugly . . .
—Boris Vian, *Mood Indigo*, 1946.

When he was seventeen Vian heard Duke Ellington in concert, and the experience so overwhelmed him that he purchased a trumpet and immediately set about mastering jazz riffs. He became a trumpeter in Claude Abadie's jazz orchestra, reviewed the latest sounds from abroad in a number of newspapers and magazines, including one he founded himself, *Jazz News*. For him this taste in music was inseparable from an interest in the social conditions in which blacks lived, particularly in the American South.

"For most of the *rats-de-cave* of St.-Germain, whether committed cafe-thinkers or not, jazz was the modern thing." Vian had attended Jean-Paul Sartre's lectures on existentialism; the two jazz enthusiasts liked each other, and soon Sartre invited Vian to write a column for his widely acclaimed magazine *Les Temps Modernes*. Jazz was the reflection of the newly fashionable philosophy. It spoke of defiance and protest. It was rude and erotic. It was supremely of the moment.

"Man simply is"—and what could be more simply "is" than the black man playing his way out of a past that had enslaved him? [Harry Belafonte as Johnny Ingram in *Odds*, discussed above, pp. 178, and below, p. 238.] The black jazz musician was man-simply-is par excellence, improvising nightly, clearing a playground of sensual delight in the existential gloom. Jazz, the black man's mastercrime of cultural defiance, was the ultimate antibourgeois art. In its very first cry of origin, from the auction blocks of the Deep South, as Vian reminded the serious readers of *Combat*, it was freedom music.[143]

At the beginning of 1958 director Louis Malle was finishing his first film, *Ascenseur pour l'échafaud* (*Elevator to the Gallows*), a film noir about a man (Maurice Ronet) who devises an ingenious plot to murder his boss with the help of the victim's wife (Jeanne Moreau). Miles Davis was playing in a Parisian club, and, as Louis Malle writes, "Boris Vian helped me convince the renowned jazz trumpeter to do the music for the film. It all took place in a single evening, Miles improvising magnificently with enthusiastic encouragement from Boris, who also wrote great liner notes for the record jacket."[144]

The use of Miles Davis's jazz score signaled a change in the artistic climate; it came to stand for something different in the post-war world, something more emphatically American and "foreign." For the generation to which Louis Malle belonged, the use of American jazz signaled rejection of the ethos (and the films) of an earlier period, the era of (in *Cahiers* terms) "*cinéma de papa*," old fogy cinema. "Now we are expected to surrender to the depiction of the new France, of motorways and glass-fronted buildings, motels and sharp suits."[145]

Odds Against Tomorrow: John Lewis's jazz score for *Odds*, released about one year after Miles Davis's work in France and about the same time of Godard's *Breathless*, reflected an American counterpart to this European nihilism. Especially resonant of the period are the images of the automobile, the bus, and, in Polonsky's words—"the geometry of traffic" [42]. Lewis's jazz underscoring for these images is relentlessly predictive of bad endings, an emotive foreshadowing of the movement toward and the dynamic of death.

Music and literature and death—the aesthetization of violence—they all coalesce in Boris Vian and the end of an era. During the controversy over *I Shall Spit on Your Graves*, Vian's own life and medical history were investigated by the press, and a grisly noir tableau was painted by *France-Dimanche*:

When he learned about the crime which he had inspired, of which he was even a kind of author by proxy, the young writer [Vian] smiled and made the following curious statement:

"A novel is meant to relieve pressure. This crime therefore suggests that my book was not violent enough. What I write next will be much more virulent."

But if this drama seems to be having little effect on Boris Vian, there is another drama in the young novelist's life.

He has a serious heart condition (so he says) and at the same time is trumpeter in an orchestra. Playing the trumpet is forbidden to him.

"If I continue, I will be dead in ten years," says he. "But I prefer to die and to go on playing the trumpet."

This (if one is to believe him) Boris Vian, murderer by proxy, is condemning himself to death: one wonders whether this, too, is a publicity stunt?[146]

Vian often predicted he would die before he reached the age of forty, and he made the deadline by a year. He died of a heart attack during a private screening of *J'irai cracher sur vos tombes*, a film version of his novel, directed by Michel Gast, that he disapproved of but was powerless to prevent. Vian's death in this fashion—watching his own screenplay being mutilated, in light of the disconcerting implication that his jazz playing was foreshortening his life—can lead to some baroque speculation about the noir connections between art and death. Louis Malle writes: "I've always thought that Boris died of shame from having seen what they'd done to his book. Like anything else, the cinema can kill."[147]

The year was 1959. Vian was dead. Within a year: Albert Camus and Michel Gallimard (the publisher of the *Série Noire*), driving together in the same car, would be dead; Richard Wright would be dead. The French *nouvelle vague*, in audacities like *Breathless* and *Shoot the Piano Player*, was employing the elements of film noir as a mechanism for personal expression, and bringing a traditional approach to genre to an end. And in the United States, *Odds Against Tomorrow*—in a marvelous amalgamation of the roman noir and the film noir and a "French connection"—was bringing the classic phase of a native film movement to an end.

The Black Protagonists of *Roman Noir*

The following is a listing of the African American noir protagonists of the literary works discussed in this section, with a summary of their defining psychological or behavioral noir traits.

Character and Work	Noir Attributes
Bigger Thomas. *Native Son.* (Wright)	Criminal perspective; fear and dread; racial hatred; alienation; violence; guilt; moral ambiguity; psychological instability; fatalism.
Saul Saunders. "The Man Who Killed a Shadow." (Wright)	Criminal perspective; fear and dread; violence; fatalism; uncertainty of motivations.
Cross Damon. *The Outsider.* (Wright)	Criminal perspective; fear and dread; racial hatred; alienation; moral ambiguity; psychological instability; violence.
Bob Jones. *If He Hollers Let Him Go.* (Himes)	Fear and dread; racial hatred; violent fantasies; sexual obsession; uncertainty of motivations; moral ambiguity; fatalism; ambiguous women; (first person pov).
Jesse Robinson. *The End of a Primitive.* (Himes)	Criminal perspective; sexual obsession; racial hatred; (eroticization of) violence; psychological instability; fatalism; ambiguous woman.
Scott Hamilton. *A Case of Rape.* (Himes)	Fear and dread; psychological instability; moral ambiguity; ambiguous woman.
Jackson. *A Rage in Harlem.* (Himes)	Criminal perspective; violence; fatalism; ambiguous woman; moral ambiguity.
Lee Anderson. *I Shall Spit on Your Graves.* (Vian/Sullivan)	Criminal perspective; (eroticization of) violence; sexual perversion; racial hatred; (first person pov).

| Johnny Ingram. *Odds Against Tomorrow*. (William McGivern) [Discussed below: pp. 245-249] | Criminal perspective; racial hatred; fear (of physical pain); fatalism; moral ambiguity; violence; alienation. |

The Black Protagonist of *Film Noir*: The Cinema Tradition

Overview. The history of black cinema can be roughly divided into four periods: Early Silent Films (1890-1920), Early Soundies and Race Films (1920-1945), Post War Films (1945-1960), and Contemporary Films.[148]

For many of those years the movies presented black men and women as subhuman, simpleminded, superstitious, submissive people who exhibited qualities of foolish exaggeration. Several writers have catalogued the American screen's black stereotypes and charted their development, but most are synthesized in the title of Donald Bogle's important study—*Toms, Coons, Mulattoes, Mammies, and Bucks*—The Good Negro (the faithful, submissive "tom" and "mammy" and the no-account, harmless "coon") and The Bad Nigger (the savage, rapacious "brute" and the rebellious, villainous "buck").[149]

Of unique historical influence was *The Birth of a Nation* (1915), which stressed the African American as menace. The black man is presented as lusting sexually for white women, grasping greedily for white property, and unwilling to accept his preordained station at the bottom of the social order. The black is portrayed as a serious danger to the established order of American society unless checked by a white force such as the Ku Klux Klan.

The film became the subject of controversy and many protests, and one of its more important consequences was what happened thereafter to the black image in film. As film critic Andrew Sarris has stated, "The outcries against *The Birth of a Nation* served merely to drive racism underground." The result was that menacing blacks, except for jungle savages, were eliminated from American-made movies, but the more demeaning caricatures continued to be presented.[150]

During the period from the advent of sound to the beginning of World War II, Hollywood films, when they bothered to recognize the existence of blacks at all, ridiculed or denigrated the race. The image of the African American remained such a composition of caricatures that in 1935 the black newspaper, *The New York Age*, in an editorial asked when the motion picture industry would have the "guts and moral courage to stop pandering to society's prejudices and fanaticism." In spite of a couple of exceptions during the war (such as Rex Ingram as Tambul in *Sahara*, 1943) and immediately after (Canada Lee as Ben in Abraham Polonsky's *Body and Soul*, 1947), the old stereotypes persisted.[151]

By the end of the 1940s the film industry seemed to begin to understand that racial attitudes were changing in the United States— Hollywood was on the verge of the most important peacetime era of race relations since Reconstruction. These changing attitudes found expression in a number of key productions that carried the central metaphor of "integrationism into the civil rights movement." What are variously called "racially aware films" or "liberal conscience films," they had in common a hero who was unobtrusive, unthreatening, who alters society by compelling it to face up to a character-defining incident, and who leaves the community the better for it. Thomas Cripps drafts a definition:

> In each the plot unfolded in a cleanlined narrative that took the viewer by the hand through issues, conflicts, and denouements between insistent blacks and their mossbacked white adversaries. At the center were ordinary folk who, like the audiences, were obliged to make up their minds by the last reel. Replacing the platoon or the submarine in this formula was the small town, hospital, or other social circle. Set down in its midst was the black protagonist, often so laden with virtue as to invite carping from critics who thought he tainted the message, yet, as [Stanley] Kramer said, so decent as to oblige the viewer to regard race as the *only* reason for discrimination. In this mode the movies asked audiences to raise their faith only a notch higher to include a black hero who teaches them that he is entitled to intrude on their monopoly of privilege, that he has been harmed by people like themselves, but that no grudge will intrude on their prospects for interracial harmony, and that the whites will be the better for the experience.[152]

The following films, in Cripps's words, "enacted shards of this liberal politics": *Home of the Brave, Lost Boundaries, Pinky, Intruder in the Dust* (all 1949), *The Jackie Robinson Story* and *No Way Out* (both 1950).

Of these titles, it is *No Way Out* (Joseph L. Mankiewicz, writer and director; Darryl F. Zanuck, producer; with Sidney Poitier in his first starring role) which pressed its point the hardest, threatening the viewer with the prospect of race riots if America remained racially inert. The film also seems to be the genesis of Poitier's lifelong role: "the restrained black who withholds himself from whites until they accept him on his merits, who commands the frame by standing apart, who demands neither hero worship nor condescension, nor even to enter the white world, but only the civility due any professional." (Thomas Cripps) "This character was the precursor of an important new black movie stereotype which would develop during the later 1950s and the 1960s: the Ebony Saint. Neither Uncle Tom nor militant, he remains nonviolent." (Dan Leab) And, appropriately, a consideration of this screen persona is vital to the process of charting the evolution of African American movie protagonists—as it is the disparity between the screen images of Sidney Poitier and Harry Belafonte that is at the heart of the distinction between the "liberal conscience" films and "film noir."[153]

In Thomas Cripps's formulation, the performance persona of Sidney Poitier lent itself to a gentle politics of the center. The behavior of Poitier's perennial hero always seems to work toward the healing of "the misfortunes of the land." He is more "the Apollonian Negro," more in control, whose inner resources assure his survival. Like Lucas Beauchamp in *Intruder in the Dust*, he is "the conscience of us all."

On the other hand, the edgy intensity of Harry Belafonte "did not commend itself to conscience-liberals in search of riskfree formulaic reprises of battles already fought." Belafonte's fewer heroes are more clearly Byronic, doomed outlaws, "Dionysian figures" ever on the edge of throwing over the traces—hellbent for outlawry and thence to their deaths.

In brief, Poitier's character worked the centers of the American ethos; Belafonte's played its rimlands.[154]

Film Antecedents. The following is a brief review of selected motion pictures which antedate the film *Odds Against Tomorrow* in their employment of African American protagonists. These are works with a certain propinquity to the crime idiom that would make cross-references to *Odds* meaningful in this analytical context. But these predecessors [*No Way Out* (1950), *Blackboard Jungle* (1955), *Edge of the City* 1957), *The Defiant Ones* (1958), *The World, the Flesh and the Devil* (1959)], with one technical exception [*Native Son* (1951)], tend to have more in common with the so-called "liberal conscience films," wherein their black leading men do not manifest the attributes or perspective of the criminally and morally ambiguous central characters of film noir.[155] The attribution of film noir's first African American protagonist, as previously emphasized, is reserved for *Odds*'s Harry Belafonte.

Character	Actor	Film
Bigger Thomas	**Richard Wright**	*Native Son* (1951)

The "technical exception" to the "liberal conscience film" generalization is this fascinating low-budget work (the first English language film made in an Argentine studio—Argentina Sono Film, Buenos Aires—directed and co-written by Frenchman Pierre Chenal), that attempted to combine the roman noir spirit of Richard Wright's powerful novel (discussed above, pp. 203-206) with the liberal-racial tradition of "protest" cinema. And, if one were to conclude that the film succeeds in capturing the noir qualities identified in the novel, especially as they are embodied in the racial anti-hero Bigger Thomas, the result indeed would be to "undermine Hollywood's dominant 'manufactured Negro-types' completely," and the work and the character would constitute notable precedents to *Odds Against Tomorrow*. However, it could be argued that these artistic constructs are not consistently sustained emotionally, conceptually, or stylistically by the film; and the film's limited distribution restricted wide exposure of what effective content it did possess.[156]

There are isolated moments of a film noir atmosphere in this work: there is a powerful sense of Bigger's desperation evoked right after the accidental killing of Mary Dalton; the lighting in the basement scene, with the furnace's flames casting shadows on Bigger's face, is moodily effective; a neon sign ironically blinks the symbolically sunlit letters of "Sunkist Oranges" against the figures of Bigger and Bessie, who are hiding in darkness from the police in an abandoned tenement building, and Bessie comments, "The sun won't shine for us anymore."

But the inferior acting by the non-professionals in the cast (including that by Wright himself), as well as by usually reliable professionals (such as Jean Wallace as Mary Dalton) is destructive to the essential requirement of a film like this to establish a believable framework in which fear, anxiety, injustice, psychic and moral passion are palpable. And the stylistic choice of employing opening and closing voice-over narration, along with some "documentary tone" musical underscoring, pitch the film in a too objective and dispassionate direction. The opening omniscient narration is stylistically suited to a sociological examination of Chicago's slums. The closing narration (not evidently the same voice as in the beginning) is by one of the film's characters, supposedly Bigger's lawyer Max (although it does not sound like him), who provides a philosophical, first-person coda: "I left Bigger feeling that everything including justice was still unsettled, and today I feel even less certain of innocence and guilt, crime and punishment, of the nature of man." The result of all this is to dissipate or neutralize most vestiges of noir sensibility, and leave a rather awkward social problem tract instead.

Representative of the critical responses to *Native Son* is one found in *The New York Times*: "the novel has emerged as a sincere but strangely unconvincing film. Perhaps Mr. Wright, who is the ill-fated hero of this screen transcription, is less of an actor than he is a novelist and playwright." [With some injury to verisimilitude, Richard Wright, who also co-wrote the screenplay, made the decision to portray—at age 50—the 20-year-old Bigger Thomas of the novel. To be fair, the Bigger character in the film is described as being 25.] "Psychologically Bigger Thomas is a man in revolt against the brutal exploitation of the white man, but that psychological basis for his subsequent actions is never made explicit by deed or nuance. . . . Bigger Thomas is a man freighted by fears, hates and ignorance. But Richard Wright's portrayal is a surface one. He is a frightened fugitive finally forced to fight for his life but little else." [Since moral and psychological complexity are cornerstones of film noir, the shallowness cited here further erodes the dimension of this film's Bigger as a noir protagonist.] "The rest of the cast illustrate the opinion of one of the reporters, who in referring to the crime says, 'it's the work of amateurs.' The stature of *Native Son* has been reduced with this exposure of film."[157]

With Wright's performance seen as embarrassingly faulty and implausible, and the film generally perceived as "awkwardly amateurish," Cripps's conclusion is that "*Native Son* could not help but seem an anachronistic, shoestring race movie."[158] Its limited distribution (by the diminutive Walter Gould Agency for Classics Pictures) restricted it to the big cities on the art house circuit. This becomes a significant point for our analysis which distinguishes race movies from large circulation studio works. For these reasons this film (though fascinating for its own eccentric filigrees) does not seem to constitute a viable challenge, other than in this exotic context, to the chronological noir priority of *Odds Against Tomorrow*.

Character	Actor	Film
Luther Brooks	**Sidney Poitier**	*No Way Out* **(1950)**

"When one thinks of how much of Luther Brooks was to remain with actor Poitier, he is tempted to ask if scriptwriters Joseph Mankiewicz and Lesser Samuels should not be credited with creating the most important black actor in the history of American motion pictures. Obviously, what they did create was the character, the screen persona that Poitier was to popularize and capitalize on. In the early days, Poitier no more molded his image than did Stepin Fetchit; he lived out Hollywood's fantasies of the American black man."
—Donald Bogle,
Toms, Coons, Mulattoes, Mammies, & Bucks

A vicious racist, Ray Biddle (Richard Widmark), accuses Dr. Luther Brooks of the murder of Widmark's brother, who has died from an undiagnosed brain tumor. Refusing an autopsy, which would clear Brooks, Biddle instead incites a race riot. Brooks is caught in the middle between black and white extremists, and Manny Farber writes: "As a colored intern moves through the *No Way Out* blizzard of anti-Negro curses, everything about him is aggressively spiked so that a malignant force seems to be hacking at him."[159]

This has the effect of defining Brooks as a guiltless victim. There is no moral ambiguity about him at all—his innocence, from the audience's point of view, is never in question. "Poitier reveals his penchant for playing characters whose attributes are superior to his fellow man, as, morally, he always keeps at least one step ahead of everyone else."[160]

He never makes a move against the dominant white culture. Instead he nourishes it. In the final scene, after having been shot by the white racist, Brooks tries to save that man's life. In a purely Christian way, he forgives his opponent, saying: "Don't you think I'd like to put the rest of these bullets through his head? I can't . . . because I've got to live too. He's sick. He's crazy . . . but I can't kill a man just because he hates me."

Odds Against Tomorrow: Ingram (Belafonte) not only makes a move against the dominant white culture, but as he sees it manifested in Slater—he obliterates it. In the grip of noir rather than Christian impulses, he *can* kill a man because he hates him.

Character	Actor	Film
Gregory Miller	**Sidney Poitier**	***Blackboard Jungle* (1955)**

Blackboard Jungle is described by Cripps as "the story of redemption in a slum school." The drama centers on Dadier (Glenn Ford), a teacher not yet worn down by the system, and Artie (Vic Morrow), a snarling, hateful kid bent on leading the class to a bad end. Between them is Miller (Poitier), who may yet be won over to civility. In their key scene, Dadier must disarm knife-wielding Artie, forcing Miller to choose. "Miller's opting for the teacher, for the good of the group, and for liberalism's faith in redemption was not so cheap a trick as to end on a happy closure, but its makers did intend a reaffirmed American faith in the worth of the individual in a possibly hospitable society."[161] His code of decency reaffirmed, Poitier's Miller "becomes the noble defender of the hero's liberal idealism, a 'positive'contribution to the triumph of good,"[162] "a hero for young and old."[163]

Odds Against Tomorrow: No redemption here; no code of decency reaffirmed; no assertion of liberal or heroic idealism. In the darkest noir context, the only moral "integrity" extant is Ingram's expression of personal dignity and revenge (in the sense of Bigger Thomas's commission of his existential murder) against Slater for his "racist sabotage" of the caper and the death of Burke.

Character	Actor	Film
Tommy Tyler	**Sidney Poitier**	***Edge of the City* (1957)**
Noah Cullen	**Sidney Poitier**	***The Defiant Ones* (1958)**

Pervasive motif and central image in both films: Sidney Poitier, the black symbol of brotherly love and self-sacrifice, extending his hand to the white man.

In *Edge of the City*, Tommy Tyler helps a troubled white man (John Cassavetes) find a job, and then as his greatest manifestation of friendship invites him home to meet his wife (Ruby Dee) and have dinner. "A Christlike figure, he stands for conscience and humaneness. But he is destroyed by his kindness and loyalty. During an argument with a fellow white worker in which Poitier defends Cassavetes, a fight breaks out. Poitier is winning. But he begs his white opponent to quit. When he turns to walk away, the white man stabs him in the back. Poitier dies in Cassavetes' arms. . . . Poitier's character falls into the tradition of the dying slave content that he has well served the massa. His loyalty to the white Cassavetes destroys him just as much as the old slave's steadfastness kept him in shackles."[164]

In *The Defiant Ones*, Poitier is Noah Cullen, a black convict handcuffed to a white, "Joker" Jackson (Tony Curtis), as the two escape the law. Cullen reacts violently to racial insults, and Jackson is a Southern bigot who dispenses them. Neither man likes the other, but before the picture ends, "something akin to love has developed. For, once they have been unchained, the good Poitier comes to the rescue of Curtis, not out of necessity but out of brotherly love. Again he sacrifices himself, this time not with his death but his freedom, all for the sake of his white friend." In a controversial train-of-freedom sequence, Cullen, who has made it onto the train, reaches out his hand to the weakened Jackson—and jumps off rather than leave his white friend behind. When the posse catches up with the two convicts they find Cullen waiting for them with Jackson cradled in his arms.[165]

Affirmation. "In retrospect, it can be said that all the Poitier films of the 1950s were important and significant. Because they were all made to please a mass white audience at a time when the main topic of conversation was school desegregation, today their messages may seem rigged or naive. But they retain a certain raw-edged bite and vigor. Audiences still respond to the actor's sophistication and charm, to his range and distinctly heroic quality. In the 1960s, Hollywood belittled and dehumanized Poitier's great human spirit by making it vulgarly superhuman. He became SuperSidney the Superstar, and he was depicted as too faithful a servant, the famous Poitier code then a mask for bourgeois complacency and sterility. But in the 1950s his work shone brightly. For black and white Americans he was a marvelous reason for going to the movies. And whether an integrationist or a separatist age likes it or not, Sidney Poitier's movie characters in the 1950s single-handedly made audiences believe things would work out, that they were worth working out. It was still just a beautiful dream, but often that's what great movies and careers are all about." (Donald Bogle, *Toms, Coons, Mulattoes, Mammies, & Bucks*, p. 183.)

Dissent. "Many of Sidney Poitier's roles in the 1950s and 1960s explore the concerns of white Americans and do not thematize a black hero. . . . They did not break the old stereotype but merely shifted the emphasis from a predominant concern with low comedy to a stoic Christianness already present in traditional cinema. The fact is that the representation of blacks as stoic Christian types coexisted with that of the low comic buffoon. However, at the historical moment of Hollywood under siege, a minor concession is made to emphasize one castrated image above the other, but no accompanying transformation of a political, economic, ideological or signifying order are made. This is why at the turn of the 1970s the resurgence of 'neo-minstrelry' would easily obliterate the stoic Christian image." (Gladstone L. Yearwood, "The Hero in Black Film.")[166]

Character	Actor	Film
Ralph Burton	**Harry Belafonte**	*The World, The Flesh and the Devil* (1959)

The problem with Harry Belafonte's pre-*Odds* movie work, according to Cripps, was that Hollywood's ways of treating unfamiliar and outlaw material was to treat it "warmly" or lay it into reverently treated classics, or, once made, to play it off quietly as a "prestige" picture. Belafonte suffered all three.[167]

His first film was *Bright Road* (1953), drawn from Elizabeth Vroman's story of a black teacher (Dorothy Dandridge) in a rural school who struggles to reach a new and alienated pupil (Philip Hepburn). "Belafonte had little to do but render his approval."

A year later Belafonte appeared in *Carmen Jones* (1954). An all-black version of Bizet's opera *Carmen*, "it seemed merely a projection of Spanish stereotypes onto blacks and therefore an easy target for critics in search of backsliding."

Island in the Sun (1957), based on the novel by Alec Waugh, was originally written as a Caribbean metaphor for American racial tensions—involving a spirit of political and social change and interracial love stories. As the work was being filmed, the texture softened. The more militant moments were cut out: the pitch of both politics and passion was lowered. "We had to fight to say the word *love*," recalled Dorothy Dandridge as a shopgirl in love with a British man with whom she chastely elopes off-camera to London. A cool love affair between Joan Fontaine (as a highly placed, liberal white woman) and Harry Belafonte (as a rakish labor boss) ended with a parting "played as though carved in stone. 'He was black and I was yellow,' Fontaine told her friends. . . . Censors neutered a political film, albeit so brassily that it escaped no critic's barbed wit. Belafonte and Fontaine agreed that it had become a 'terrible' case of 'what might have been.'"[168]

An analysis of *The World, The Flesh and the Devil* (released May 1959) occurred above (pp. 187-188, and note 64). Similar discussion about the film, especially from Belafonte himself, eventually pauses at its shortcomings, as in: "a preposterously paltering retreat from racial issues that any TV viewer had come to see as urgent."[169] The notions of racial tension and sexual competition between the black man Ralph Burton (Belafonte) and the white man Benson Thacker (Mel Ferrer) for the white woman Sarah Crandall (Inger Stevens), and the volatility of a violent showdown at the end, had the potential for a tough and provocative noir narrative. But, in an exact reversal of what happens in *Odds Against Tomorrow* (wherein a fury of racial hate causes the men to destroy each other), the men here come to some kind of moral reconciliation.

Burton reads an antiwar inscription from the Bible, throws down his weapon, and confronts the still armed white. Thacker, unable to kill the black man, disposes of his rifle, "and the final shots of the film slam the tolerance theme home when the woman is shown taking Burton by the hand and calling the white man to join them," to move heroically, hand-in-hand—embodying the essence of 1950s liberal-humanist ideology—towards a brave new world.

Dissent from Harry Belafonte. "In the late 1950s the figure of the black man as romantic idol still had to be wholly contained. I had tried to do things in Hollywood, but every idea was rejected. In every script that was sent to me I had no woman. I always had to be reliant on some white hero to come in and save my moment. We were still emasculated. We couldn't just get out there and be.

"I guess what happened to me on *The World, the Flesh and the Devil* was my first real exposure to Hollywood studio chicanery. The original script was written with greater honesty for two white guys, and the metaphor was laborer versus capitalist. But then they said let's take it to another level, let's make it racial so it's a black man versus a white man. They wrote the first half of the script, up to the moment that [Burton] meets the girl, and they shot that—while [writer-director] Randy MacDougall was working on the second half. When I read the new material, my heart sank, because they'd taken out all the truth that would have made the film really admirable.

"I could not have a relationship with the white girl. We spoke in tongues. The only man in the world talking to the only woman in the world—he happens to be black and she happens to be white—they're both gorgeous and nobody's talking about loving. Nobody's talking about getting together, holding, embracing. It was just so false.

"But Hollywood was no more than a reflection of the nation. It was saying no more and doing no more than America was saying and doing. If Hollywood was to change, then America had to change. We had to then change the way America was doing business: to let Hollywood understand that it had to do business on different terms. The upheaval took place and the struggle took place, and in that climate Abe and I then saw the opportunity to put a point of view on the screen that was very different from any of the others around. This would be *Odds Against Tomorrow*." (Interview with Author, 2 September 1998.)[170]

Without the Consolation of Tears

An event that spurred me to write of Bigger: I had written *Uncle Tom's Children* [1938]. When the reviews of that book began to appear, I realized that I had made an awfully naive mistake. I found that I had written a book which even bankers' daughters could read and weep over and feel good about. I swore to myself that if I ever wrote another book, no one would weep over it; that it would be so hard and deep that they would have to face it without the consolation of tears.

—Richard Wright,
"How 'Bigger' Was Born"

The Negro always has played the same film part, or a variation on the same part. Take my good friend Sidney Poitier; he always plays the role of the good and patient fellow who finally wins the understanding of his white brothers. Well, I think the audience is ready to go beyond even films like *The Defiant Ones*. I think they would be terrifically relieved to see on the screen the Negro as he really is and not as one side of a black-and-white sociological argument where brotherhood always wins in the end.

—Harry Belafonte,
New York Times, 15 March 1959

For a couple of years in the late 1950s Harry Belafonte was, as posited in an essay by Henry Louis Gates, Jr., "arguably the most desirable man in the Western world. He was the first artist (of any color) in the history of the recording industry to have a platinum album. As a live performer, he was unrivalled both in the size of the crowds he attracted and in the size of his contracts. . . . Each week brought more articles in newspapers and magazines, biographical sketches in *Life* and *Time* and the *Saturday Evening Post*. And this declaration from *Look*: 'Singer-actor Harry Belafonte, one of the most acclaimed entertainers in America today, has also become the first Negro matinee idol in our entertainment history."[171]

According to Maurice Zolotow (10 May 1959), Harry Belafonte "has a single-minded, concentrated obsession about his work and about holding on to the success he has already achieved and increasing it in terms of prestige and power. Given his character, his talent and his drive for success, it is quite possible that Harry Belafonte will become the richest and most famous entertainer that the Negro race has ever produced."[172]

This image of Belafonte as the extraordinarily successful mainstream entertainer is important as contextual reference, but when this charismatic persona becomes integrated into the fabric of *Odds Against Tomorrow*, another commentary isolates in the filmic character of Johnny Ingram additional facets: "The Negro that bullets from the screen is a young Belafonte—proud, belligerent, defiant, unyielding, and attractively hostile.

"'When Harry first began singing folk songs,' novelist Bill Attaway has said, 'he had this tremendous feeling of protest. It was something an audience sensed the moment he came on-stage. He was the visual embodiment of Poe's dramatic statement: "Endure? no—no—defy!" I don't know any performer who was so magnificent in his anger.'"[173]

Ebony magazine (July 1959), responding to this energy, proclaimed that Belafonte "emerges as a major independent movie producer, whose HarBel Productions is a weapon against stereotyped portrayals of the Negro in films and a socially constructive force in the film industry. 'I want to make films that show Negroes just as we are, as people with the same hopes and loves, weaknesses and problems as other people,' Belafonte says. 'These films will show Negroes working, succeeding, failing, loving, hating and dying."

Arguably, Belafonte's most completely realized effort in this regard is *Odds Against Tomorrow*. (For the record: the film had a budget of $1,100,000, most of which was provided by United Artists;[174] HarBel Productions contributed $250,000 and Belafonte's talent as a fee waiver, for which he received 50% of the picture's net profits. Polonsky was paid $35,000 "for writing" and for "changes.") Belafonte's portrayal of Johnny Ingram (his cool, tough, and elegant relationship with those around him)—as conceived by Abraham Polonsky—is at the heart of that realization.

HARRY BELAFONTE: My own personal desire was to put things on the screen that reflected the deeper resonance of black life, things that had never been approached before, even within the United Artists realm. I saw in McGivern's novel, *Odds Against Tomorrow*, a host of possibilities, if only it could be put into the hands of a writer and craftsmen who would bring the proper dynamics to it. I met Abe through a mutual lawyer friend, Sidney Davis, who represented both of us.

Abraham Polonsky and the Blacklist. I liked what I saw in Abe, what he stood for. He was blacklisted. He was uncompromising in how he speaks on his life and his beliefs. He was to be the writer, but we debated our tactics of how to do this in the face of the world, the studio, and the [House Un-American] Committee, as the blacklist was very fresh. We could not confront them head-on, because a lot of people were standing up and declaring themselves and were being shot out of the water. And not much was getting accomplished. Because it was not only McCarthy himself. There were dozens of vigilante groups. The whole industry was doing it, even the unions. Nobody was exempt from some relationship to the purges. So many lives were being destroyed, since the Committee seemed to be so omnipotent: they could haul people in, ruin them through innuendo and what not. It came right down to either you were for them or you were against them. So, this called for a different strategy, much like guerrilla warfare.

Max Youngstein [production executive at United Artists] had no problems at all with this, as United Artists had already been the conduit for using blacklisted artists, who were doing work with Burt Lancaster and others. They just needed to be sure they kept all these different stories in their right place. Everything we did in the fronting process was hugely inventive. This part began to be fun, but in its complication it became almost as full time an effort as the work of doing the movie itself.

Robert Wise. He was chosen as director for two reasons. One was that he was just a great filmmaker. Two, he had evidenced in quiet ways his disapproval of how politics was affecting the industry's treatment of artists, and he wanted to take part in undermining the existing forces. I sent him the material without telling him who wrote it, just to find out whether or not he had any interest in the subject matter. He did. And then I had to approach him with the facts, anticipating that there may be some hesitancy. I certainly was not ready for the way he sparked when he heard that this was going through some underground method. He got right into it and said okay. He said that the blacklist situation and the content of the film itself escalate this thing; he then had to find how to put it through his own process. Bob and Abe came together and hit it off. (Interview with Author, 2 September 1998.)

The Front: John Oliver Killens. The black writer John Oliver Killens (1916-1987) has had a major influence on African American literature through the use of its folklore. His novels are replete with traditional jokes, folktales, legends, beliefs, blues, ballads, and spirituals. He fashioned his career in the protest mold of Richard Wright. For both of these writers the primary purpose of art is to attack and ultimately change society for the better. On one occasion, he said, "Art is life and life is art. All art is social, all art is propaganda, not withstanding all propaganda is not art. The ultimate purpose of art is to teach man about himself and his relationship with other men."

His novels, such as *Youngblood* (1954), *And Then We Heard the Thunder* (1964), *'Sippi* (1967), and *The Cotillion or One Good Bull Is Half the Herd* (1971), protest American racism in its social, economic, and political forms. Killens singled out for ridicule those African Americans ashamed of their color or who deny their rich African and African American heritage. Philosophically, he protested against the concept of nonviolence as a means of liberating African Americans from the restrictions of American racism. His writing affirms black manhood, a concept defined by Killens as the ability to think and act independently of white social pressure or physical intimidation.

From 1954 through 1970 Killens was active in the civil rights movement, along with Martin Luther King, Harry Belafonte, and many others. He came to believe that passive acceptance of racial oppression only encourages more racial violence. He eventually grew more attracted to Malcolm X and fully embraced black nationalism.

His novel *'Sippi* reflected his new militancy; it takes its title from the folk story about a stubborn black man who refuses to honor Mississippi with the title "Missis" anymore—he calls her just plain 'Sippi. Set in the 1960s, *'Sippi* chronicles the black college student voting-rights struggle of that era. Malcolm X, Stokely Carmichael, Paul Robeson, Martin Luther King, and Harry Belafonte are some figures whom Killens weaves into the fabric of this protest novel.[175]

Killens's vehement position on the American feature film is asserted in his essay, "Hollywood in Black and White":

Hollywood is a Southern-oriented city, as is all of Greater Los Angeles. This statement should surprise no one, since Hollywood, more than any other institution, has been responsible for the glorification of the South, past and present, and for creating the image of black inferiority. It created the lying, stealing, childish, eyeball-rolling, feet-shuffling, sex-obsessed, teeth-showing, dice-shooting black male, and told the world this was the real Negro in the U.S.A. It invented the Negro "mammy" whose breasts were always large enough to suckle an entire nation, and who always loved old massa's chilluns more than she loved her own. The men of Fake-town have brainwashed America and the entire world with the brush of white supremacy.

I accuse Hollywood of being the most anti-Negro influence in this nation in the 20th century. With *Birth of a Nation*, Hollywood fired its first big gun in its war against the black American, and the gunfire has continued unabated ever since.[176]

Given the form and content of *Odds Against Tomorrow* and the nature of this Killens profile, it would seem predictable, almost inevitable (if Killens were a screenwriter), that he would be the author of the film—his view of art as a medium for social protest, his affirmation of black manhood and the resistance to white intimidation, his advocacy of black violence as a response to white violence, his indictment of Hollywood's traditional portrayal of blacks, his association with Harry Belafonte. Killens was indeed the perfect front—but he did not write one word of the script. As it happens, these artistic and ideological attributions are also a perfect match for Abraham Polonsky—who *is* a screenwriter.

HARRY BELAFONTE: "If Abe and the rest of us were getting off on being clandestine in using this [film] mechanism more effectively than it had been, then we had to find a player [to act as a front] who would be able to protect our campaign. John Killens was not only already a rebel, but he was looking to skim the system. So he was invited in to become part of the illusion that we were creating. He went with 100% of everything Abe had written." (Interview with Author, 2 September 1998.)

As a result of the Polonsky-scripted illusion that was created, Killens garnered quite a few plaudits for his résumé. The following come under the heading of IRONIES OF THE BLACKLIST:

"*Odds Against Tomorrow*. The tension builds well to the climax—thanks partly to director Robert Wise (*I Want to Live*), partly to an able Negro scriptwriter named **John O. Killens**." (*Time*, 26 October 1959.)

"Belafonte gave a first-rate performance in the melodrama *Odds Against Tomorrow* as a young singer in conflict with a southern drifter. New York location scenes were skillfully shot, and the cops-and-robbers scenario by black novelist **John O. Killens** was excellent."

(James P. Murray, *To Find an Image: Black Films from Uncle Tom to Super Fly*, p. 24.)

Biologically Essentialist View of Black Cinema. The biological version of essentialist black cinema privileges films about black people, produced by a black filmmaker, for a black audience. Killens was among those who believe that the image of blacks generally in American motion pictures cannot be improved significantly without the involvement of black writers: "There's never been a crop of black writers for film or television. If you don't work in these two media, you do not reach the multitudes. Hollywood makes great pretensions of doing controversial movies. But the great debate in America today is *Negro freedom*. This is the fundamental controversy. How does the Negro artist break through this wall of censorship?"[177]

Albert Johnson, in "Beige, Brown, or Black," an essay written the same year that *Odds Against Tomorrow* was released, shares Killens's assessment: "American drama has suffered from a lack of Negro playwrights (not to mention Negro screenwriters) who are able to present their characters in authentic and dramatically informative situations."[178]

But the contrary view holds "that it is misguided to suppose that a filmic work of art, or entertainment, has black audience appeal simply because it aims for a black audience by promoting certain black aesthetic values. . . . It has become extremely difficult to maintain that either a black filmmaker or a black audience is required for a film with a black orientation."[179]

HARRY BELAFONTE: *Odds Against Tomorrow* is not a black movie. It is not about black culture or white culture. It is about two people coming together in a circumstance where race plays a part. They're both trying to work through this fitting that has trapped them into place. As men they speak to a drama that's taking place in their lives. It doesn't beg for racial authenticity. It's a film that discusses the issue of race within its context and circumstance.

I've made the point that I was *colored* when I was born, not long after the 1920s I became *Negro*, and then not too long after that I became *black*. And the issue is not about preference or which word is correct. The point of this is that it demonstrates that words mean nothing, and what's more important is the reality that we are people still looking for definition. I think today people wrestle with these words and wonder because the greater truth has never been discussed.

The family scenes that came out of this film were not written to satisfy a social critique as to whether this is an authentic black family or not. That's not what the movie's about so it doesn't have to concern itself with that fact. After all, what is the authentic black family? On the one end, the black family is Colin Powell, General of the United States Army, graduate of West Point, of West Indian heritage who speaks, eats, drinks, and does everything in a completely different way from the black family made up of the unemployed, the unwed mother who sits in Harlem and has another kind of rhythm altogether. Which of these is authentic?
(Interview with Author, 2 September 1998.)

Black Women & the Black Family. Regardless of their ethnic functionality, the familial moments in *Odds Against Tomorrow* are dramaturgically substantial enough to deserve comment. The domestic glimpses into Slater and especially Ingram's relationships outside of the robbery plot are revelatory of not only Polonsky's writing approach, but also remarkable for communicating an unusual cultural nuance. This was an aspect noted at the time in *Variety* (7 Oct 59): "The home life of Belafonte's estranged wife is a unique view (for films) of a normal, middle-class Negro home—with an integrated Parent-Teachers Assn. meeting going on."

The character of Ruth (Kim Hamilton), Ingram's ex-wife, is a compelling presence. What traditional images of black women should be used in an analysis of her persona? In "Black Women in Fiction & Nonfiction," Jacqueline Bobo identifies five notable mass media characterizations of black women that have been perpetrated over time: the sexually promiscuous black woman; the overbearing black matriarch; the domineering black woman known as "Sapphire;" the domestic servant; and the welfare mother. "Although the matriarch, Sapphire, and the overly sexed black woman are not generally considered powerful images, they *do* open up the potential for subversive readings, since each characterization contains some element of control. The domestic servant and the welfare mother, on the other hand, are classic representations of powerlessness: passive victims, long-suffering and at the mercy of forces they do not understand."[180]

For this period under discussion—labeled "The Fifties: Racial Liberalism" in *Blacks in Films*—Jim Pines states dramatically: "It is interesting to note that the image of black women, the role of black women, has no significant place in the liberal cinema. In contrast with the earlier racist syndrome where the 'mammy' figure prominently did her bit (alongside numerous black male icons), the black man receives total attention in the contemporary 'progressive' liberal trend. . . . The cinematic image of the black woman remains to this day vulgar and despicable." (p. 80)

For a significant contrast, consider the CBS News social report about the black urban underclass, *The Vanishing Family: Crisis in Black America*, filmed in Newark, New Jersey, which aired January 1985. Through interviews and narration by CBS senior correspondent Bill Moyers, the report examines the lives of unwed mothers and fathers, detailing their education, employment, welfare history (especially across generations), hopes, frustrations, and disappointments.

The documentary's four segments are organized around three major themes, with each segment profiling unmarried couples. By the end of the four segments, the dominant message of the report is evident: "self-help, individual responsibility, and community accountability are required to survive the crisis. . . . The mothers in these segments are caring, responsible, and conscientious; they raise the children and provide for them. (Where women talk of their children's futures, men speak in individual terms about their frustration and unrealistic aspirations.) In each case, black women are assertive and responsible within the contexts of their various households. Thus, even within the constraints of underclass poverty, this moment can be read as an appeal to the utopian ideal of strong and liberated black women."[181]

It is quite evident that Polonsky's Ruth Ingram—described thus in the screenplay: "Everything about her points to an almost excessive pride in self, an excess of dignity" [58]—has a more clear lineage to these liberated black women from real life than to the stereotypes of regular Hollywood fiction. She represents solid, responsible, parental concern, and, like the women in the documentary, speaks of her child's future:

> RUTH
> (calm and reasoned)
> You know, Johnny, I didn't mind what you did to
> me. . . I mean I minded, but I would've gone on.
> But I couldn't do it to Eadie. A child can't have a
> father who lives your life.
> (flaring)
> I'm trying to make a world fit for Eadie to live in.
> It's a cinch you're not going to do it with a deck of
> cards and a racing form. [82]

Ruth's reasoned somberness is bluntly opposed to Johnny's demeanor, which expresses—like the real men in the documentary—frustration, individual obsession, and unreasonable aspirations: "I've got five hundred on the nose of Lady Care today. Can't lose forever." [34]

Film and Literature

ABRAHAM POLONSKY: Harry, you brought McGivern's novel to me, and do you remember what your first words were?

HARRY BELAFONTE: Fix it.

William P. McGivern (1922-1982), author of the source novel of *Odds Against Tomorrow* (1957), wrote over 20 works covering the gamut of crime—homicide detection, espionage, political corruption, the world of the psychopath and the crooked cop. As a police reporter for the *Philadelphia Evening Bulletin* (1949-1951), he became interested in policemen and detectives and how they function in an environment of big-city corruption. The experience provided the details and factual basis for several of his crime novels. Three of these novels, in addition to *Odds*, have resulted in rather distinguished film noir adaptations: *The Big Heat* (1953, Fritz Lang), *Shield for Murder* (1954, Edmund O'Brien and Howard W. Koch), and *Rogue Cop* (1954, Ray Rowland).

The McGivern protagonist is generally at the crux of a moral dilemma, wrestling with problems of ethical, moral, even spiritual responsibility. Although formidable and independent in his interaction with others, the central character struggles with an inner world of psychological complexity and moral peril. In novels such as *The Big Heat* and *Rogue Cop*, the protagonists are in solitary confrontation with the seemingly overwhelming power of an underworld that thrives on duplicity.[182]

Odds Against Tomorrow, published in 1957, the year *Sputnik* was launched by the USSR, is a flawed investigation of racial and class tensions in an era of Cold War uniformity and civil rights activity. Published three years after Malcolm X arrived in Harlem, and the same year in which Arkansas Governor Faubus defied a court order to desegregate Little Rock schools, the novel is as much about McGivern's attitude towards the era's racism as it is about the era itself.[183] The following is a brief analytical summary:

> The first half of McGivern's narrative is devoted to the robbing of a bank in Crossroads, Pennsylvania, with the same characters of Ingram, Slater, and Burke, but with the addition of the caper's mastermind, Frank Novak. The scheme is predicated on the involvement of an African American impersonating a real waiter, whose delivery of food and coffee is a device to gain access to the bank. Novak is notably succinct in describing Ingram's participation: "I need a colored guy to make it work. A colored guy is the shoehorn that gets us into the bank. That's you, Johnny. A nice shiny shoehorn."[184]
>
> Slater's racial bigotry is there as a complication. "The man was ready to get them all killed through his dumb suspicions and hatred. Instead of concentrating on what was coming, he was indulging his prejudice like a spoiled child." (pp. 114-115) But it is *not* a factor in the failure of the bank robbery attempt, which is foiled by the astute police work of a Sheriff Burns. Burke is killed. Slater is wounded and is rescued by Ingram, who helps Earle into the getaway car and drives them both out of town. They rendezvous with Novak, but when he learns of the debacle, he drives away abandoning Ingram and the wounded Slater to stare at each other in the rain and darkness.
>
> The second half of the novel is concerned with McGivern's rendition of the brotherhood theme: Ingram and Slater

amazingly are able to develop psychic connections, to bond over their status as fellow veterans of the war, to reach a basis for certain (military) loyalties, and—as in *The Defiant Ones*—to achieve an astonishing racial rapprochement. [They] "had done something together and they had the right to keep it alive." (p. 203) In the end, the police kill Slater, who is cut down while he is actually attempting to rescue Ingram! Tears then stream from Ingram's eyes and a lonely sadness wells up in his breast, and, while squeezing Slater's hand tightly, he embraces the dead spirit of the racist with a compassion that defies credulity.

Ultimately, the essence of the Johnny Ingram character—as he evolves from novel to film—must be evaluated on the basis of his interactions with Earle Slater, as these moments define his authentic self. Accordingly, on the flaccid end, here is William McGivern's etching of Ingram:

"The over-all projection of his personality was neither shrewd nor arrogant; he seemed merry rather than clever, as if he were dressed for a masquerade party and realized his costume was an outrageous contradiction of his true station in life." (p. 45) "His manner was a parody of shuffling conciliation . . . a pose [that] was also a weapon; he could exaggerate it if necessary, broadening the smile and accentuating the obsequious head-bobbings, until his manner became a derisive burlesque of terrified humility." (p. 47)

The Roman Noir Continuity of Racial Fear. Within the pattern established by Wright's Bigger Thomas, Saul Saunders, and Cross Damon; Himes's Bob Jones and Scott Hamilton, McGivern's Ingram [had] "a fear that lurked within him that was as ineradicable as a child's fear of darkness or strangers." [The knowledge that someone was staring at him] "with revulsion and hatred always caused an uneasy stir in him, made him feel nervous and vulnerable. The look was always the same, a mixture of disgust and contempt and anger. That was how [Slater] was looking at him, and it made Ingram feel frightened and helpless. But worst of all it made him feel guilty and ashamed of himself, as if he deserved to be looked at that way." (pp. 59-60) [It was this primal fear that motivates Ingram's participation in the robbery scheme—an immediate fear of the gangster Tenzell, to whom he owes $6000 in gambling debts]: "It wouldn't be a bullet, that's what made him sick with terror. They'd come into his room on a dark night or catch him in an alley, and there was no telling what they'd do to him—enjoying it, laughing at him. He had a terror of being beaten; it was an old fear; it had been with him all his life." (p. 52) During the aborted robbery attempt, trapped by the police, "Ingram couldn't force himself to move; he stared out the door, helpless with fear . . . fighting down a hysterical compulsion to laugh." (pp. 119-120)

Slater consistently dominates Ingram by force. Note two parallel passages:

> "He was on Ingram like an animal, slamming him back against the wall with a spine-numbing crash. He slapped Ingram savagely with his open hand then, and the impact of the blow was like a pistol shot in the room.
> "'That's right, ain't it, Sambo? We understand each other now, don't we?'
> "Ingram touched his bruised lips gently. 'I read you,' he said in a soft, empty voice.'
> "Earl nodded at Novak. 'See? There won't be any more trouble. It's like training a dog. You need a stick and a little time. That's all.'" (pp. 65-66)

> "Earl shifted his position, and removed the gun from the pocket of his overcoat. 'You see this?' he said, watching Ingram steadily. 'It means you don't have any rights at all. Get this straight now; we aren't partners in this deal. We don't vote on things. You got a chance just as long as you jump when I tell you. You got that, Sambo?'
> "Ingram saw the dashboard light flickering along the blue barrel of the gun. 'I got it,' he said, looking up into Earl's dangerous eyes. 'Yeah, I got it.'" (p. 129)

There is an almost preternatural aspect to the Ingram of the novel, which violates reasonable verisimilitude. Ingram is absurdly tolerant of Slater, eventually even acceding to his racial epithets. Slater: "You mind me calling you, Sambo?" Ingram: "It's as good a name as any." (p. 230)

Instead of resisting, fighting back, eradicating the racist, Ingram "wanted to help the man; that was the fact of it, the senseless, pointless fact of it." (p. 159) "Ingram understood himself at last. In a confusing way he had been closer to [Slater] than anyone else in his whole life." (p. 255)

The novel concludes with Ingram's astonishing elegiac assessment: With "a sense of lonely, irretrievable loss" [over the death of Slater], there is in Ingram "a darkness made up of pain and fear and loneliness, but through it all the memory of Earle blazed with a brilliant radiance. Without one you couldn't have the other, he realized slowly. Without the darkness there wouldn't be any stars. It was worth it then. Whatever it cost, it was worth it." (pp. 272-273)

It is difficult to know whether this was McGivern's paean to passive resistance, or a canonization of Uncle Tomism. Certainly these narrative convolutions were incompatible with Polonsky and Belafonte's idea for Ingram and their less sententious inclinations for the film. Whatever were McGivern's original intentions, this was the text that Abraham Polonsky confronted—as he proceeded to "fix it."

The Screenplay by Abraham Polonsky

James Baldwin once wrote that the protest novel is undertaken out of sympathy for the African American, but through its need to present him merely as a social victim or a mythic agent of sexual prowess, it hastens to confine the African American to the very tones of violence he has known all his life. Compulsively re-enacting and magnifying his trauma, the protest novel proves unable to transcend it. So choked with rage has this kind of writing become, it cannot show the African American as a unique person or locate him as a member of a community with its own traditions and values, its own "unspoken recognition of shared experience which creates a way of life."[185]

Baldwin's indictment provides an insight into Polonsky's approach to the screenplay. The key to the approach is shown in Polonsky's Johnny Ingram and his location in the noir world.

Bigger Thomas & Johnny Ingram. Johnny Ingram is the African American protagonist of film noir, as Bigger Thomas, the black "bad man" of Richard Wright's *Native Son*, is the African American prototype of the roman noir. (For the various reasons discussed, Wright's own *cinematic* counterpart is not as valid a precursor.) An understanding of the essence of film noir's native son, Johnny Ingram, can be approached by analogies to Bigger Thomas—an interpretive point certainly not being made on the basis of the book and film's dissimilar narrative content. There is, however, a certain tough and unsentimental *noir sensibility* which both entities share: a specific noir landscape, atmosphere, and tone—blended with a racially charged, nihilistic, and existential vision—with black central characters who struggle to create their individual identities in a socially flawed world.

The analytical implications are these: *Native Son* and *Odds Against Tomorrow* are not "protest works" centering on a social dilemma that is neatly resolved by a simplistic political thesis. Bigger and Johnny's situations are too complex to be understood by philosophical or political abstractions. But it would be equally misleading to read the works in an entirely personal way, interpreting their central themes as a categorical rejection of politics and a celebration of the isolated individual. Wright's novel and Polonsky's screenplay offer a vision of life in which their protagonists are both strongly conditioned by environment and able in certain ways to transform themselves and their environments through consciousness and free will. They are therefore both typical figures who, in Marxist terms, represent the dispossessed masses, and also fully particularized individuals who, in existential terms, have autonomous selves.

Again, a note on antecedents: before the occurrence of these two seminal works, there was really no substantial depiction (as defined in these pages) of the noir African American in fiction.

LITERATURE: "My race possessed no fictional works [before *Native Son*] dealing with such problems, had no background in such sharp and critical testing of experience, no novels that went with a deep and fearless will down to the dark roots of life." (Wright, "How 'Bigger' Was Born.")

CINEMA: "The idea of depicting black men as willing to engage in violent acts toward whites was virtually taboo in Hollywood films [except for *Odds*] all the way through the 1960s." (Lott, "A No-Theory Theory of Contemporary Black Cinema.")

HARRY BELAFONTE: Abe wanted to create a character which would be significantly different from the way black men had been portrayed, but not to take it to the extreme where you so deified the black character that he lost his humanity, texture, or believability. We did not want it to be predictable. Abe took on the task of creating a black man's relationship to the world that had never been seen before. The basis for equality in the relationship is seen in how he talked to white people. He had to have a certain confident ability in who he was and where he was and what he was doing, even if he has flaws. He moved with a certain kind of strength and a certain kind of ease through life, and made decisions about what to do with an independence that black characters in film had never expressed before.

Belafonte on "Noir Heroism": In the way that Ingram was written, it became evident that the way he was "heroic" is based upon the very way he was trapped in his skin and trapped in his environment. It wasn't that he did acts of greatness. Just trying to work his way through the morass of stuff that black people have to work their way through is in itself a heroic act. Take the guy: he really loves his wife; he really loves his daughter; he pleads with them to have a relationship with him and let him back into their lives.

He's also trapped, however, in that the only way he can deal with life is caught up in this addiction of his—gambling. Because what he has to go through as a man to be able to survive—having his job in the night club—is a greater indignity to him than trying to make a buck the fast way. It wasn't so much that he was a gambler as that he was trying to break his way out of this economic suffocation that existed.

A Noir Ethic: Ingram's wife is working to accommodate the rules of the system. Ingram rejects the rules of the system, which he felt were sucking us dead. Violate the system. I'm outside the system. We've got to hustle the system. If we can't make America work inside the law, because the laws are stacked against us, we work outside the law, and we'll set up our own moral code as to what we will and will not do. We won't kill, we won't sell cocaine, but we will be in the numbers business, we will go into bootlegging. The black community completely understood this. (Interview with Author, 2 September 1998.)

Henry Louis Gates, Jr., in "Literary Theory and the Black Tradition," writes: "The commonplace observation that black literature with very few exceptions has failed to match pace with a sublime black music stems in large measure from a concern with statement. Black music, by definition, could never utilize the schism between form and content, because of the nature of music. Black music, alone of the black arts, has developed free of the imperative, the compulsion, to make an explicit political statement."[186]

This perspective is essentially a celebration of form; or at least a recognition that style and technique are as equally important as content. In Gates's words: "a specific mastery of technique cannot be separated from 'poetic insight.'" Enter the formal signifiers of the film's Johnny Ingram:

> BELAFONTE: [Polonsky] wrote him in a way that made him hugely different in how he was talking to the white characters. He walked in and he demanded his equality *by just his presence*. "What do you want? Run it by me and I'll think about it. I understand the power of my vote." No black guy ever talked to white guys that way in films.

> When he turns to this red neck who's giving him a hard time, they look at each other and you know there's no quarter here. There'll be no massa. Already the character's heroic and he hasn't done anything except just *play his dignity and his strength as a person*.

> He further creates the heroics of his character through his intellectual superiority, by solving the problem with the chain on the bank door. It was just a simple thing—the box. If the box is big enough, they have to open up. He became central to anything that was going to happen from that moment on, because he was the thinking force that saw with richer clarity than the white characters. The audience's senses were being bombarded *by the way this character moved through his part*.
> (Interview with Author, 2 September 1998.)

> POLONSKY: [From an existential perspective,] "the moral authority resides in Ingram's self-esteem—in the undestroyed element left in human nature which wants to look at itself and say, 'This is myself, I believe in myself, I have a good opinion of myself. I have a self that I can recognize, that's mine.'"[187]

Style is an existential determinant.

> Harry [Belafonte] does *look* cool—he started a new trend in American dress by wearing a heavy turtleneck, sportjacket and

shades throughout most of the movie. Though not as pervasive as James Dean's red windbreaker, a lot of guys affected that turtleneck look in the early '60s.

—Barry Gifford, *The Devil Thumbs a Ride*

Furthermore, given the inherent significance of jazz to the film, musical tropes for Ingram's personal style seem inevitable. As, analogously, in the way blues musician Skip James asserts his sense of autonomy: "I don't sing other people's songs, I don't sing other people's voices. I can't." As in the similar use of musical vernacular by Ralph Ellison: "Like a jazz musician who creates his own style out of the styles around him, I play by ear." As in the way Toni Morrison structures her novel, *Jazz* (1993), like the music of the title, around the lyric play of elemental themes, and who recognizes the symbolism of jazz as "an incredible kind of improvisation, a freedom in which a great deal of risk is involved."[188] Indeed, learning to sing one's own songs at some considerable risk—as understood by Polonsky and Belafonte and Wise—is the goal of every artist and, demonstrably, the resolve of this film's noir protagonist.

The Polonsky Motifs. There are present in *Odds Against Tomorrow* elements that link it to the rest of Abraham Polonsky's extraordinarily personal and thematically coherent body of work. The following précis underscores these structural motifs and narrative compatibilities.

1. Both Ingram and Slater try to take a short cut to the American dream. (Slater: "You've been sniffing around trying to find a hole in the fence just like everybody else." [23]) Polonsky's **protagonists** of both *Body and Soul* (1947) and *Force of Evil* (1948) become casualties of their desire for success. They seek the all-American dream, but are corrupted in the process. They can only attain status by throwing fights, aligning themselves with lawbreakers. Fame and money, fancy hotels and snazzy suits, come not by hard work and honesty but by cheating, throwing the fight, fixing the books—the real American way. Polonsky's heroes are cocky, cynical loner-losers, estranged from society's mainstream, who break the rules and cause others extreme sorrow—not the moral, honest, often comic-book caricatures of American manhood that dominated Hollywood cinema.

In addition, Polonsky created a character in *Body and Soul*, a washed-up boxer (lovingly played by Canada Lee), who was one of the earliest portraits of a black man as a human being with emotions and feelings, a man exploited.[189]

> Obviously it was Garfield's movie, but at its moral and dramatic center was the chiaroscuro performance by Canada Lee as Ben, dancing his ballet of death, the clarity of which provided the ethical bridge between the complaisant Charley and the resolute Charley. Without the sacrificial presence of the trainer, *Body and Soul* would have been only another prize ring melodrama. But a black role had made a movie *work*. . . . Polonsky's *Body and Soul* had introduced a black protagonist to the center of the frame, and given him a moral authority to which white people must respond.
>
> (Thomas Cripps, *Making Movies Black.*)

2. The past and present **social environment** of *Odds* which circumscribes both Ingram and Slater, and which functions with such slippery contagion ("I got rid of a headache. Now I got cancer."), also provides "the shadings and nuances which were filling in Bigger Thomas's picture." Richard Wright wrote about how he felt the pinch and pressure of the environment as a factor in the creation of his noir character: "I don't mean to say that I think that environment *makes* consciousness . . . but I do say that I felt and still feel that the environment supplies the instrumentalities through which the organism expresses itself, and if that environment is warped or tranquil, the mode and manner of behavior will be affected toward deadlocking tensions or orderly fulfillment and satisfaction." (Wright, "How 'Bigger' Was Born.")

In Polonsky's film scripts, from *Body and Soul* through *Tell Them Willie Boy Is Here*, and in his novels, *Season of Fear* and *Zenia's Way*, the social environment has played a dramatic and defining role. And perhaps the cynosure of this shaping vision can be located in his most ideologically dense novel, *The World Above* (1951), articulated by its scientist/psychiatrist hero, Dr. Carl Myers: "There is no wickedness in all history that did not come from the social environment, and there is not an act of heroism or goodness that did not issue from the social cause. . . . The task of science is to help undo the misery of history. Science is one of the social forces that must liberate the human spirit from its social prisons."[190]

Ingram and Slater, however, receive no amelioration from science.

3. The partnerships of Burke-Ingram-Slater, Ingram-Ruth, and Slater-Lorry parallel and intersect each other in their tragic futility. The integration of **multiple and parallel sets of characters and family relationships** is a structural signature of Polonsky screenplays. Joe Morse's relationship with his brother Leo, in *Force of Evil*, has a primal influence on every other relationship in his life, especially those with his partner in crime, Ben Tucker, and his partner in love, Doris Lowry.

Madigan (1968), Polonsky's first officially credited film after 17 years of blacklisting, is especially rich in this regard. At least five narrative threads or sets of relationships weave through the film:

a. Detectives Madigan and Bonaro in pursuit of murderer Benesch, after allowing him to escape in the beginning (the spine of the overall narrative);

b. Madigan and his wife, Julia, who feels neglected due to her husband's professional zeal;

c. Police Commissioner Russell, whose pristine code of ethics is challenged by his friendship with Chief Inspector Kane, who is a victim of syndicate extortion;

d. Russell, whose code is further undermined by his love affair with a married woman, Tricia Bently;

e. Russell and Madigan throughout—Russell (troubled by Madigan performing the dirtier side of police work in the streets): "I always get the feeling he's out there . . . doing something I'd rather not know about."; Madigan (whose individualism is explicitly pragmatic): "If it works, it's good. If it doesn't, it's lousy."

A strong sense of collective guilt pervades the film, a feeling that an inability to give the "right" answer or a surrender to human weakness is finally responsible for harm to someone else. Symbolically, Benesch slays a policeman with the revolver he had previously taken from Madigan, laying the ultimate guilt for the killing on Madigan, who lost Benesch when he had the chance to take him.

Another powerful example (interestingly, post-*Odds*) occurs within an additional relationship thread involving Russell and a Dr. Taylor, a black clergyman whose son has been arrested for a crime he did not commit. "During the Harlem riots," Taylor tells Russell, "I was called an Uncle Tom for using whatever influence I had to bring about peace and understanding. Was I wrong?"

"You were right, Doctor," the Commissioner replies.

"Prove it, Commissioner," Taylor responds. "Prove it to me."

Though Russell is certain the policemen who questioned Taylor's son did not exceed their authority, the accusation by this black man, a living symbol of the guilt Russell shares with the white community, seems unanswerable.[191]

> QUESTION: *Madigan* is made up of several narrative relationships, and it is most interesting when they cross each other, as when the police commissioner meets the detective at the ball, and so on . . . the way the function together. Was this the intention?

> POLONSKY: Absolutely and deliberately so. The point of the structure was to leave everything unfinished so that the culminations were always interstitial and never major. One of the key elements or discoveries in the modern aesthetic is the unfinished work. In this film there's a whole bunch of unfinished stories going on with plenty of push behind them because of what's hanging on the characters. And never any attempt to tie anything up, ever. Things just kind of go on, and bounce off one another, and suddenly the film is over.[192]

Then, ultimately, the centerpiece of *Tell Them Willie Boy Is Here* (1969) is the reciprocity of relationships among the two white protagonists, Sheriff Cooper and Elizabeth Arnold, and the two Indians, Willie Boy and Lola. The entire film narrative—in its language, imagery, and editing—emphasizes their interconnectedness.

> QUESTION: I find it interesting that the flaw in Joe Morse's development as a fictional character [in *Force of Evil*] is his desire to maintain the sense of family, to protect his brothers, and it brings his ultimate downfall. In *Willie Boy* you have a hero who refuses to participate in the family relationships of, let's say, a tribal society. And this also brings his downfall. What are you saying about families?

> POLONSKY: In the older Jewish environment, the family center was a source of strength, because it formed a cooperative effort in a hostile society. We were able to draw force from it. The tribal structure of the Indians is a disaster for them today. It's a disaster for the Africans, too, isn't it? Because in the context of modern technology, it has no strength to win.[193]

4. Out of chaos some meaning must emerge. Ingram eventually is driven to definitive action. Ultimately, a philosophical **existential vision** is decisive. **Pride, self-vindication, the assertion of one's manhood**—these are recurrent themes in Polonsky films. The individual effort is always in opposition to a cold and indifferent universe. Within this universe, man is in search of a socially and personally fulfilling use of his manhood. There is always significance to the struggle, but these are qualities that inevitably lead men to destruction. "There is no secret formula," says Polonsky. "The formula, as always, is simply passion, indignation, and necessity."[194]

In *Body and Soul*, the boxer is willing to renounce the money (and probably his life), rather than obtain it on somebody else's terms.

In *Force of Evil*, the lawyer commits to the destruction of those who destroyed him and his brother, even if the revenge he is taking includes himself.

In *Madigan* and *Tell Them Willie Boy Is Here*, the noir cop and the western sheriff are individualists who rely on their own wits and abilities in the pursuit of their men. As professionals, their motive is not so much a search for "truth" as it is a commitment to completing the job whatever the cost.

But, always, at the ambiguous core of each moral conflict, there is paradox:

POLONSKY: [*Tell Them Willie Boy Is Here*]   Willie Boy is not a reservation Indian; he's not a white man either, although he's a partial success in the white world. He's a success in the white world by refusing to be white, and he's a success in the Indian world by refusing to be an Indian, and in that sense is able to exist as himself. But the moment the event starts, which he sets off, and he does an Indian thing, he runs off with the girl who's now his wife, now the old rituals and habits of his particular inherited myth, which is disaster for the Indians, begin to operate. And the more he becomes an Indian, the more impossible it becomes for him to live. And when he's really and truly an Indian in the end, he's like all the Indians, he's dead.[195]

Not with a whimper but a bang.

We're in a struggle for the soul of this country. We're in a struggle for America's moral center. And unless that can be made straight, I'm not sure any of the other battles are winable.

How do you end racism in the midst of a place that is so morally collapsed? How do you end poverty in a place so spiritually poor? How do you end hunger in a place so driven by greed and avarice?

We will ultimately arrive at a place, I think, where there will just be an *explosion*, because despair will be so vast among so many.

—Harry Belafonte,
New York Times, 9 September 1993

The matrix of Polonsky motifs has a certain Darwinian coherence. Polonsky's Johnny Ingram is a character in the same evolutionary tableau that includes: Charley Davis and Joe Morse in their process of revenge against their betrayers; Dan Madigan and Sheriff Cooper in their rituals of professional redemption; Willie Boy in his conscious choice of self-sacrifice. It is left to our imaginations what violent retribution will be meted out to Charley Davis as he exits the boxing arena. Joe Morse has lost everything but a sense of revenge. Dan Madigan and Sheriff Cooper's notions of professionalism are sustained at extreme costs. Willie Boy and Johnny Ingram are literally incinerated on the biers of racial intolerance. Indeed, imbuing all these characters is the metaphor or the literal act of *immolation*. Again, this is the nature of the Polonsky paradox—that the ceremony of self-sacrifice can result in the creation of self and the liberation of the spirit.

Richard Wright, a literary progenitor of these racial themes and stylistic motifs, has incorporated this existential paradox into his novels and his roman noir protagonists:

Bigger's accidental killing of Mary Dalton "made him free, gave him the possibility of choice, of action, the opportunity to act and to feel that his actions carried weight." As Bigger says, "I didn't know I was really alive in this world until I felt things hard enough to kill for 'em." (*Native Son*, pp. 461, 501.)

"It was not because he was a Negro that he had found his obligations intolerable; it was because there resided in his heart a sense of freedom that had somehow escaped being dulled by intimidating conditions. Cross had never been tamed." (*The Outsider*, p, 503.)

Indeed, if a dominant theme in twentieth-century literature is the search for identity, then Polonsky reinterprets this theme for his own work by electing to have his characters search for their freedom in ways as complex and ironic as the history of capitalism and racism itself. Polonsky desires to explore human reactions to oppression and domination and to find a way perhaps to mirror his own feelings of marginality, political exile, and spiritual alienation.

Thus, in *Odds Against Tomorrow*, Ingram's controversial upsurge of racial hatred and violence at the end of the film needs to be confronted on several levels: as the climax of a *naturalistic* text, it is, given the equation of the men involved, the pre-determined result of economic and racial forces beyond Ingram's control; as an integral part of an *existential* text, it is, at the cost of character sympathy, the assertion of individual (violent, destructive) free will against unshakable racism; as an expression of an *eschatological* text, with an etiology of the apocalypse, it reveals an uneasiness with Western civilization.

NOTES TO THE CRITICAL COMMENTARY

[1] Alain Silver and Elizabeth Ward, *Film Noir: An Encyclopedic Reference to the American Style*, Third Edition (Woodstock, New York: The Overlook Press, 1992), p. 216; Foster Hirsch, *The Dark Side of the Screen: Film Noir* (San Diego: A.S. Barnes & Company, Inc., 1981), p. 199. Hirsch also includes *Psycho* (1960) in this context, as part of his discussion of "noir's legacy." *Odds Against Tomorrow* receives the longest filmic annotation in the "Chronology" section of Manohla Dargis's "N for Noir" ("*Sight and Sound* A-Z of Cinema"), *Sight and Sound*, July 1997, p. 31. The *Odds* entry for the year 1959 closes out the classic period category of the chronology. A "Neo-noir" segment follows, with 1960 marking the beginning of the modern noir era.

    Some studies have regarded *Touch of Evil* (1958) as the film noir genre's epitaph—the title of Robert Ottoson's *A Reference Guide to the American Film Noir: 1940-1958* (The Scarecrow Press, 1981) sums up its chronological orientation. Raymond Borde and Eugene Chaumeton write that the American noir "series" began in 1941 and ended in 1953 [*Panorama du Film Noir Américain, 1941-1953* (Paris: Editions du Minuit, 1955)], but in a postscript to the 1969 edition, they move the end of noir along to 1955. While acknowledging 1958 as the "outer limits," Paul Schrader, "Notes on Film Noir," *Film Comment* (Spring 1972), feels, even more severely, that the classic period ends in 1953. Further film noir periodization references are to be found in James Naremore, "American Film Noir: The History of an Idea," *Film Quarterly*, Winter 1995-96, p. 12 and in Note 2, p. 26.

    But, in the overall pattern, the presence in *Odds Against Tomorrow* (1959) of so many defining film noir motifs cogently justifies its characterization as the culminating work of the classic phase.

[2] William P. McGivern, *Odds Against Tomorrow* (New York: Dodd, Mead & Company, 1957).

[3] Thomas Cripps, *Making Movies Black* (New York: Oxford University Press, 1993), p. 266.

    "The title [*Odds Against Tomorrow*] refers to the inevitable doom that lies ahead when people cannot live in harmony together. The fact that the black and white combatants here are each criminals—of different degrees—adds texture to the proceedings." [James Robert Parish and George H. Hill, *Black Action Films* (Jefferson NC: McFarland & Co., 1989), p 225.]

    John Springer's *Forgotten Films to Remember* (Secausus NJ: Citadel Press, 1980) concerns films which gave great pleasure to their audiences when they were first released, but which are seldom revived theatrically and only occasionally turn up on television. In his discussion of "Forgotten Films of 1959," Springer writes this about *Odds Against Tomorrow*: "Vividly explored the conflict between two bankrobbers—one black, one a vicious bigot. Nobody could play that latter character as well as Robert Ryan. Nobody could be more attractive than Harry Belafonte. So they gave an extra dramatic dimension to a tough crime drama . . ." (p. 250)

[4] *Ibid.*, p. 267.

[5]Note the **"informer"** or **"betrayer" theme** in Polonsky's feature film screenplays of *Body and Soul* (1947) and *Force of Evil* (1948). [See *Force of Evil: The Critical Edition* (Los Angeles: Sadanlaur Publications, 1996), pp. 137-139.] This subject is explicitly engaged by Polonsky in his fronted teleplays for the CBS series *You Are There*, specifically "The Fate of Nathan Hale" (Air Date: 30 Aug 53), "The Recognition of Michelangelo" (15 Nov 53), "The Vindication of Savonarola" (13 Dec 53), and "The Tragedy of John Milton" (30 Jan 55). [See *You Are There Teleplays: The Critical Edition* (Los Angeles: Sadanlaur Publications, 1997), pp. 100-101.] The investigations of Hollywood by The House Committee on Un-American Activities (HUAC) are clearly the subtext for the medical panel's examination of Dr. Carl Myer's "subversive" scientific theories in Polonsky's novel *The World Above* (Little, Brown and Co., 1951), pp. 455-465. *A Season of Fear* (New York: Cameron Associates, 1956) is an Abraham Polonsky novel devoted in its entirety to loyalty oaths, intellectual orthodoxy, and censorship— the cold war era's version of "political correctness."

The critical commentary will be developing the notion of a reciprocity between American and French cultural predilections—between Hollywood and French film noir, between *Odds Against Tomorrow* and the French director Jean-Pierre Melville (see Note 34). In this context, and in terms of the employment of the "betrayal" motif, note the following statements by Melville:

QUESTION: In your *films policiers* people spend their time "doubling" each other, while the hero reacts like a jackal or a wounded tiger. Why?

MELVILLE: Because if there are two of you, one betrays. Why do you think I have chosen solitude? (*Laughter.*) Commerce with men is a dangerous business. The only way I have found to avoid being betrayed is to live alone. Do you know two men who have lived and worked together as good friends and who are still on amiable speaking terms a few years later? I don't. Friendship is a sacred thing, like the existence of God for those who believe in it. As soon as you realize things "aren't going too well," it opens the way to all kinds of betrayal. I believe that betrayal is one of the basic motivations behind men's actions—much more than love. Love is what makes one live, they say in *Carmen*. It isn't true. It's betrayal. [*Melville on Melville*, edited by Rui Nogueira (New York: The Viking Press, 1972), p. 116.]

[6]Franklin Jarlett, *Robert Ryan: A Biography and Critical Filmography* (Jefferson NC: McFarland & Co., 1990), p. 238.

[7]The film noir corpus which has been constituted by film critics since the 1940s comprises a bewildering heterogeneity of crime-film cycles and generic hybrids. As noted by Frank Krutnick, *In A Lonely Street: Film Noir, Genre, Masculinity* (London: Routledge, 1991), pp. 188-189: "Motifs, scenarios, stylistic strategies, narrative conventions, etc., are extensively set in play, not within any individual, discernible category but across a complex range of Hollywood productions of the period." In addition to the "tough thriller," which occupies most of his attention, Krutnick discusses the following major crime-film cycles related to film noir: the rogue-cop thriller, the "women's-picture" crime thriller, the gangster film, the "semi-documentary"/police-procedural thriller, the outlaw-couple film, and the **"social-problem" crime film**. The Hollywood social-problem film focuses with a seriousness of purpose on contemporary issues such as alcoholism, the treatment of mental disorders, juvenile delinquency, and racial prejudice. While Krutnick is concerned only with 1940s films in his analysis, with an examination of such social-problem noirs as *Crossfire* (1947) and *Knock on Any Door* (1949), it is within this social-problem context that *Odds Against Tomorrow* could be accommodated if the discussion were extended to later films.

Raymond Durgnat's "Paint It Black: The Family Tree of the Film Noir," in *Film Noir Reader*, edited by Alain Silver and James Ursini (New York: Limelight Editions, 1996), pp. 39-43, delineates "imperfect schematizations for some main lines of force in the American film noir. They describe not genres but dominant cycles or motifs, and many, if not most, films would come under at least two headings, since interbreeding is intrinsic to motif processes." The first category listed is **Crime as Social Criticism,** with one of its cycles labeled "The Sombre Cross-Section," in which "a crime takes us through a variety of settings and types and implies an anguished view of society as a whole. . . . Certain conspicuous social malfunctions impose a black social realism." Again, employing Durgnat's taxonomy, this would seem a likely niche for *Odds Against Tomorrow.*

Thom Andersen's configuration of the so-called *film gris* hybrid, based on a body of films which may be distinguished from film noir because of "its greater psychological and social realism," is relevant here. Significantly, the initial works he identifies as helping define this cycle are two films by Abraham Polonsky—*Body and Soul* (1947, screenplay) and *Force of Evil* (1948, screenplay and direction). *Odds Against Tomorrow*, informed by Polonsky's socially conscious screenplay, would seem to be a logical continuation of the assumptions and attributes of film gris. [Andersen, "Red Hollywood," in *Literature and the Visual Arts in Contemporary Society.* Edited by Suzanne Ferguson and Barbara Groseclose. (Columbus: Ohio State University Press, 1985), p. 183.]

[8]Colin McArthur, *Underworld U.S.A.* (New York: The Viking Press, 1972), p. 53.

"The big caper film is a sub-genre of the adventure-process film, the film in which any small group of individuals of diverse ability (often social outcasts), comes together to confront a massive establishment, be it prison, army, or secret installation. Such films can, perhaps, be traced far back in mythology to stories of communal quests requiring cooperation of men with special powers. Certainly the story of Jason and the golden fleece is an archetypal caper, or process quest." [Stuart M. Kaminsky, *American Film Genres: Approaches to a Critical Theory of Popular Film* (New York: Dell Publishing Co., 1977), pp. 100-101.]

A representative list of caper or heist films, **pre**-*Odds,* would include: *Criss Cross* (1949), *The Asphalt Jungle* (1950), *Armored Car Robbery* (1950), *The Lavender Hill Mob* (1951), *The Hoodlum* (1951), *Touchez pas au Grisbi* (1953), *Rififi* (1954), *Six Bridges to Cross* (1954), *Five Against the House* (1955), *Violent Saturday* (1955), *The Good Die Young* (1955), *The Killing* (1956), *The Big Caper* (1957), *The Burglar* (1957), *Plunder Road* (1959).

[9]Jim Pines, *Blacks in Films: A Survey of Racial Themes and Images in the American Film* (London: Studio Vista, 1975), p. 87.

[10]Barry Gifford is the author or editor of more than 30 books, the best known of which is probably *Wild at Heart,* adapted into an unparaphrasable film by David Lynch (1990). As an editor for Black Lizard Press, Gifford was significantly responsible for the revival of the lurid *roman noirs* of Jim Thompson and David Goodis, as well as the more sophisticated thrillers of Charles Willeford, a revival that extended to films. In this regard, his collection of essays on his favorite thrillers and B-movies, *The Devil Thumbs A Ride & Other Unforgettable Films* (New York: Grove Press, 1988), has helped to foster the image of Gifford "as some kind of Elmore Leonard for those raised on Jack Kerouac." According to Allen Barra ("Folks Who Go Bump in the Night," *Los Angeles Times,* 27 December 1992), "Gifford has been skirting around the edge of 'major' status for years with virtually no help from fashionable academic circles." With an

acknowledgment, therefore, of the possibly dubious nature of the inclusion of the following in an "academic" publication, here is Gifford's rather baroque, but entertaining, analytical summary of *Odds Against Tomorrow*:

A tough, bitter movie superbly rendered by Wise who broke in with the Jacques Tourneur/Val Newton gang (*The Body Snatcher, The Seventh Victim, Cat People, I Walked With A Zombie*). Wise knew how to string the viewer along—pull him in and play him off—and McGivern's story of a botched hold-up has the perfect tension for him. Robert Ryan as Earle, the southern racist, is brilliant. He keeps his lip curled like Elvis and antagonizes Belafonte to a logical conclusion. Those two with Begley are to rob a small Pennsylvania [*sic*. this is the location in the novel; it is New York in the film] bank. What we get on the way is one of the great moments in American *noir* when Ryan comes on to Grahame, his easy mark neighbor: they play, paw, vie for control and finally she says—they're both married, Ryan to the frowzy Winters—'Well, just this once.' Those famous first words.

Begley tries to keep Harry and Ryan cool, and Harry does *look* cool—he started a new trend in American dress by wearing a heavy turtleneck, sportjacket and shades throughout most of the movie. Though not as pervasive as James Dean's red windbreaker, a lot of guys affected the turtleneck look in the early '60s. Begley's planned the whole thing perfectly, of course. He needs a black man to get them in the back door of the bank at night, to impersonate the colored coffee delivery boy. Ryan has the souped-up old woody for the getaway. But it all blows up—Begley's gunned down, wounded badly, and rather than go to jail again (they're all [*sic*] ex-cons), he shoots himself in the head. Belafonte and Ryan run for it and the cops catch up to them in time to watch the ending stolen directly from *White Heat*.

Odds is a seedy, unpleasant take on life in America in the late 1950s. Almost as if *It's A Wonderful Life* were going on somewhere in the background, in the same town, with Gloria Grahame as the link between them: the bad girl in the nice little town, and we get a peek at her life on the underside. The French like this one, what with racial hatred, hair-trigger violence, tramp wives, the cool spade in shades, bleak highways, lonesome landscape, wet, dark streets. The U.S.A. at its best. There is a great deal of truth in this one, though, and, as usual, that's hard to take. (*The Devil Thumbs A Ride*, pp. 117-118.)

[11]Pines, *Blacks in* Films, pp. 87-88.

[12]T.S. Eliot, *The Waste Land* [1922] (New York: Harcourt, Brace & World, Inc., 1962), lines 60-63.
This section on poetry and film has been influenced by many sources. Of special merit for its primacy and lucidity is Robert Richardson's *Literature and Film* (Bloomington IN: Indiana University Press, 1972), pp. 91-132.

[13]Nathanael West, *Miss Lonelyhearts* [1933] (New York: New Directions Publishing Corporation, 1962), p. 5.

[14]Peter Hogue, "Melville: The Elective Affinities," *Film Comment*, November-December 1996, p. 22.

"The virtue of the picture [*Odds Against Tomorrow*] is the photography [by Joseph Brun]. The natural theatricality of the city and the river in upstate New York where the film was shot, under the cold light of racing cloud banks, has been brilliantly caught with no arch artiness. It is a background of almost percussive tension." (Robert Hatch, *The Nation*, 29 November 1959.)

[15]William Carlos Williams, "The Red Wheelbarrow" [1923], *Collected Earlier Poems* (New York: New Directions, 1951), p. 277. Italics added.

[16]Vladimir Nabokov, "A Guide to Berlin" [1925], quoted in Alfred Appel, Jr., *The Art of Celebration: Twentieth-Century Painting, Literature, Sculpture, Photography, and Jazz* (New York: Alfred A. Knopf, Inc., 1992), p. 112. Italics added.

[17]Quoted in Naremore, "American Film Noir," p. 18.

Naremore's emphasis in his essay on the French (Paris 1946-1959) influences on the history of the "idea" of film noir makes it extraordinarily valuable to this discussion of *Odds Against Tomorrow* and the "history" of *its* idea. His analyses have had a wide-ranging impact on the design and conceptual framework of this critical commentary—considerably beyond the individual citation of his work in these notes. His book-length study of noir cinema—*More than Night: Film Noir in Its Contexts* (Berkeley: University of California Press, 1998)—from which the "American Film Noir" essay was abstracted, must now be considered, in my view, the first choice of texts on the subject.

[18]First published in French as "Une expérience utopique," *Présence du Cinéma*, No. 14, June 1962, pp. 5-7. The complete English text is printed in Polonsky, *Force of Evil: The Critical Edition*, pp. 186-188.

[19]Robert Wise, Interview with Author, 11 February 1998.

Infrared light is that portion of the electromagnetic spectrum adjacent to the long wavelength, or red end of the visible light range. Invisible to the eye, it can be detected as a sensation of warmth on the skin. Infrared photography involves taking photographs in infrared light. The process requires the use of film that is sensitive to such light, and lens systems in the camera that will transmit it. If these are employed, objects may be photographed through haze and mist and even apparent darkness. Infrared photography is seldom utilized in normal filming but is very useful in conditions of low illumination and for achieving a variety of special effects, including the simulation of a night scene while filming in broad daylight.

Joseph Brun, the cinematographer for *Odds Against Tomorrow*, writes of the technical aspects of photographing the film. "Filters were used in all possible combinations and I was greatly helped by the variety of film emulsions which are put at the disposal of cameramen nowadays. We jumped from Background-X, to Plus-X, or Tri-X, and used a large quantity of infrared film. The make-up men changed the make-up of the principal actors several times a day to accommodate the change from panchromatic emulsions to infared." (Joseph Brun, "*Odds Against Tomorrow*," *American Cinematographer*, August 1959, p. 479.)

"One is dazzled by the technical virtuosity with which the film is put over. The camera work of Joseph Brun is superb, there is no other word for it. The grey landscapes of wintry New York state, the smoky jazz club and the austere apartment houses as handled by Brun's camera are almost more expressive than the actors. The cutting is a model of cinema craftsmanship, and the music score by the Modern Jazz Quartet's John Lewis is expert." (Derek Conrad, *Films and Filming*, November 1959.)

[20] Appel, Jr., *Art of Celebration*, p. 54.

[21] Edmund Wilson, *The Shores of Light* [1952] (New York: The Noonday Press, 1967), pp. 54-56.

[22] William Carlos Williams (1883-1963) was a poet, novelist, short-story writer, and a physician. His poetry is without rhyme or conventional meter, usually written in short graceful lines and in what the poet calls an "American rhythm." *Paterson*, his most ambitious work, which appeared in five books from 1946 to 1958, is an attempt to apprehend the essence and the experience of his city and at the same time to use its river as an entrance into the general stream of time.
Polonsky: "The allusion to William Carlos Williams is very interesting. I had read all of the modern poets, of course, but Williams is a favorite writer *for* me—he's very good. He's got a lot of interesting stuff, and I've got all his books here." (Interview with Author, 11 June 1998.) Polonsky's choice of the words "*for* me" (italicized for emphasis) takes a predilection for Williams beyond mere literary enjoyment to possible professional resource.

[23] There are instances when the film does impose an order and accessibility on the wasteland debris in a somewhat routine manner. For example, the provocative images of the quoted passage are followed by an explication of the symbolism: "The figure is being dragged along, and then snagged behind a piling. The mass is drifting in toward him now, closer, and has turned to reveal an old rag doll caught in it. Ingram stares, his mind far away, the doll reminding him of his own little girl." [112]
Similarly, the burst balloon at the zoo [69], symbolizing Ingram's vulnerability to circumstance, is uncharacteristically explicit for a screenplay of such usual poetic indirection, as Polonsky himself points out. (Interview with Author, 25 July 1997.)

[24] Interview with Author, 11 June 1998.
Poetry and Science. Polonsky's juxtaposition of aesthetics and mathematics has an intriguing corollary in William Carlos Williams's reference (in *Paterson, Book III*) to the figure of Marie Curie who, with her husband Pierre, discovered radium in 1898. In an early typescript of *Paterson*, Williams notes the ways in which a lecture on atomic fission suggested to him how the "antennae of the poet and the yardstick of the scientist" work on the same subject: "The lecture on uranium (Curie), the splitting of the atom (first time explained to *me*) has a literary meaning . . . in the splitting of the foot . . . (sprung meter of Hopkins) and consequently is connected thereby to human life or death. . . . Three discoveries here: 1. radium. 2. poet's discovery of modern idiom. 3. political scientist's discovery of a cure for economic ills." [Quoted in John Malcolm Brinnin, *William Carlos Williams*, University of Minnesota Pamphlets on American Writers, Number 24 (Minneapolis: University of Minnesota Press, 1967), p. 40.]

[25] **The Poetic Ambiance of *Noir*.** Eliot's poetry portrays the world from which he is isolated and alienated—with images of the sordid, the disgusting, and the depressing. In the poems of "The Waste Land" group there are "the one-night cheap hotels and sawdust restaurants, the vacant lots, faint stale smells of beer, a thousand furnished rooms and the yellow soles of feet, the dead geraniums,

the broken spring in a factory yard, all the old nocturnal smells, the basement kitchens, and the damp souls of housemaids." [Leonard Unger, *T.S. Eliot*, University of Minnesota Pamphlets on American Writers, Number 8 (Minneapolis: University of Minnesota Press, 1970), pp. 17-18.]

[26]The song, "That Shakespearian Rag" (music by Dave Stamper, lyrics by Gene Buck and Herman Ruby), was popular in 1912, during Eliot's graduate-student days, and contains the following chorus:
"That Shakespearian rag,—
Most intelligent, very elegant,
That old classical drag,
Has the proper stuff, the line 'Lay on Macduff,'"
[and, then, note the next lines—]
"Desdemona was the colored pet,
Romeo loved his Juliet—"

[27]Appel, Jr., *Art of Celebration*, pp. 38-39.

[28] Dyer, "Entertainment and Utopia," *Movie* 24, Spring 1997, cited by Robin Wood in "Servants and Slaves: Brown Persons in Classical Hollywood Cinema, *CineAction*, No. 32, p. 87.

[29]Analogous utilizations of jazz music as metaphor or thematic device are recognized in this critical commentary's discussion of Richard Wright's dramatic usage of "demonical jazz" in *The Outsider*, pp. 208-209; in its references to the inextricability of jazz in Boris Vian's career and personal life, pp. 222-224; and in its focus on the linkage between jazz & personal style and artistic technique, pp. 253.

[30]This is section IV of "The Waste Land," "Death by Water," in its entirety, lines 312-321.

[31]**The Poetic Ambiance of *Noir*.** In "The Waste Land" there are verbal echoes of several of Joseph Conrad's works, such as the allusion to Conrad's title in the phrase "heart of light." This suggests Conrad as a source and an influence. The following passages from "Heart of Darkness," from Marlowe's comments on his experience after Kurtz's death, may indicate some of the facets of not only Conrad's impact on Eliot's work, but also of his profound influence on the ambiance of literary and film noir.

"I have wrestled with death. It is the most unexciting contest you can imagine. It takes place in an impalpable grayness, with nothing underfoot, with nothing around, without spectators, without clamour, without glory, without the great desire of victory, without the great fear of defeat, in a sickly atmosphere of tepid scepticism, without much belief in your own right, and still less in that of your adversary. . . .

"No, they did not bury me, though there is a period of time which I remember mistily, with a shuddering wonder, like a passage through some inconceivable world that had no hope in it and no desire. I found myself back in the sepulchral city resenting the sight of people hurrying through the streets to filch a little money from each other, to devour their infamous cookery, to gulp their unwholesome beer, to dream their insignificant and silly dreams. They trespassed upon my thoughts. They were intruders whose knowledge of life was to me an irritating pretence, because I felt so sure they could not possibly know the things I knew." [Quoted in Unger, *T.S. Eliot*, pp. 20-21.]

[32]The "cures" Eliot proposes are those found in the *Brihadaranyaka—Upanishad*, 5, 1: *Datta* (Give), *Dayadhvam* (Be Compassionate), *Damyata* (Restrain Yourselves). ("The Waste Land," lines 402ff.)

[33]Cripps, *Making Movies Black*, p.267; Jarlett, *Robert Ryan*, p. 237.

[34]The character, vision, and style of French film director Jean-Pierre Melville (born Jean-Pierre Grumbach) are embodied in a trio of mid-1960s gangster films—*Le Doulos* (*The Fingerman*), *Le Deuxième Souffle* (*Second Breath*), and *Le Samourai*—which constitute the core of his achievement in cinema. "Drawing on his 1930s viewing and his adolescent reading of American thrillers, Melville manipulated the whole mythology of the gangster film. His criminals are idealized figures, their appearance stylized with emphasis on the belted raincoat, soft hat, and ever-present handgun. Their behavior oddly blends violence and ritualized politeness, and lifts them out from their settings. He used his stars to portray timeless, tragic figures caught up in ambiguous conflicts and patterns of deceit.

"Melville's reputation will rest largely on his ability, almost unique in French cinema, to contain deeply-felt personal attitudes within the tight confines of commercial genre production. Certainly his thrillers are unequaled in European cinema." [Roy Armes, "Jean-Pierre Melville," *The St. James Film Directors Encyclopedia*, edited by Andrew Sarris (Detroit: Visible Ink Press, 1998), p. 338.]

"Jean-Pierre Melville's idiosyncratic favorites among American directors—Wyler, Welles, Huston, Robert Wise—were not crime movie specialists, and he understood that movies are about light, movement, and primal dreams. He was devoted to 'holy terrors.'" (Hogue, "Melville: The Elective Affinities," p. 22.)

[35]*The Village Voice*, 6 July 1982.

Volker Schlondorff was Jean-Pierre Melville's assistant director from 1959 to 1964, working especially on *Le Doulos* and *Léon Morin, Prêtre*. He also served as assistant director to Alain Resnais and Louis Malle. Intellectual, literate, and fluent in several languages, Schlondorff, as a director of his own films, has been chiefly attracted to the adaptation of literary works—*The Tin Drum* (1979), *Swann in Love* (1984), *Death of a Salesman* (1985), *The Handmaid's Tale* (1990).

[36]Rédecouvir l'Amérique," *Cahiers du Cinéma* 54, Christmas 1955, in *Cahiers du Cinéma: the 1950s*, edited by Jim Hillier (Cambridge MA: Harvard University Press, 1985), translated by Liz Heron, p. 91.

Rohmer continues: "The charm of these [American novels and films] lies in the delirious romanticism of their heroes and the modernism of their technique. Hollywood, shy of them for so long, suddenly noticed their existence, and a breath of the avant-garde made the studios tremble."

Eric Rohmer is usually classified with Francois Truffaut, Jean-Luc Godard, Claude Chabrol, and Jacques Rivette as a member of the French New Wave. He joined the others on the staff of *Cahiers du Cinéma* in 1951; he had already spent three years as a film critic with such prestigious journals as *La Révue du cinéma* and Jean-Paul Sartre's *Les Temps Modernes*. At *Cahiers* he encountered an environment in which film criticism and filmmaking were thought of as merely two aspects of the same activity. Consequently, the critics who wrote for *Cahiers* never doubted that they would become film directors. Rohmer's receptive tone to "vice and the neon lights," quoted in the text, is certainly compatible, at this stage of his career, with a critical sensibility that enlivened his authorship, with Claude Chabrol, of a seminal book on Alfred Hitchcock, *The First Forty-Four Films* (1957).

[37]*Melville on Melville*, pp. 53-54, 99.

[38]*Film Quarterly*, Winter 1995-96, p. 14.

[39]Quoted in Roger Asselineau, "French Reactions to Hemingway's Works Between the Two World Wars," in *The Literary Reputation of Hemingway in Europe*, edited by Roger Asselineau (New York: New York University Press, 1965), p. 56.

[40]Sheldon Norman Grebstein, "The Tough Hemingway and His Hard-Boiled Children," in *Tough Guy Writers of the Thirties*, edited by David Madden (Carbondale IL: Southern Illinois University Press, 1968), p. 18.

[41]*Ibid.*, p. 19.

[42]Asselineau, "French Reactions to Hemingway's Works," p. 57.

[43]Quoted in David Madden, *James M. Cain* (New York: Twayne Publishers, Inc., 1970), p. 171.
  Sergio Pacifici, in *A Guide to Contemporary Italian Literature* (1962), describes the influence of tough writers on Italians: "At the end of the last war, several prominent Italian intellectuals readily confessed that their encounter with American literature had been one of their most significant and rewarding experiences. Strange as it may seem, the violence and deep pessimism of Faulkner, Cain, Caldwell, and Steinbeck, whose works were widely read in Italy in the Thirties, had actually given them the measure of hope and courage they needed to continue living and writing. Through the fiction of the American, they kept in touch with the free world, and were delivered from the sterile conventionality of Fascist 'culture.'" [This partially explains the appearance in the late 1940s of the tough (neo)realism of Italian cinema—*Open City, Paisan, Bitter Rice*.] "The effects achieved by such novelists as Cain and Steinbeck, Hemingway and Saroyan, were eventually first imitated then thoroughly assimilated by Pavese, Vittorini, and, through their example, Berto and Calvino." [Quoted in Madden, *Cain*, p. 170.]

[44]Madden, *James M. Cain*, p. 171.

[45]Asselineau, "French Reactions to Hemingway's Works," p. 55.

[46]Quoted in Madden, *James M. Cain*, p. 174.

[47]*Ibid.*

[48]*Ibid.*
"However the pessimism of these films and their treatment of sexual relationships made them seem un-American to critics at that time. 'Where you see something that makes every Senator, every businessman, every employer a crook and which destroys our belief in American free enterprise and free institutions, that is communistic,' according to writer [Rupert] Hughes. . . . Whatever else they may have been, the 1940s thrillers were not 'good American stories.'

[The negative response of Hughes to stories that he considers "un-American" is a logical reaction from a founding member of The Motion Picture Alliance for the Preservation of American ideals, a bellicose right wing, anti-Communist organization founded in 1944.]

"This is partly why they appealed so strongly to European audiences as cynical views of an urban jungle that was also the future for Europe: the appeal of American culture in the post-war years had that ambivalence. If you wanted to be modern, you adopted it, including a measure of its own disillusionment with itself." [Robin Buss, *French Film Noir* (London: Marion Boyars, 1994), p. 119.]

[49]Truffaut, *The Films in My Life* (New York: Da Capo Press, 1994), p. 4.

[50]*Rififi* (*Du Rififi Chez Les Hommes*, 1955), directed by Jules Dassin; scripted by Dassin, Rene Wheeler, and Auguste Le Breton, from Le Breton's novel. An ingenious caper film, it was made in France, where Dassin settled after being forced out of Hollywood by the blacklist. It is famous for a meticulously enacted and tense 22-minute robbery sequence played with no dialogue and only ambient sound effects, and for the sleazy view of the Montmartre underworld. It also possesses, as Georges Sadoul points out in his *Dictionnaire des Films*, an element of wry humor.

[51]"Victoria Presents A Grim Melodrama," *New York Daily News*, 16 October 1959.

[52]Hogue, "Melville: the Elective Affinities," p. 17.

[53]Robert Bresson made three films in the 1950s which firmly established his reputation as one of the world's most rigorous and demanding filmmakers: *Diary of a Country Priest* (1950), *A Condemned Man Escapes* (1956), *Pickpocket* (1959). As a whole Bresson's films constitute a crucial investigation of the nature of cinematic narration. All three films of the 1950s are variations on the notion of a written diary transposed to a voice-over commentary on the visualized action. Other films include *The Trial of Joan of Arc* (1962), *Au hasard Balthazar* (1966), *Lancelot du Luc* (1974).

[54]P. Adams Sitney, "Robert Bresson," *The St. James Film Directors Encyclopedia*, p. 61.

[55]*Ibid.*

[56]Speaking of suicide—and the French connection—it is worth mentioning that at least two of Jean-Pierre Melville's films end with symbolic suicides staged similarly to Polonsky's: Alain Delon in *Le Samourai* (1967) aims an empty gun and is shot by the police; Richard Crenna in *Un Flic* (1972) makes a gesture as if to pull out a gun (though he has none), and is shot by cop Alain Delon. Both films are bitter meditations on disenchantment and defeat.

[57]Wheeler Winston Dixon, *The Early Film Criticism of Francois Truffaut* (Bloomington IN: Indiana University Press, 1993), p. 137.

[58]Andre Bazin discusses a "revolutionary humanism" that he claims characterizes Italian neo-realism, in "The Evolution of the Language of Cinema," in his *What is Cinema? Volume 1*. Essays selected and translated by Hugh Gray (Berkeley CA: University of California Press, 1971).

Luc Moullet has "a strong aversion to would-be philosophers who get into making films in spite of what film is, and who just repeat in cinema the discoveries of the other arts, people who want to express interesting subjects with a certain artistic style. If you have something to say, say it, write it, preach it if you like, but don't come bothering us with it." ("Sam Fuller: In Marlowe's Footsteps," *Cahiers du Cinéma* 93, March 1959, in Hillier, ed., *Cahiers du Cinéma: 1950s*, translated by Norman King, p. 145.)

[59]Claude Chabrol, "Little Themes," *Cahiers du Cinéma*, 100, 1959, in *The New Wave*, edited by Peter Graham (Garden City NY: Doubleday & Company Inc., 1968), p. 73.

[60]This film was released by Metro Goldwyn Mayer, and was copyrighted by Loew's Incorporated, Sol C. Siegel Productions Incorporated, and Belafonte's own HarBel Productions.

[61]Chabrol, "Little Themes," pp. 74-75.

François Truffaut: "The great problems of our time? I don't know the answers to them; many more intelligent, cultivated, and able people than I have broken their heads on these things you want me to mix into. Let me tell you of my contempt for certain 'great subjects.' For me Stanley Kramer is an outrageous schemer and his film, *The Defiant Ones* or the other about the atomic bomb [*On the Beach*], are the work of an ass. Can a white love a black and vice versa? Don't make me laugh! The person who treats a subject like that must not be very convinced himself of the answer; if he were, he wouldn't make the film. I'll go further: to talk about things like that is indecent because talking gives the feeling that the problem exists. Naturally, if the same subject had been done by Renoir, it would interest me just the same." [Robert Wise would probably be given the same exemption. See Truffaut on Wise in these pages, 185-186.]

Penelope Houston, in a response to Truffaut, writes: "No one expects the filmmaker dutifully to sit down with a list of 'big subjects' and tick them off one by one. What one could say is that his understandable retreat from the intimidating difficulty of the social subjects needn't lead him all the way to a private fantasy world of his own. We can't, again, presume to tell him that he ought to be concerned with some aspect of social reality; but we can ask why he isn't, what is the condition of the society he's living in which makes him so unwilling to come to grips with it."

[François Truffaut, " Should Films Be Politically Committed?" and Penelope Houston, "Uncommitted Artist?" in *Focus on Shoot the Piano Player*, edited by Leo Braudy (Englewood Cliffs, NJ: Prentice-Hall, 1972), pp. 135-136, 141.]

[62] Abraham Polonsky, *"The Best Years of Our Lives*: A Review," *Hollywood Quarterly*, Volume 2, Number 3, April 1947, p. 257.

[63] Albert Maltz, "What Shall We Ask of Writers?" *New Masses*, 12 February 1946, pp. 19-22.
That Maltz essentially recanted the thrust of this essay, under political pressure from the Communist party in "Moving Forward," *New Masses*, 9 April 1946, pp. 8-10, 21-22, does not diminish the independent validity of the initial polemic.

[64] "Scenario: After a total atomic war, life has disappeared from the face of the earth. The sole survivor is a Negro, all alone in New York. He organizes his life as best he can, but suffers from loneliness. After a couple of months he realizes that another human being, a white woman, has survived the catastrophe. He meets her. Soon he falls in love with her, but his racial complexes make happiness impossible for him. Two months later, a white man appears in a dinghy [*sic*]. He too wants the woman. At first the Negro acts self-effacingly, then he reacts and challenges the other man. The white man decides on a duel to the death, and in the deserted city, in front of the United Nations building, the two last men on earth throw themselves into the final struggle. For it is, of course, war, man's folly, that is 'the apocalypse of our time.' . . . The result is the biggest load of tripe for years." (Chabrol, "Little Themes," pp. 73-74.)

[65] Pines, *Blacks in Films*, p. 86.

[66] Polonsky, *"Best Years* Review," p. 258.

[67] Maltz, "What Shall We Ask of Writers?" p. 22. Emphasis in original.

[68] Chabrol, "Little Themes, " p. 77.

[69] Thomas Cripps, *Hollywood's High Noon: Moviemaking & Society before Television* (Baltimore: The John Hopkins University Press, 1997), p. 180.

[70] Manny Farber, *Movies* (New York: The Stonehill Publishing Company, 1971), pp. 71-83, 113-124, 134-144.
Farber, in his typically cranky and eccentric fashion, is irritated by what he calls **white elephant art**: "Masterpiece art, reminiscent of the enameled tobacco humidors and wood lawn ponies bought at white elephant auctions decades ago, has come to dominate the overpopulated arts of TV and movies. The three sins of white elephant art: (1) frame the action with an all-over pattern, (2) install every event, character, situation in a frieze of continuities, and (3) treat every inch of the screen and film as a potential area for prizeworthy creativity." (p. 137) And he favors art that, "termite-like, feels its way through walls of particularization, with no sign that the artist has any object in mind other than eating away the immediate boundaries of his art, and turning these boundaries into conditions of the next achievement. . . . The best examples of **termite art**

appear in places other than films, where the spotlight of culture is nowhere in evidence, so that the craftsman can be ornery, wasteful, stubbornly self-involved, doing go-for-broke art and not caring what comes of it." (pp. 135-136) Termite art aims at: "buglike immersion in a small area without point or aim, and over all, concentration on nailing down one moment without glamorizing it, but forgetting this accomplishment as soon as it has been passed; the feeling that all is expendable, that it can be chopped up and flung down in a different arrangement without ruin." (p. 144)

In the anthology of his writings, *Movies* (original title: *Negative Space*), Farber does not discuss *Odds Against Tomorrow* and, in light of these somewhat perverse quotations, it is difficult to determine how completely accepting he would be of the film's various focuses. He, like Pauline Kael (see her "Trash, Art, and the Movies"), is highly antipathetic to even a hint of social consciousness—"art-infected projects where there is unlimited cash, studio freedom, an expansive story, message, heart, and a lot of prestige to be gained. . . . the prize picture, which has philosophical undertones, panfried domestic sights, risqué crevices, sporty actors and actresses, circuslike gymnastics, a bit of tragedy like the main fall at Niagara."

His famous paean to "Underground Films" (1957) celebrates male action films which are "slicing journeys into the lower depths of American life: dregs, outcasts, lonely hard wanderers caught in a buzzsaw of niggardly, intricate, devious movement." The qualities he prefers are: "unscrubbed action, masculine characterization, violent explorations inside a fascinating locale; stiff, vulgar, low-pulp material; cold mortal intentness; striking photography, a good ear for natural dialogue, an eye for realistic detail, a skilled inside-action approach to composition." His champion directors are Howard Hawks, Raoul Walsh, William Wellman, Anthony Mann, Phil Karlson, John Farrow, Robert Aldrich— "perfect examples of the anonymous artist, who is seemingly afraid of the polishing, hypocrisy, bragging, fake educating that goes on in serious art."

Into which category would Manny Farber place *Odds Against Tomorrow*—underground/termite art or white elephant/masterpiece art? The film reflects many "underground" characteristics, and Farber describes director Robert Wise as "a sometime member of the underground," and especially admires portions of *Born to Kill*. But *Odds* does possess a racial theme and an obvious moral message, and Farber was put off by what he described as "the bloated philosophical safe-crackers in Huston's *Asphalt Jungle*." ("Underground Films," pp. 12-24, in *Movies*.)

[It seems to me that *Odds Against Tomorrow* reconciles the dichotomous elements of Manny Farber's film types. I am also prepared to predict the likely possibility of Claude Chabrol finding the film compatible with the guidelines of his "Little Themes" essay. But whether Manny Farber, given the quirky nature of his linguistically dazzling criteria, would unqualifiedly embrace it is another matter. With Farber all bets are off.

CRITICAL EXERCISE: Students of film may find it profitable to analyze *Odds Against Tomorrow*—or any film which combines characteristics of a commercial genre with a social realist theme—by employing the definitional terms of Farber's essays to refine more precisely the nature of an individual work. Is it termite or white elephant art? Does it have to be either/or?]

[71]Cripps, *Hollywood's High Noon*, p. 215; Naremore, "American Film Noir," p. 23.

[72]Mike Davis, *City of Quartz: Excavating the Future in Los Angeles* (New York: Vintage Books, 1992), p. 41.

[73] David Ansen, "The Neo-Noir '90s," *Newsweek*, 27 October 1997, p. 70.

[74] Chipps, *Hollywood's High Noon*, p. 181.

[75] All bulleted citations are from Borde and Chaumeton, *Panorama du Film Noir Américain*, excerpted in *Film Noir Reader*, translated by Alain Silver, pp. 17-25. All cross-references to *Odds Against Tomorrow* are by the author.

[76] Jean-Pierre Coursodon, "Robert Wise," *American Directors, Volume II* (New York: McGraw-Hill Book Company, 1983), p. 371.
Political liberalism is the subtext here: the failed robbery is a metaphor for a stalled society, impeded in its progress by bigotry.

[77] Edward Mapp, *Blacks in American Films* (Metuchen NJ: The Scarecrow Press, 1972), p. 49.

[78] "Symposium: Writers' Views on Creating Black Characters," in Frankie Y. Bailey, *Out of the Woodpile: Black Characters in Crime and Detective Fiction* (New York: Greenwood Press, 1991), p. 133.

QUESTION: *Does the portrayal of sordid, foolish, and criminal black characters help to convince the reading public that this is how blacks "really are"?*

DOLORES KOMO [*Clio Browne: Private Investigator*, 1988]: "I do not believe that an intelligent reader would be convinced by such portrayal any more than he/she would characterize all Italians by how they have been portrayed in *The Godfather*." (p. 123)

RICHARD MARTIN STERN [*You Don't Need an Enemy*, 1971]: "If a writer goes *out of his way* to treat black characters as sordid, foolish, or criminal, yes, I do believe that he/she is then trying to plant in the reader's mind the idea of stereotype. That I find not only reprehensible but also inane because there are no stereotypical blacks, whites, hispanics, or other races; each ethnic group or background has its share of admirable, abominable, foolish, heroic, untrustworthy, and thoroughly dependable persons, and to believe otherwise, in my opinion, is to wear blinders." (p. 125)

ROBERT B. PARKER [*Crimson Joy*, 1988]: "I doubt it. The portrayal of clean, wise, law-abiding characters doesn't convince the public either. I suspect it depends on the reader." (p. 127)

MARGARET MARON [*Bloody Kin*, 1985]: "Of course not. This is not to say there aren't any sordid, foolish, and criminal elements among blacks; nor to say that such traits can't be given to one's black characters if the story demands it. The lies—and they are lies even if unintended and unconscious—come when one portrays *only* blacks with these characteristics." (p. 129)

SARA PARETSKY [*Deadlock*, 1984]: "I believe the answer is yes. I believe racism is at the heart of almost every major problem the United States faces because it is racist attitudes that enable the white majority to feel that blacks are not fully human and therefore do not have to be accorded dignity. This lack of respect is translated into a hundred different social and economic problems. And when writers create sordid, foolish, or criminal black characters, they only underscore these attitudes—which in my opinion flourish perfectly adequately without needing additional fertilizer. I find the same thing to be true of Jewish characters (being Jewish myself I have some sensitivity there). There are sordid, foolish, and criminal Jews just as there are sordid, foolish, and criminal blacks— but presenting them in fiction just serves to fuel the hostility of the white, gentile majority." (p. 129)

MICHAEL JAHN [*Night Rituals*, 1982]: "I don't know that there is *a* reading public.

"Were I writing a mass-market paperback original to be sold mainly in supermarkets, I would imagine that the depiction of sordid, foolish, or criminal black characters would *reinforce* stereotypical attitudes among readers who already held those opinions. There's nothing to be done about them anyway.

"But the mystery genre, especially hardcover mysteries, is hardly a mass-market commodity. I prefer to think that mystery readers are well informed about racial matters, as they are about many other matters.

"There's so much stereotyping on the airwaves and in the movies that all those likely to believe such things have plenty of material. The convinced racists have their opinions fixed, and those likely to join that camp get their information from the television and tabloids.

"Maybe it's my own prejudice, but I believe that racists don't read mainstream books and that serious readers aren't likely to believe off-the-wall depictions of blacks. Books bought in bookstores and books bought in Greyhound Bus terminals attract vastly different readerships." (pp. 135-136)

LES ROBERTS [*An Infinite Number of Monkeys*, 1987]: "Most people who read for recreational purposes are fairly intelligent. I doubt if one negative black character in a book will convince that reader that all blacks are like that. However, small-minded people believe what they want to believe. If a reader already thinks all blacks really are foolish, criminal, lazy, and sit around all day eating watermelon, then a portrayal of that kind of black in drama or literature will reinforce his beliefs. And a black judge, humanitarian, or hero in a book is not going to convince him that such blacks really exist at all. However, a writer who creates a silly, lazy, criminal, or sordid black must ask himself why he made the character a black in the first place—just as if he had made that character any other ethnicity. I believe we write viscerally—that our true beliefs surface in our work. If I looked over a body of my work and found that inadvertently *every* black character I had created was a negative stereotype, I would certainly examine my own feelings closely.

"But in crime fiction most of the characters, excluding the sleuth, have negative aspects to them—it comes with the genre. And I will not be 'limited' to writing only about wonderful, saintly, or heroic blacks any more than I would limit myself to writing about them as pimps, illiterate basketball players, and Stepin Fetchits or Uncle Toms." (p. 139)

Summing Up. The following definition of **stereotype** seems to be in keeping with what has been written about stereotypes of African Americans in crime and detective fiction:

> "When an author makes Chinese immigrants launderers and characterizes them as violent and emotional only because they are Chinese by ancestry, these qualities are stereotypes. If an author creates a well-motivated, individually characterized Chinese immigrant who launders clothes because of legal and economic restraints which bar him from other occupations, that character is an artistic creation of the

author placed in an accurate historical context, not just a stereotype taken from an imprint of earlier expressions in society or literature. The word *stereotype* refers to descriptions of Chinese Americans that are based on race and ethnicity rather than on serious attempts by the author at characterization." [William F. Wu, *The Yellow Peril: Chinese Americans in American Fiction 1850-1940* (Hamden CT: Archon Books, 1982), p. 4.]

[79]Hirsch, *Dark Side of the Screen*, p. 163.

[80]*Ibid.*, p. 157.

[81]Donald Chase, "In Praise of the Naughty Mind: Gloria Grahame," *Film Comment*, September-October 1997, p. 58.

[82]Throughout Borde and Chaumeton's study there is a celebratory tone for a kinky irrationality. They place great emphasis on the essential affective qualities of noir, which they list in the form of five adjectives typical of surrealism: "oneiric, bizarre, erotic, ambivalent, and cruel." Sometimes, however, the traits are unevenly distributed, with the "noir aspect" manifesting itself in a fragmentary or tangential form. Interestingly, in light of Robert Wise's direction of *Odds*, another film of his is used to make a point in this regard: "*The Set Up* is a good documentary about boxing: it becomes film noir in the sequence where accounts are settled by a savage beating in a blind alley." (Naremore, "American Film Noir," p. 19.) There is no fragmentary or tangential aspect to *Odds*. The noir elements are pervasive.

[83]Donald Bogle, *Blacks in American Films and Television: An Encyclopedia* (New York: Garland Publishing, Inc., 1988), p. 158.

[84]Borde and Chaumeton's *Panorama* criteria have been used to structure an analysis of *Odds Against Tomorrow*, because of the importance of the French connection. But as a further comparison, note another respected set of guidelines in *The Classical Hollywood Cinema: Film Style and Mode of Production to 1960* by David Bordwell, Janet Staiger, and Kristin Thompson (New York: Columbia University Press, 1985), p. 76. This approach defines film noir by four challenges to the mainstream Hollywood cinema: an assault on psychological causality, a challenge to the prominence of heterosexual romance, an attack on the motivated happy ending, and a criticism of classical technique. Even based on the listing of the category headings alone, it is evident that *Odds Against Tomorrow* accommodates the specifications of these criteria as well.

[85]Pauline Kael, "Raising Kane," *The Citizen Kane Book* (Boston: Little, Brown and Company, 1971), p. 20.

[86]Michael L. Stephens, *Film Noir: A Comprehensive, Illustrated Reference to Movies, Terms, and Persons* (Jefferson, NC: McFarland & Company, Inc., 1995), p. 381.

[87]The discussion in the main text will be devoted to what will be defined as *roman noir* literature by African American authors that pre-dates *Odds Against Tomorrow*. The narrowing of the focus to this segment of black writing seems

justified by *Odds*'s status as film noir, but the title of Vattel T. Rose's essay—"Afro-American Literature as a Cultural Resource for a Black Cinema Aesthetic"—connotes the spirit and the overall importance of *intertextuality* [i.e., the manner by which texts (poems, novels, films) respond to other texts] that inspired this portion of the critical commentary. Rose writes: "The Afro-American literary tradition can serve as both a general and specific resource for a black cinema aesthetic." [In *Black Cinema Aesthetics: Issues in Independent Black Filmmaking*, edited by Gladstone L. Yearwood (Athens OH: Ohio University Center for Afro-American Studies, 1982), p. 28. Also see the following by Henry-Louis Gates (another proponent of this type of intertextual criticism): "Preface to Blackness: Text and Pretext," in *Afro-American Literature: The Reconstruction of Instruction*, edited by Dexter Fisher and Robert B. Stepto (The Modern Language Association of America, 1978).]

In light of the commentary's contextual review of black roman noir, literary comparisons with *Odds Against Tomorrow* will remain imprecise, since William McGivern, the writer of the source novel of *Odds*, is white. Nevertheless, there are insights to be learned from a comparison of the differences—novel versus film—in the portrayal of the black Johnny Ingram character: Polonsky's reworking of McGivern's stereotype resulted in a striking shift in the concept of the character and in the dramaturgy of the narrative. (See pp. 246-253.)

AFRICAN AMERICAN CRIME FICTION. Crime, mystery, and suspense fiction by African American writers—with central black protagonists of any kind, **pre-***Odds Against Tomorrow* (1959)—is not extensive. The following is a fairly complete listing:

Pauline E. Hopkins in 1900 publishes two short stories with mystery themes: "The Mystery Within Us," a tale of magical realism and spirituality, and "Talma Gordon," a locked-room mystery with themes covering miscegenation and the "tragic mulatto." Her *Hagar's Daughter* (1901-1902) introduces Venus Johnson, a black female detective. ["Venus's positive relationship with her mother and grandmother in the novel generally enlarge the capacities of the detective novel genre while establishing the bedrock of the black detective tradition. Venus's status as a domestic and her use of her blackness to help solve a murder and kidnap case indicate important tropes of black detection enlarged upon in future black detective novels." (Soitos)]

"The Black Sleuth" (1908-1909) **by John Edward Bruce** is serialized in *McGirt's Reader*; an early detective story featuring a black protagonist. ["Bruce showed ways in which blacks could use the detective persona to illustrate the inherent intelligence, nobility, and pride of the black race. His emphasis on the positive aspects of black identity coupled with a militant attitude toward black self-expression, dignity, and survival brought a new awareness of black nationalism to the detective novel. Bruce followed Hopkins's lead in having a detective character use his blackness as well as disguise to solve the case." (Soitos)]

The Haunting Hand (1926) is published by Jamaican-born W. Adolphe Roberts; it is the first mystery novel by a black writer, although it does not feature black characters.

George S. Schuyler, Harlem Renaissance journalist, novelist, and critic, writes over a dozen mystery and thriller stories serialized in the *Pittsburgh Courier* (1933-1939), including "Black Internationale," "Black Empire," and "The Ethiopian Murder Mystery." ["While these stories have black characters and feature black detectives, they did little to contribute to the black detective tradition." (Soitos)]

The Conjure-Man Dies **(1932) by Rudolph Fisher** is published, the first mystery novel by an African American to feature black characters. ["Fisher's main achievement was his clever demonstration of how hoodoo elements might be used in a novel to reinforce black pride in important Afrocentric areas. Fisher deserves his reputation as a primary black detective writer who introduced Harlem Renaissance themes to black detective fiction." (Soitos)]

Chester Himes, while serving a prison term for armed robbery, publishes his first crime stories, including "His Last Day," "The Meanest Cop in the World," and "Prison Mass" (all 1933).

The Trial of Dr. Beck **(1937), a play by Hughes Allison,** opens on Broadway; it relates the story of a physician on trial for the murder of his wife, the founder of a hair care empire.

Flour Is Dusty **(1943) by Curtis Lucus** is published; the crime novel focuses on drugs and crime in Atlantic City's black community.

The Street **(1946) by Ann Petry** is published, the first best-seller by an African American woman.

"Corollary" by Hughes Allison is published in the July 1948 issue of *Ellery Queen's Mystery Magazine*; it is the first short story published by an African American in this magazine.

[Sources for this material are: *Spooks, Spies, and Private Eyes: Black Mystery, Crime, and Suspense Fiction of the 20th Century*, edited by Paula L. Woods (New York: Doubleday, 1995); Stephen F. Soitos, "Crime and Mystery Writing," *The Oxford Companion to African American Literature* (New York: Oxford University Press, 1997), pp. 182-184; Frankie Y. Bailey, *Out of the Woodpile: Black Characters in Crime and Detective Fiction* (New York: Greenwood Press, 1991).]

[88]See Barry Gifford, "The Godless World of Jim Thompson," printed as the introduction to many of the Jim Thompson novels published by Black Lizard; for example in *The Getaway* (Berkeley CA: Creative Art Book Company, 1984), pp. v-vii.

[89]Quoted in Richard Bradbury, "Sexuality, Guilt and Detection: Tension between History and Suspense," in *American Crime Fiction: Studies in the Genre*, edited by Brian Docherty (New York: St. Martin's Press, 1988), p. 90.

[90]*Ibid.*

[91]Geoffrey O'Brien, *Hardboiled America: Lurid Paperbacks and the Masters of Noir* (New York: Da Capo Press, 1997), pp. 147, 151.

[92]Chabrol in Gordon Gow, *Suspense in the Cinema* (New York: Castle, 1968), p. 20; Highsmith in her *Plotting and Writing Suspense Fiction* (Boston: The Writer, 1966), p. 144. Both are quoted in Charles Derry, *The Suspense Thriller:*

Films in the Shadow of Alfred Hitchcock (Jefferson NC: McFarland & Company, 1988), p. 19.

[93]."During the Depression, the situation of blacks, who suffered the highest unemployment rates in the North and the worst sharecropping conditions in the South, was least improved by the New Deal. Farm aid went chiefly to whites. Work relief programs such as the CCC were segregated, and the NRA paid lower wages to blacks, when it hired them at all. Nor would Roosevelt commit himself to a federal law abolishing lynching." [William Marling, *The American Roman Noir* (Athens GA: The University of Georgia Press, 1995), pp. 60-61.]

[94]Irving Howe, "Black Boys and Native Sons," *A World More Attractive: A View of Modern Literature and Politics* (New York: Horizon Press, 1963), pp. 100-102.

[95]Wright delivers a talk, "How 'Bigger' Was Born," at Columbia University on 12 March 1940 (later published as a pamphlet by Harper, then added to future printings of *Native Son*).

[96]Quoted in Howe, "Black Boys and Native Sons," p. 103.

[97]Margaret Walker, *Richard Wright, Daemonic Genius* (New York: Amistad Press, 1988), pp. 237-238; Edward Margolies, *The Art of Richard Wright* (Carbondale IL: Southern Illinois University Press, 1969), p. 3.

[98]Wright, "The Man Who Killed a Shadow," in *Spooks, Spies, and Private Eyes*, p. 90.

[99]Wright, *Native Son* (New York: Harper Perennial edition, 1993 [1940]), p. 9.
See also Robert Porfirio, "No Way Out: Existential Motifs in the Film Noir," in *Film Noir Reader*, pp. 77-93.

[100]Wright, "The Man Who Killed a Shadow," pp. 90, 92, 98.

[101]Ross Pudaloff, "*Native Son* and Mass Culture," in *Bigger Thomas*, edited by Harold Bloom (New York: Chelsea House Publishers, 1990), p. 96.

[102]*Ibid.*

[103]Harold Bloom, "Introduction," *Bigger Thomas*, p. 2.

[104]Michel Fabre, *The Unfinished Quest of Richard Wright*, translated by Isabel Barzun (New York: Morrow, 1973), p. 171; quoted in Pudaloff, p. 97.
And, as if to emphasize the inextricable political undertones of African American noir writing, Addison Gayle finds Bessie's murder "the weakest incident in the novel " because it violates the black nationalism he sees as the basic thrust of the work. [*The Way of the New World: The Black Novel in America* (Garden City: Doubleday, 1975), p. 171.]

[105]Margolies, *The Art of Richard Wright*, p. 139.

The alliterative chapter headings for *Savage Holiday* are "Anxiety," "Ambush," and "Attack." It is as if there exists an inexorable flow of consequences stemming from the first letter of the first word of the titles of these sections. *Savage Holiday* is not a primary source for analysis in this study, because the protagonist of this Wright novel, Erskine Fowler (who ends up murdering a woman whom he perceives in a Freudian fantasy to be his mother), is *white*. But, according to Margolis, "despite the color of his skin and his relatively high social position, Fowler reminds one of nothing so much as Wright's broken and humiliated southern Negroes. Like them Fowler is forced outside of life and made a despairing, frustrated onlooker of activities in which he is unable to participate. And like them too, he is a living repository of fear, shame, and concealed hate that he is unable to vent properly." (p. 147)

[106]Richard Wright, *The Outsider* (New York: Harper Perennial edition, 1993 [1953]), p. 504.

[107]At least two roman noir cross-references are relevant here: the novel by Cornell Woolrich [published as by William Irish], *I Married a Dead Man* (1948), adapted into a Barbara Stanwyck film, *No Man of Her Own* (1950), involves switching identities with a dead person; in the "Flitcraft"/"falling beam" episode from Dashiell Hammett's *The Maltese Falcon* (1930), the Flitcraft character has an existential insight ["He felt like somebody had taken the lid off life and let him look at the works."], abandons his present life, and takes up another.

Wright, *The Outsider*: "Was there a slight chance here of his being able to start all over again? To live a new life? . . . These questions made him feel that the world about him held countless dangers; he suddenly felt like a criminal, and he was grateful for the nervous flakes of snow which screened his face from the eyes of passersby. (p. 105) . . . He had to break out of this dream, or he would surely go mad. He had to be born again, come anew into the world. To live amidst others without an identity was intolerable. In a strict sense he was not really in the world; he was haunting it for his place, pleading for entrance into life." (p. 167)

[108]Wright, *The Outsider.*, pp. 466-467.

See Richard Lehan, *A Dangerous Crossing: French Literary Existentialism and the Modern American Novel* (Carbondale IL: Southern Illinois University Press, 1973), p. 103.

[109]Wright, *The Outsider*, p. 111.

[110]*Ibid.*, p. 178.

The symbolic function of jazz music is powerfully illustrated in both the literary and the film texts. The movement from "the frightened ecstasy of the unrepentant" to a feeling of the "culpability of jazz" is experienced by Cross Damon as an indication of shifts in his behavior. Likewise, note the tonal shifts in Johnny Ingram's two musical numbers [46-47; 55-57], as the result of darkening circumstances in his life; discussed above, pp. 178.

[111]Abraham Polonsky, "The Emergence of Jazz," *You Are There*, Air Date: 5 Sep 54; in *You Are There Teleplays: The Critical Edition*, pp. 249-250.

African American writer Chester Himes sees a connection between music and literature: "My writing is very close to the improvisation of jazz. The jazz musician thinks, he feels, he rehearses, he performs, he scores, he improvises until he gets a beat. With it, he is playing jazz. That is what we all have in common. Good jazz is pure art." ["Conversation with Chester Himes," by French abstract painter Jean Miotte, 1977; in *Conversations with Chester Himes*, edited by Michel Fabre and Robert E. Skinner (Jackson: University Press of Mississippi, 1995), p. 124.]

[112]Chester Himes, "Dilemma of the Negro Novelist in U.S.," in *Beyond the Angry Black*, edited by John A. Williams (New York: Cooper Square Publishers, 1966), p. 57. This text was originally delivered as a paper at the University of Chicago in 1948.

According to James Sallis, in an Introduction to Himes's *A Case of Rape* (First Carroll & Graf edition, 1994), when Himes concluded his "Dilemma" presentation, "his stunned audience sat transfixed. There was no applause, no reaction at all. Slowly, one by one, they stood and left the room, avoiding one another's eyes.

"I submit to you that this has always been the fate of what Chester Himes had to say.

"And I submit also, *not* in contradiction, that without Himes there would today be little recognition for the work of novelists such as Toni Morrison, Alice Walker, and Ishmael Reed, that there would be no movies like *Boyz N the Hood*, *Do the Right Thing*, *Menace II Society*—movies where I've noticed, among white viewers, much the same sort of stunned silence that met Himes's address." (p. viii)

[113]The Johnny Ingram character in William McGivern's novel *Odds Against Tomorrow* is established from the beginning as being haunted by fear—"a fear lurked within him that was as ineradicable as a child's fear of darkness or strangers." (p. 59)

Polonsky's reworking of the character for the film dramatically reduces this aspect, but Harry Belafonte relates (during a *60 Minutes* profile, 28 Sep 1997) a personal experience that is remarkably consistent with these fictional examples. During a 1955 tour of the South, getting off the bus for a rest stop, Belafonte is about to enter the men's room: "I heard a voice behind me, 'You let go a drop: you're a dead nigger.' I turned around and took a look, and there was a state trooper. I looked at him: the humiliation of it! I never had a feeling like that before in my life. I guess my urine had better sense than I did, because it just backed up. And I didn't let go a drop. And I walked back on that bus, and I just sat there for the rest of that tour—devastated by the experience."

[114]Davis, *City of Quartz*, p. 42.

Not as relevant to this study as Himes, but black writers Langston Hughes and Countee Cullen are also sometimes cited in this Los Angeles-as-nightmare context, especially in terms of their employment by the film studios. Hughes, for example, found that the only studio work for a black writer was furnishing demeaning dialogue for cotton-field parodies of black life. After a humiliating experience with the film *Way Down South*, he declared that "so far as Negroes are concerned, [Hollywood] might just as well be controlled by Hitler." (Arnold Rampersad, *The Life of Langston Hughes*, p. 371; quoted in Davis, *City of Quartz*, p. 42.)

In *If He Hollers Let Him Go*, Chester Himes has his protagonist Bob Jones watching a movie: "I never found out the name of the picture or what it was about. After about five minutes a big fat black Hollywood mammy came on the screen saying: 'Yassum' and 'Noam,' and grinning at her young white missy; and I got up and walked out.

"I was down to a low ebb. I needed some help. I had to know that Negroes weren't the lowest people on the face of God's green earth. I had to talk it over with somebody, had to build myself back up. The sons of bitches were grinding me to the nub, to the white meatless bone." [Himes, *If He Hollers Let Him Go* (New York: Thunder's Mouth Press, 1986 [1945]), p. 79.]

[115]Chester Himes, *The Quality of Hurt*, quoted in Woody Haut, *Pulp Culture: Hardboiled Fiction and the Cold War* (London: Serpent's Tail, 1995), p. 36.

[116]In Ernest Hemingway's "A Pursuit Race" (*Men Without Women*, 1927), protagonist William Campbell refuses to come out from under his bedsheets because of his existential fear—because, in Hemingway's sports parlance, "I can't slide."

[117]Himes, *If He Hollers Let Him Go*, p. 4.

[118]Himes, *If He Hollers Let Him Go*, p. 203; *Tell Them Willie Boy Is Here* (1969), written and directed by Abraham Polonsky.

[119]Chester Himes: "I wrote *The End of a Primitive* in 1953 and 1954 while living with an American white woman in Majorca who had a husband and four daughters far away in Central Europe. . . . I decided to write a book . . . which would be an affront and challenge to all white American editors. I incorporated all of my own emotions into the book to demonstrate how a black American rids himself of fear, but in the book it cost the black protagonist his life. Which is its theme, rid yourself of fear, if you are a black man, and die."
When William Targ, Himes's editor at the World Publishing Company, read the material, he responded: "The manuscript appears to me as a night of Walpurgis, a nightmare of alcohol, frantic and deviant sex, scatology, nymphomania and many other things." An incensed Himes fired back, "What can one expect from a culture as chaotic as ours?" (The work was rejected.) A year would pass before if was finally accepted by the New American Library, but then only in a significantly abridged version as *The Primitive* (1955). The unexpurgated edition of *The End of a Primitive* was published in 1997 by W.W. Norton & Company. [These notes are taken from the Introduction to this volume.]

[120]These are extracts from the English version of interviews Fabre made in the 1970s, published as "Chester Himes Direct" in *Hard-Boiled Dicks*, Nos. 8-9 (December 1983), pp. 5-21; they are anthologized in *Conversations with Chester Himes*, pp. 133-134.

[121]Robin Wood, "Servants and Slaves: Brown Persons in Classical Hollywood Cinema," *CineAction*, No. 32, Fall 1993, pp. 81-82.

[122]Gladstone L. Yearwood, "Towards a Theory of a Black Cinema Aesthetic," in *Black Cinema Aesthetics Issues in Independent Black Filmmaking*, edited by Gladstone L. Yearwood (Athens OH: Ohio University Center for Afro-American Studies, 1982), p. 80.

^{123}James Snead, *White Screens/Black Images: Hollywood from the Dark Side*, edited by Colin MacCabe & Cornel West (New York: Routledge, 1994), p. 123.

^{124}Himes, *The End of a Primitive*, p. 206.

^{125}*Little Big Man*: novel by Thomas Berger (Dial Press, 1964); film (1970)—screenplay by Calder Willingham, directed by Arthur Penn.

^{126}**On the Linguistics of "White" and "Black" (and "Noir"):**
"You think that goodness is light and darkness evil," says a character in Henri-Georges Clouzot's *Le Corbeau* (1943). "But where is the light? Where is the darkness?" For reasons of suspense and political insight, the mechanics of film and roman noir involve the blurring of distinctions between "light" and "dark" characters. [Buss, *French Film Noir*, p. 16.]
   In *Malcolm X* (1992, screenplay by Arnold Perl, Spike Lee; direction by Spike Lee), Malcolm Little (Denzel Washington) ends up in Charleston State Prison, where fellow inmate Baines (Albert Hall) introduces him to the Islamic religion and the teachings of Elijah Muhammad. The following is part of his education:

> BAINES: Did you ever look up the word "black" in a dictionary?
> **Black:** Destitute of light. Devoid of color. Enveloped in darkness, hence utterly dismal or gloomy . . . as the future looked black. Soiled with dirt. Foul. Sullen. Hostile. Forbidding . . . as a black day. Foully or outrageously wicked . . . as black cruelty. Indicating disgrace, dishonor, or culpability. And there's others: **blackmail** . . . **blackball** . . . **blackguard** . . . Let's look up "white" . . .
>
> MALCOLM: **White:** Of the color of pure snow. Reflecting all the rays of the spectrum. The opposite of black. Free from spot or blemish. Innocent. Pure. Without evil intent. Harmless. Honest, squaredealing, and honorable. Wait a minute . . . this is written by white folks, right? This is a white folks' book.
>
> BAINES: This sure ain't no black man's book.
>
> MALCOLM: So what're we reading this one for?
>
> BAINES: 'Cause the truth is lying there . . . if you read behind the words. You got to take everything the white man says and use it against him.

   Within the context of great world literature and certain novelistic precursors to the roman (& film) noir—for example, Emile Zola's *Thérèse Racquin* (1867), and *La Bête Humaine* (1889); Dostoyevsky's *Crime and Punishment* (1866) —Stendhal's *The Red and the Black* (1830) might be noted because it is structured in noir fashion around a protagonist who is a villain, and because of its linguistic employment of **color symbolism**. Not attempting any racial signification, however, Stendhal denounces the selfishness, greed, and power of the Church ("the Black"), in a decidedly negative image, which attracts unscrupulous and ambitious young men, like protagonist Julien Sorel, who, some years earlier, would have donned a military uniform ("the Red") and fought under Napoleon. According to Joyce Carol Oates, "*The Red and the Black* stands at the beginning of so much of modern literature that its influence can no longer be isolated." The essential loneliness of the hero, his tragic split between egoism and love—these make Julien a predecessor to Meursault in Albert Camus's *The Stranger*. And the noir cross-references in world literature continue. [See Joyce Carol Oates, "Man Under Sentence of Death: The Novels of James M. Cain," in *Tough Guy Writers of the Thirties*, edited by David Madden (Carbondale: Southern Illinois University Press, 1968), pp. 112-113.]

As James Naremore writes, "we need a close examination of the metaphor of darkness. This discourse on noir grew out of a European male fascination with the instinctive (a fascination that was evident in most forms of high modernism), and many of the films admired by the French involve white characters who cross borders to visit Latin America, Chinatown, or the 'wrong' parts of the city." ("American Film Noir," p. 15.)

127"Interview with Chester Himes" by Michel Fabre (1970), in *Conversations with Chester Himes*, p. 88.

128Himes, *A Case of Rape* (New York: Carroll & Graf Publishers, 1994 [1956]), pp. 25-27.

129*Ibid.*, p. 86.

130*Ibid.*, p. 65.

131*Ibid.*, p. 101.

132*Ibid.*, p. 105

133Quoted in Bailey, *Out of the Woodpile*, pp. 64-65.

Himes's recitation of an existential commitment to violence as a means of survival in prison is reflected years later in Michael Mann's neo-noir *Thief* (1981), when Frank (James Caan) discusses his similar manner of prison survival.

134Himes, *A Rage in Harlem* (New York: Vintage Crime/Black Lizard, [1957] 1991), p. 93.

Himes's original prose text is transposed here into poetic form by the critical commentary author.

135Manthia Diawara, "Noir by Noirs: Toward a New Realism in Black Cinema," in *Shades of Noir*, edited by Joan Copjec (London: Verso, 1993), p. 263.

136This is a favorite film noir metaphor; q.v., *Quicksand* (1950, screenplay by Robert Smith, directed by Irving Pichel).

137James Campbell, *Exiled in Paris: Richard Wright, James Baldwin, Samuel Beckett, and Others on the Left Bank* (New York: Scribner, 1995), p. 240.

138Given the popularity of American hard-boiled fiction in the 1940s, Jean-Paul Sartre had returned from New York with a roster of best-selling novelists he'd signed on for French editions by Gallimard. Since Boris Vian was proficient in English, he was recommended by Sartre and was commissioned by Gallimard to translate the following noir titles: *The Big Clock* by Kenneth Fearing, *The Lady in the Lake* by Raymond Chandler, *Ladies Won't Wait* by Peter Cheyney, *Young Man with a Horn* by Dorothy Baker, *Love's Lovely Counterfeit* by James M. Cain, *The Man with the Golden Arm* by Nelson Algren.

Translating this genre of American fiction helped Vian to polish his own writing style for the Vernon Sullivan series. In addition to *J'irai cracher sur vos tombes*, Vian published the following novels, all Editions du Scorpion, as Vernon Sullivan: *Les Morts ont tous la même peau* [*The Dead All Have the Same Skin*, 1948: this novel featured a deeply confused character, whose overriding fear in life is that he may have Negro blood in his veins; blackmailed by a man who claimed to be his brother, and who threatens to denounce him in his prim white community, he kills him, which leads to his doom]; *Et on tuera tous les affreux* (1948), and *Elles se rendent pas compte* (1950).

"During the fourteen years Vian was under the Paris Big Top, he produced at least 10 novels, 42 short stories, 7 theater pieces, 400 songs, 4 poetry collections, 6 opera libretti, 20 short story and novel translations; sang on records; acted in films; and wrote about 50 articles on as many subjects." [Julia Older, "Introducing Boris Vian," in Boris Vian, *Blues for a Black Cat & Other Stories*, edited and translated by Julia Older (Lincoln: The University of Nebraska Press, 1992), p. ix.]

Another valuable source for this brief profile of Vian: Zvjezdana Rudelic, "Boris Vian," *Dictionary of Literary Biography, Volume 72. French Novelists 1930-1960*, edited by Catharine Savage Brosman (New York: Gale Research, 1988), pp. 384-396.

[139] Boris Vian as "Vernon Sullivan," *I Shall Spit on Your Graves* (Paris: The Vendome Press, 1948), Preface (no page number). All subsequent page references to the novel will be in the text.

Clearly attempting to accommodate itself to the roman noir stylistic of first person point of view, Vian in his Preface invokes the influence of James M. Cain: "We meet in these pages the extremely clear influence of Cain, in spite of the fact that the author does not seek to justify, by an artifice, written or otherwise, the use of the first person." Indeed, Cain, in *The Postman Always Rings Twice* (1934) and *Double Indemnity* (1943), employs the first person by way of "the fable of the man under sentence of death, writing to us from his prison cell or from the cell of his isolated self." Both novels sustain the unity of the device by having the personal narratives conclude just before the protagonists go to their deaths— execution (*Postman*) or suicide (*Indemnity*).

But Jim Thompson in *The Killer Inside Me* (1952), *Savage Night* (1953), or *After Dark, My Sweet* (1955), for example, employing something of the "artifice" to which Vian refers, maintains the first person narrations through the last lines of the novels, in spite of the technical absurdity of having the characters relate the moments of their own deaths.

Vian (Sullivan) in *I Shall Spit on Your Graves* utilizes a combination of first and third person narration—first person is utilized for most of the novel, until the protagonist is physically incapable of continuing the storytelling.

[140] **Roman Noir Cross-References.** These aggressive, unmediated final words may have influenced the ending of Chester Himes's *The End of a Primitive*, as that novel concludes with its black noir protagonist, Jesse Robinson, having the final say in his phone call to the police: "'I am a nigger, and I've just killed a white woman,' Jesse said, giving the address on 21st Street, and hung up. 'That'll get the lead out of his ass.' he thought, half-amused." (p. 207)

In terms of a literary influence on Vian, James Campbell devotes some attention to the chronology of the publication of Richard Wright's *Native Son* and its potential artistic impact: "Had Vian read *Native Son*? *J'irai cracher* was written in August 1946 while Wright was in Paris. *Native Son* would not be published in its French translation until several months after the appearance of the pseudo-American novel, but Vian read English, was up-to-date in things American—especially Afro-American—and it seems unlikely that he would have ignored the major work of the black American everyone was talking about.... The theme of the 'black' novel is almost identical [sic] to that of *Native Son*, in which a young Negro kills a white girl, half accidentally, but also with feelings of triumphant revenge—'it made him feel free for the first time in his life'—for the slow death he has suffered throughout his entire life." [*Exiled in Paris*, p. 17.]

[141]The success of the novel was enhanced by the scandalous affair of Edmond Rougé, a salesman who in April 1947 strangled his mistress, Marie-Anne Masson, in a cheap hotel room next to the Gare Montparnasse, leaving next to the corpse a copy of *J'irai cracher sur vos tombes*, opened to the page describing the death of one of the women. The press immediately accused the novelist of having inspired the murder. Vian, who was brought to trial for offending public morals (the first such French trial since that of *Madame Bovary* in 1857), denied authorship until late 1948. On 3 July 1949 the government forbade the sale of the book, and in 1951 Vian and his publisher were each sentenced and fined one hundred thousand francs (about $200.). [Rudelic, "Boris Vian," p. 385.]

[142]In the book, "a black man who can 'cross the line' sets out to avenge the murder of his younger, darker brother; and the primary tool of this vengeance is—his tool.... He is caught, and hanged—hung, like a horse, his sex, according to Vian, mocking his murderers to the last. [sic. Vian's English translation reads: "his black-white *bottom* stuck out mockingly at the world."] Vian did not know that this particular nigger would almost certainly have been castrated: which is but another and deadlier way for white men to be mocked by the terror and fury by which they are engulfed upon the discovery that the black man is a man: 'it hurt,' says T.E. Lawrence, in *Seven Pillars of Wisdom*, 'that they [the negroes] should possess exact counter-parts of all our bodies.'.... Vian cared enough about his subject to force one into a confrontation with a certain kind of anguish. The book's power comes from the fact that he forces you to see this anguish from the undisguised viewpoint of his foreign, alienated own." [James Baldwin, *The Devil Finds Work* (New York: The Dial Press, 1976), pp. 38-39.]

[143]Campbell, *Exiled in Paris*, p. 15; Older, "Introducing Boris Vian," pp. xiv-xv.

[144]Louis Malle, "Foreword" to Vian's *Blues for a Black Cat*.
Malle writes of Vian: "In Paris in the 1950s Boris Vian was everything —poet, fiction writer, singer, subversive, actor, musician, and jazz critic. He was my friend, and I admired him passionately for his eclecticism, devastating irony, and taste for provocation."

[145]Buss, *French Film Noir*, p. 52. Buss continues: "What is wrong with the working-class killer [in *Ascenseur pour l'échafaud*] is not that he kills, but that he is so incompetent about it. His outlook is that of the old *régime*: accordions, not Miles Davis."

^{146}*France-Dimanche*, 4 May 1947; quoted in Campbell, *Exiled in Paris*, pp. 83-84.

^{147}Louis Malle, "Foreword" to Vian's *Blues for a Black Cat*.

^{148}Tommy L. Lott, "A No-Theory Theory of Contemporary Black Cinema," in *Representing Blackness: Issues in Film and Video*, edited by Valerie Smith (New Brunswick NJ: Rutgers University Press, 1997), p. 85. Various periodizations have been offered by other scholars, but they all have a rough compatibility.

DEFINITIONS. *"Black film* may be defined as those motion pictures made for theater distribution that have a black producer, director, and writer, or black performers; that speak to black audiences or, incidentally, to white audiences possessed of preternatural curiosity, attentiveness, or sensibility toward racial matters; and that emerge from self-conscious intentions, whether artistic or political, to illuminate the Afro-American experience. . . . [As] almost every black film, from production through distribution, was affected by whites [even the most independent producers of race movies—those films made for exclusively black audiences between 1916 and 1956—relied on white sources of capital, distributors, bookers, and exhibitors] . . . our definition must necessarily be broader so as to include film [though rare] produced by white filmmakers whose work attracted the attention, if not always the unconditional praise, of black moviegoers and critics." [Thomas Cripps, *Black Film as Genre* (Bloomington IN: Indiana University Press, 1978), pp. 3-4, 7.]

All-Colored films, Ghetto-Oriented films, Jim Crow films. Daniel J. Leab uses these terms [in "A Pale Black Imitation: All-Colored Films: 1930-1960," *The Journal of Popular Film*, Volume IV, No. 1, 1975] in the following evaluation: "Hollywood has produced a large number of stinkers over the years. But few of the movies turned out by the studios have been as bad as the ghetto-oriented films made by both black and white filmmakers. Whether these people were in the industry or only on its fringes, their productions were of very poor quality both technically and artistically. These cheaply produced, quickly made Jim Crow movies were inferior to almost everything produced by the industry." (p. 57) ["Jim Crow" was the name of a minstrel routine (actually "Jump Jim Crow") performed beginning in 1828 by its author, Thomas Dartmouth ("Daddy," "Jim Crow") Rice, and by many imitators, including Joseph Jefferson. The term came to be a derogatory epithet for African Americans and a noun designating their segregated life. It is to be inferred that it is in this second sense that Leab uses the term "Jim Crow movies," as he writes: "ironically and tragically, these movies were designed to be shown in separate and inferior movie theaters." (p. 75)]

Leab continues: "In the sound era, despite considerable rhetoric about 'better moving pictures of the Negro' and 'giving actors and actresses a fighting chance,' most makers of Jim Crow films were interested only in exploiting at the box office the desire of ghetto moviegoers to see blacks on-screen. In large part this attitude can be traced to white control of distribution and of most productions, but whatever the race of the filmmakers, commercial considerations governed their activities." (pp. 57-58) "Even before World War II strong dissatisfaction had been expressed in the black community with these films and with white producers who tried to 'palm off a lousy production on Negroes who attend through sheer race pride' in the performers. During the boom times of World War II and immediately thereafter the all-Negro quickies did well, but then they rapidly faded away as blacks began to get better roles in major studio films and as integration became a major concern in American life." (p. 74)

Harry Belafonte has been quite explicit that he was not making a "race picture" in the above sense, when he produced *Odds Against Tomorrow*—and the budget, the major distribution company, the group of front line Hollywood professionals involved all support this contention. (Interview with Author, 2 September 1998) Therefore, the comparative analysis in the main text of the images and personas of African American protagonists—and the conclusion that Belafonte in *Odds Against Tomorrow* is the first such film noir embodiment—is conducted on the basis of evidence found in major studio productions.

[149]Donald Bogle, *Toms, Coons, Mulattoes, Mammies, and Bucks* (New York: Continuum, 1989). Other indispensable works, from which this overview of black cinema is derived: Thomas Cripps, *Slow Fade to Black: The Negro in American Film, 1900-1942* (New York: Oxford University Press, 1977) and his previously cited *Making Movies Black* (1993); Dan Leab, "Blacks in American Cinema," in *The Political Companion to American Film*, edited by Gary Crowdus (Lakeview Press, 1994), pp. 41-50; Peter Roffman and Jim Purdy, *The Hollywood Social Problem Film: Madness, Despair, and Politics from the Depression to the Fifties* (Bloomington: Indiana University Press, 1981), pp. 242-252.

[150]Leab, "Blacks in American Cinema," pp. 42-43.

[151]*Ibid.*, p. 44.

[152]Cripps, *Making Movies Black*, pp. 220-221.

[153]Leab, "Blacks in American Cinema," p. 45; Cripps, *Making Movies Black*, pp. 244-245.

Poitier vs. Brown: Leab develops an analyis contrasting Sidney Poitier to **Jim Brown**, an examination which is valuable in elucidating the cinema of a future decade. Brown is used to express the intensity of the black revolution in America which peaked in the late 1960s. Brown "usually played strong-willed men of action—sure of themselves, aggressive, self-disciplined—and in many of these films he was paired with white actresses. Now there was no question about interracial coupling, nor was there any question of Brown's characters eschewing violence or being self-effacing.
"Brown's films—such as *100 Rifles* (1969) and *El Condor* 1970)—paved the way for the veritable avalanche of productions with black superheroes that descended on American movie screens in the early and mid-1970s. These 'blaxploitation films,' as they were dubbed, were filled with sadistic brutality, sleazy sex, venomous racial slurs, and the argot of the streets [attributes which help define them decisively as *neo-noir* films with black protagonists]. Important issues such as racial discrimination of the basest sort, police brutality, and economic exploitation of ghetto blacks were touched on but social commentary was kept to a minimum.
"'Sambo' gave way to 'Superspade.'. . . Superspade was a violent man who lived a violent life in pursuit of black women, white sex, quick money, easy success, and a cheap joint, among other pleasures. In these films [such as *Super Fly* (1972) and the *Shaft* series] white was synonymous with every kind of

conceivable evil and villainy. Whites were moral lepers, psychologically antiblack, whose vocabulary was laced with the rhetoric of bigotry." (p. 46)

Pauline Kael, in her "Notes on Black Movies" (*The New Yorker*, 2 December 1972) writes that "these [Superspade] films say that the smart black man gets what the white man has: the luxury goods of a consumer society, including luscious broads. These films say that there is nothing but consumerism, so grab what you can; what's good enough for the white man is good enough for you. The message is the exact opposite of the Martin Luther King message; he said, in essence, that you must not let the white man degrade you to his level. King wanted something better for blacks than the consumer-media society. Since his death, if black people have been dreaming of something better the media have blotted it from sight. That dream has been Shafted, Hammered, Slaughtered."

Poitier vs. Belafonte: Thomas Cripps's comparison of Poitier's screen image to that of Harry Belafonte's (emphasized in the main text) is more pivotal to the thesis of this commentary—which maintains the primacy of Belafonte in *Odds Against Tomorrow* as film noir's first black protagonist. In the context of these two actor comparisons to Poitier, the Belafonte priority is a somewhat self-evident observation, due to Belafonte's antecedence to Jim Brown and the scholarly distinction that is usually made between the film noir and the neo-noir eras.

[154]Cripps, *Making Movies Black*, pp. 251, 262.

[155]None of these films is included in Silver and Ward's *Film Noir*, and only *No Way Out* (1950) is in the other two studies which are considered to contain the most comprehensive listings of film noir titles: Ottoson's *A Reference Guide to the American Film Noir* and Spencer Selby's *Dark City: The Film Noir* (Jefferson NC: McFarland, 1984). The film's inclusion in both is for reasons *other* than the nature of its African American protagonist; for example, Ottoson: "The chief noir element operative here, as in *The Sound of Fury* and *The Lawless*, is the depiction of the violent instability of the masses." (p. 127)

[156]The distribution of *Native Son* in the United States was handled by the tiny Walter Gould Agency. By the time of its release, the film was severely mutilated. The New York State Board of Censors demanded that over a half hour be cut prior to the opening. Even then, the states of Pennsylvania, Wisconsin, and Ohio refused to allow the film to be shown.

Wright wrote a bitter letter to his agent in August 1951: "People everywhere know that the film was cut, that the killing of the rat was cut, that making of the homegun was cut, that the real heart of the boys' attempt at robbery was cut, that most of the dialogue between the newspaper men was cut. But the cut that did the greatest damage was the cutting of the trial. . . . The trial is shown with arms waving and mouths moving but nothing is heard."

These extrinsic circumstances, as well as other aspects intrinsic to the novel's adaptation to film, were, according to Peter Brunette, "insurmountable barriers that keep *Native Son* on film from playing the theaters, even in this tamed and emasculated version." [Peter Brunette, "Two Wrights, One Wrong," in *The Modern American Novel and the Movies*, edited by Gerald Peary and Roger Shatzkin (New York: Frederick Ungar Publishing Co., 1978), pp. 136, 142.]

[157]A.W., "Richard Wright Plays Hero in Movie Adaptation of His Novel, 'Native Son,'" *New York Times*, 18 June 1951.

When the film was being made, the *New York Times* reported that the production was aimed primarily at the United States. "Asked why he came to Argentina to make 'Native Son,' Richard Wright explained that 'it just happened that way.' He would gladly have gone to Hollywood. He would have been delighted to make the picture in France, Italy or England. But Hollywood, he is convinced, would insist upon watering the story down and it is his opinion that no nation receiving substantial aid from the United States would risk offending that country by making a movie which deals with the Negroes' dilemma in a pretty uncompromising manner. Since Argentina seemed completely indifferent to the potential complications along that line, Mr. Wright came along happily to Sono Film's studio." (Virginia Lee Warren, "Argentina Doubles as Chicago Locale for 'Native Son,'" *New York Times*, 21 May 1950.)

Interestingly, in light of the film being heralded as "Argentina's first English-spoken film made expressly for distribution abroad," *Variety*, in its 25 April 1951 review, asserted that it "stands little chance in the U.S. but shapes good for [the Latin American] market." Writer *Nid.*, reviewing the film from Buenos Aires as *Sangre Negra* , felt that the work was made with the intention to create anti-U.S. feeling: "It is rather sad that a number of British and U.S. residents in Argentina should have been enticed into collaborating in this underhand stab at the U.S. . . . so slanting it, by touches of exaggeration or caricature, as to give Richard Wright's message against racial intolerance plenty of anti-U.S. twist. . . . The anti-U.S. impact likely will be strongest when it is distributed in Latin-America, particularly Panama, Brazil and other countries with a large proportion of colored population. Presumably, it is for that public that contrasts between the rich sections of Chicago and those of the Negro slums are shown with crude sensationalism."

The most negative attributes of the film are summarized in Darr Smith's review: "The movie sinks to the level of a low-grade, uninteresting chase. Wright is unbelievably bad as an actor. There seems to be a fetish that has arisen out of the success of a handful of foreign films, that if you use amateurs as actors you will thereby attain realism. This thesis becomes true only by accident. 'Native Son' is the dull proof that it should be discarded in most cases. [Director Pierre Chenal] could do no more with his actors than make them sound as though they were reciting. [The photography by Antonio Merayo] is unknowingly jerky and out of focus. The script is as bald and blatant and obvious as a propaganda leaflet." (*Los Angeles Daily News*, 13 August 1951)

But, as amelioration in the most positive response, *The Saturday Review of Literature* (7 July 1951) admired the film's "unwillingness to compromise with standard entertainment patterns . . . while it is a bit uneven, it is by no means without interest. Richard Wright has drawn here a highly sympathetic Bigger and leaves it to the audience to search out the social implications of Bigger's tragedy. As an actor Wright is amazingly persuasive—particularly when you consider that this was his initial try at it. His Bigger in uneducated but not unintelligent, frightened and desperate yet still appealing. . . . The whole, in spite of its technical defects, proves to have been very much worth doing—even if it meant going all the way to the Argentine to do it."

[158]Cripps, *Making Movies Black*, p. 279; Bogle, *Toms, Coons . . .*, p. 184; Pines, *Blacks in Films*, pp. 84-85.

[159]Farber, "Ugly Spotting," *Movies*, p. 62.

[160] Ottoson, *Guide to Film Noir*, p. 128.

161Cripps, *Making Movies Black*, pp. 286-287.

162Pines, *Blacks in Films*, p. 81.

163Bogle, *Toms, Coons . . .*, p. 180.

164*Ibid.*, p. 181.
The ending of the film left the audience to conclude "that white well-being hinges on black sacrifice, a point not lost on black critics, who began to carp at Poitier's work. Indeed director Martin Ritt recalled that Tommy's death stirred 'a goddamned riot in the theatre.'" [Cripps, *Making Movies Black*, p. 289.]
"The film was praised for its honesty, but its conclusion was disturbing: audiences wanted to know *why* the Negro had to be killed in order for the hero to achieve self-respect." [Albert Johnson, "Beige, Brown, or Black," in *Black Films and Film-Makers: A Comprehensive Anthology from Stereotype to Superhero*, edited by Lindsay Patterson (NY: Dodd, Mead & Company, 1975), p. 37.]

165Bogle, p. 182; Pines, *Blacks in Films*, p. 76.

166Gladstone L. Yearwood, "The Hero in Black Film: An Analysis of the Film Industry and Problems in Black Cinema," *Wide Angle*, Vol. 5, No. 2, 1982, pp. 46-47.

167Cripps, *Making Movies Black*, p. 262.

168*Ibid.*, pp. 262-265.

169*Ibid.*, p. 266.

170**An Ambivalent Conclusion:** "[On the one hand] one cannot rightfully separate the dominant tendency to erect 'safe' as well as vacuous and malleable Negro models from the persistent and profound impact the Sidney Poitier character and image have had on the cinema screen and on contemporary American culture at large. The cinematic definition and solution of the so-called 'Negro problem,' both in social and moral terms, is heavily based on this factor. **But** [on the other hand] it also represents liberal cinema's major failure, in that the establishment of the one-star racial system (revolving as it [did] round Poitier, which is really another form of racism), evolved directly out of liberal-humanitarian ideals. In this context, such films as *The World, the Flesh and the Devil* (1959) and *Odds Against Tomorrow* (1959), possibly *Native Son* (1951) . . . also are marginally more interesting—if only because they manage to evince strong social comment with a fair degree of perceptiveness, and with none of the mystique and predictability that abound in Poitier-centered presentations."
[Jim Pines, *Blacks in Films*, p. 84.]

171Henry Louis Gates, Jr., "Belafonte's Balancing Act," *The New Yorker*, August 26 & September 2, 1996, pp. 134, 139.

172Maurice Zolotow, "Harry Belafonte," *The American Weekly*, 10 May 1959, p. 14.

¹⁷³Arnold Shaw, *What Is the Secret Magic of Belafonte?* (New York: Pyramid Books, 1960), p. 280.

¹⁷⁴**Sidebar on Independent Production and Distribution.** A discussion about the mechanism of how films get financed and distributed is relevant to a fuller understanding of the authorship and production of *Odds Against Tomorrow.* From the point of view of black filmmaking, here is Mark A. Reid [*Redefining Black Film* (Berkeley: University of California Press, 1993)]: "I distinguish three forms of distribution networks: major studios such as Columbia Pictures, United Artists, and Metro-Goldwyn-Mayer; major independent distributors such as Cinemation, American International Pictures, and Dimension Pictures; and black independent distributors such as Black Filmmakers Foundation, Chamba Educational Films, and Mypheduh Films. Black-American independent productions that are distributed by major studios or major independent distributors cannot be considered black independent films because they rely on the major studios' distribution outlets. (p. 150)

"This distinction between independent distribution and distribution by major or mini-major companies is significant to any analysis of black independent film because black filmmakers may alter their scripts to aim for distribution by major studios." (p. 82) Reid then proceeds with examples, from which he infers two conclusions which are reconciled with some fragility. One (example): "Melvin Van Peebles probably altered his *Sweetback* in several ways to aim for major distribution, since he hoped that his film would 'be able to sustain itself as a viable commercial product.' [Van Peebles] writes, 'The [white] Man . . . might go along with you if at least there is some bread in it for him. But he ain't about to go carrying no messages for you, especially a relevant one for free.'" This seems to imply some degree of artistic compromise, but Reid follows by recognizing aspect two (the ameliorating tradeoff): "Even though he realized that he would have to satisfy Cinemation's tastes, Van Peebles undoubtedly gained for *Sweetback* more visibility and more bookings in theaters throughout the nation and took in more money than if he had depended on nonprofit distribution organizations." (p. 83)

United Artists. The formation of United Artists Corporation (UA), 15 January 1919, marked the first time that a group of artists rather than businessmen joined to create a major distribution company for their films. The four principals in this new enterprise were Mary Pickford, Douglas Fairbanks, Charles Chaplin, and D.W. Griffith. (A fifth artist, William S. Hart, was involved in the original configuration but later dropped out.) This prompted Richard A. Rowland, president of Metro Pictures, to make his famous remark, "So the lunatics have taken charge of the asylum."

United Artists was concerned only with the distribution function until the early 1950s, when the company was taken over by Arthur Krim and Robert Benjamin. They hired a new management team which included such men as Arnold Picker, Robert Blumofe, and Max Youngstein. This group implemented a concept which the original UA organization never ventured to adopt: the financing of independent producers. As Arthur Krim put it: "Our approach is to alter the structure of the company so that we are no longer distributing exclusively for the benefit of producers. The pictures that are now handled by United Artists are being distributed for our own benefits and interests as well."

In essence, UA went into partnership with its producers. Together, the company and producer would reach agreement as to story, cast, director, and budget; afterwards, the producer had complete autonomy in the making of the picture. Also, the producer was allowed to own a share of the picture and to participate in its profits. As a result, UA's producers would often defer salary considerations to collaborate in the distribution process. [See Tino Balio, *United Artists: The Company Built by the Stars* (Madison: The University of Wisconsin Press, 1976); Anthony Slide, *The American Film Industry* (New York: Limelight Editions, 1990); Ronald Bergan, *The United Artists Story* (New York: Crown Publishers, 1986).]

This arrangement greatly appealed to Harry Belafonte: "Arnold Picker, Arthur Crim, and Bob Benjamin were on the board at United Artists. They were liberal and they had a vision of America's future in certainly more upscale terms than anybody else in the picture business I'd known. They provided an environment that permitted us to be more adventuresome, with a studio name, than any other entity.

"I did not consider the so-called race films, made for the black community exclusively, the proper venue for what I wanted to do. They were never connected to mainstream Hollywood and the film industry as it was. In their limited exposure, very little is known about that work—except in pockets where black communities had theaters that they controlled. What I wanted to do was to establish a black presence on the production end of the major film industry, to articulate a richer point of view than what was presently being expressed. I was encouraged in this effort by a young man at United Artists by the name of Max Youngstein, the fourth man in the equation." (Interview with Author, 2 September 1998.)

[175]William H. Higgins, Jr., "John Oliver Killens," *Dictionary of Literary Biography: Volume 33. Afro-American Fiction Writers After 1955.* Edited by Thadious M. Davis and Trudier Harris (Detroit: Gale Research Co., 1984), pp. 144-152.

[176]John Oliver Killens, "Hollywood in Black and White," in *The State of the Nation,* edited by David Boroff (Englewood Cliffs NJ: Prentice-Hall, Inc., 1965), p. 102. This essay also appeared in *Nation,* 201 (20 September 1965), pp. 157-160.

[177]*Ibid.,* p. 106.

[178]Albert Johnson, "Beige, Brown, or Black," in Patterson, *Black Films and Film-Makers,* p. 36.

[179]Tommy L. Lott, "A No-Theory Theory of Contemporary Black Cinema," *Representing Blackness,* pp. 88, 90.

[180]Jacqueline Bobo, "Black Women in Fiction & Nonfiction: Images of Power & Powerlessness," *Wide Angle,* Volume 13, Number 3, July 1991, p. 73.

[181]Herman Gray, "Television, Black Americans, and the American Dream," in *Mediated Messages and African-American Culture,* edited by Venise T. Berry & Carmen L. Manning-Miller (Sage Publications, 1996), pp. 136-138, 144.
See also: Bishetta Merritt and Carolyn A. Stroman, "Black Family Imagery and Interactions on Television," *Journal of Black Studies,* Vol. 23, No. 4, June 1993, pp. 492-499.
"Black women have long responded to the need to transform their social situations and to reconstruct the ways in which they are represented. The first codified stage of this process began in the nineteenth century. In 1880 the first of

the Black women's political organizations was formed, and by 1896 the two largest groups had consolidated into the National Association of Colored Women. "Two black women who had a significant impact on the movement were Ida B. Wells and Anna Julia Cooper. Wells led the fight against lynching while Cooper worked extensively for the right of black women to be educated. They were influential in shaping a wider movement of black women. This is a crucial point, one that is especially important today: that black women have not docilely submitted to their imposed social conditions." (Bobo, "Black Women in Fiction & Nonfiction," p. 80.)

[182]Richard Keenan, "William P. McGivern," *Critical Survey of Mystery and Detective Fiction*, edited by Frank N. Magill (Salem Press, 1988), pp. 1154-1155.
"McGivern's books constitute crime fiction of a high order. In each, the actual crime and its concomitant details serve primarily as a point of departure for his highest interest: the texture of humanity that emerges with the creation and development of character. McGivern writes in the third person, combining spare prose and taut dialogue with an economical, highly selective use of descriptive detail. The situation in which the McGivern protagonist finds himself may be remote from the average reader's experience, but the reader readily empathizes; the angst McGivern depicts is universally felt and understood." (Keenan, p. 1158.)

[183]See Woody Haut, *Pulp Culture: Hardboiled Fiction and the Cold War* (London: Serpent's Tail, 1995), pp. 140-142.

[184] McGivern, *Odds Against Tomorrow*, p. 51. All subsequent page citations from the novel will be made in the main text.

[185]Baldwin, "Everybody's Protest Novel," in *Bigger Thomas*, edited by Harold Bloom (New York: Chelsea House Publishers, 1990), pp. 5-6.
And there are those (Rose, "Afro-American Literature as a Cultural Resource for a Black Cinema Aesthetic," pp. 37-38) who would extend Baldwin's perspective to cinema: "Just as Afro-American literature has, over the course of time, moved from one-dimensional protest—(important though this was)—a black cinema aesthetic that satisfies itself with relatively easy protest against the system and mere opposition to the regular fare of Hollywood cinema will have failed both its own possibilities and the black community. At their deepest levels, Afro-American arts must explore the full dimensions of the Afro-American experience in all its complexity, contradictions, vitality, triumphs. No less can be demanded." [It is maintained here that *Odds Against Tomorrow* fulfills these requirements.]

[186]Henry Louis Gates, Jr., *Figures in Black: Words, Signs, and the "Racial" Self* (New York: Oxford University Press, 1989), p. 31.

[187]Polonsky, quoted in Barbara Zheutlin and David Talbot, *Creative Differences: Profiles of Hollywood Dissidents* (Boston: South End Press, 1977), p. 80. These are words that Polonsky used in describing Joe Morse's situation in *Force of Evil*, but which can be applied with equal validity to Johnny Ingram.

[188]Gates, *Figures in Black*, p.57; Ralph Ellison, "The Essential Ellison (Interview)," *Y'Bird* 1, No. 1 (1978), pp. 130-159; Toni Morrison, *Jazz* (New York: Penguin, 1993); see Dana Micucci, "An Inspired Life: Toni Morrison Writes and a Generation Listens," *Chicago Tribune*, 31 May 1992.
"Words came to Morrison in arias and choruses; she constructs tragic scenes of love and violent death while pushing her characters 'toward the abyss somewhere to see what is remarkable, because that's the way I find out what is heroic.'" (Betty Fussell, "All that Jazz," *Lear's* 5.8 (1 October 1992), p. 68. [Both Morrison citations can be found in *Conversations with Toni Morrison*. Edited by Danille Taylor-Guthrie (Jackson, Mississippi: University Press of Mississippi, 1994.)]

[189]Rob Edelman, "Abraham Polonsky," *The St. James Film Directors Encyclopedia*, pp. 393-394.

[190]Polonsky, *The World Above* (Boston: Little Brown, 1951), pp. 360-361.

[191]See Ed Lowry's insightful CinemaTexas Program Notes on *Madigan*, Vol. 9, No. 3, 30 October 1975, pp. 47-54.

[192]Unpublished interview, n.d., Polonsky Collection, California State University, Northridge.

[193]Interview with James D. Pasternak and F. William Howton, in *The Image Maker* (Richmond VA: John Knox Press, 1971), p. 27.

[194]Polonsky, in *Creative Differences*, p. 99.

[195]Polonsky, in *The Image Maker*, p. 27.

Black Women & the Black Family. *Odds Against Tomorrow* departed from the prevailing stereotype of the role of the black woman in the cinema at that time, described by Jim Pines (*Blacks in Films*, 1975) as having "no significant place in the liberal cinema," of an image that "remains vulgar and despicable." Ruth Ingram (Kim Hamilton, right), by contrast, is caring, responsible, and conscientious; she protects and nurtures her child, Eadie (Lois Thorne, left). Where Ruth talks of Eadie's future, Johnny (Belafonte, center) speaks in individual terms about his frustration and unrealistic aspirations: "I've got five hundred on the nose of Lady Care today. Can't lose forever." Ruth is assertive and accountable. "This moment can be read as an appeal to the utopian ideal of strong and liberated black women." (See Herman Gray, "Television, Black Americans, and the American Dream.")

Revolt and Brutal Despair: The French Connection. "As for the Americans, it was not their cruelty or pessimism which moved us. We recognized in them men who had been swamped, lost in too large a continent, as we were in history, and who tried, without traditions, with the means available, to render their stupor and forlornness in the midst of incomprehensible events."
—Jean-Paul Sartre, *What Is Literature?*

Third-Phase Film Noir: The End-of-the-Line. "These films [like *White Heat* (1949), *Kiss Me Deadly* (1955)] were painfully self-aware; they seemed to know they stood at the end of a long tradition based on despair and disintegration and did not shy away from the fact. The third phase is rife with end-of-the-line heroes. It's just a matter of when these doomed characters [Slater (Ryan), top of the stairs; Ingram (Belafonte), below] are finally going to explode . . . and take the world with them. It's the end of the line. You can't go much further."
—Paul Schrader, "Notes on Film Noir."

This is the way the world ends. "Strange angular piles of smoking metal . . . a shattered, not quite real world." Two central motifs established in the first shot of the film—the music and the wind— continue through the ending to complete a symmetry of the modern wasteland theme. Existential markers depict a world of obsessive return, dark corners, and *huis clos.*

"I had not thought death had undone so many."
—T.S. Eliot, "The Waste Land."

John Lewis & the Film Score
for *Odds Against Tomorrow*: I

by Martin C. Myrick

The selection of John Lewis as the composer for the musical score of *Odds Against Tomorrow* reveals the socio-political savvy of the film's creators. At a point in time when tensions between black and white communities were building to a boiling point, the cross-cultural appeal of Lewis's music would serve as a vehicle for the film's message, gaining access to both communities in general. Lewis was both a member of the Modern Jazz Quartet, famed for setting the standards for "Cool Jazz" in the 1950's, and the principal architect of the group's style and sound, which found a broad appeal among whites as well as blacks.

While the origin of Cool Jazz stems from various sources, most critics agree that its formal birth announcement can be credited to a group of recording sessions in 1949 and 1950 which featured Miles Davis, Gil Evans, and Claude Thornhill. Lewis was a part of those sessions. In 1949, he joined the Miles Davis Recording Group through his association with army buddy and prominent be-bop drummer, Kenny Clarke. The songs which they recorded were later reissued as a collective known as "The Birth of the Cool."

> Some of the interesting things about this particular group (the Davis nonet) were the exclusion of the tenor saxophone and the addition of both the tuba and the French horn. The musicians refrained from using the characteristic vibrato found in most be-bop, instead eliciting a drier tone. Some of the instruments lent a character to the music that was characterized as "pastel bop."[1]

John Aaron Lewis was born in La Grange, Illinois in 1920, and grew up in Albuquerque, New Mexico. At the age of seven he began playing piano and later attended the University of New Mexico where he studied anthropology and music, playing several instruments in the school band.

Lewis's introduction to jazz improvisation was a 1920's Louis Armstrong recording, and later, a radio broadcast of the Jay McShann Orchestra that featured saxophonist Charlie Parker. Parker's playing fascinated Lewis: ". . . every time he played a solo, it was perfect," Lewis recalls.[2]

Lewis met Kenny Clarke in 1942 when he had joined the army big band, and, after the war, Clarke was instrumental in securing Lewis as the new pianist/arranger for the Dizzy Gillespie Band, replacing Thelonius Monk. The rest of Gillespie's rhythm section included Clarke on drums, Ray Brown on bass, and Milt Jackson on vibraphone. Members of this rhythm section recorded with the Miles Davis Group as well, and after awhile struck out on their own to become known as the Milt Jackson Quartet.

The musicians were richly talented and nomadic. Milt Jackson was thought of by some critics to be the finest vibe player ever. While playing with Gillespie's band, Lewis had studied at the Manhattan School of Music, where he received two degrees and developed his interest in Baroque counterpoint. In 1952, Ray Brown left the quartet, due to his marriage to Ella Fitzgerald and his commitment to her as her music director, and he was replaced by Percy Heath. In 1955 Clarke left the group to move to Europe and he was replaced by Connie Kay.

The premier "cool jazz" groups of the 1950's were the Modern Jazz Quartet, the George Shearing Quintet, and the Dave Brubeck and Gerry Mulligan quartets. The styles of these groups were perceived by their audiences as understated, subdued, and emotionally detached.

Cool Jazz occupied a very short time in jazz history, from about 1948 until the late 1950's. Some historians will argue that it came about because white people, who had the money to buy records, objected to the rowdiness and general lack of morality associated with jazz.[3]

While touring as the Milt Jackson Quartet, Lewis and his fellow musicians gradually became disturbed at the lack of attentiveness they found with audiences in night clubs and decided to create a new image for themselves. They changed their name to the Modern Jazz Quartet, began dressing in tuxedos, and took their music to concert and recital halls—resulting in a new respect for jazz and an elevation of its status among "serious music" listeners in the U.S. and especially in Europe.

The group was so different in many ways from the other small bands around that the term "chamber jazz" may have been coined to describe them. Under the influence of John Lewis, who was a composer and the group's music director, as well as its pianist, they explored classical forms. They played concert halls and colleges rather than clubs. They were flawlessly dressed in white tie or business suits. David Harrington, founder of the Kronos Quartet, acknowledges the MJQ as a model. One thing that made the MJQ unique among small groups of the bebop era (other than piano trios) was the absence of a horn. This also led to their aura of refinement—no one blows or spits in the Modern Jazz Quartet.[4]

After the group was established, Lewis began to concentrate on compositions which were a synthesis of the traditional jazz element of collective improvisations and the element of classical form. "The fugue is Lewis's favorite form. He uses it very effectively to integrate written lines with single and collective improvisations."[5] Probably more than any other composer of his time, John Lewis advanced the use of classical elements in jazz. "John Lewis has been said to be one of the few people who really understands the similarities between jazz and classical and who helps bridge gaps between these disciplines."[6] This synthesis of classical and jazz was given the name **Third Stream Music** by composer Gunther Schuller. Third stream music had been evolving for sometime. Charles Ives and Claude Debussy had both been inspired in their compositions by ragtime, as had Stravinsky who had even composed the "Ebony Concerto" for the Woody Herman band.

The popularity of jazz (and ragtime before it) has caught the ears of classical composers throughout this century. And jazz artists, for their part, have at times returned the compliment. But the strongest case for jazz/classical crossover music was made by pianist/composer/arranger John Lewis and composer/arranger Gunther Schuller. Schuller, who played French horn for both the Metropolitan Opera orchestra and various modern jazz bands, teamed in 1955 with Modern Jazz Quartet founder Lewis to form the Jazz and Classical Music Society. Its goal was, according to Schuller, "to bring classical music and jazz together conceptually, technically, and in the performance practices."[7]

The historical and aesthetic importance of Lewis's film score for *Odds Against Tomorrow* is that it is one of the earliest, and most likely the first, example of a true third stream film score, and while it is now commonplace to find scores with elements of classical, jazz, and even rock music, it was John Lewis's ground breaking compositions which led the way to the future.

Lewis's first film composition was *No Sun in Venice* in 1956, released in 1958, and, although it could be classified as third stream due to its mixture of jazz with fugue form, it was composed for the quartet. Lewis said at the time: "Jazz is often thought to be limited in expression. It is used for 'incidental music' or when a situation in drama or film calls for jazz, but rarely in a more universal way apart from an explicit jazz context. Here it has to be able to run the whole gamut of emotions and carry the story from beginning to end."[8]

Though it is certain that Lewis uses definitive elements of classical and jazz music in *No Sun in Venice*, it is not as easily classified "Third Stream" in the same context as *Odds Against Tomorrow*. The film score for *Odds Against Tomorrow*, first of all, was composed not only for the quartet, but for a 22-piece chamber orchestra as well. In order to truly convey the aesthetic and the feel of third stream music, the composition must include, in its instrumentation, a mixture of instruments or groups of instruments which are representative of jazz and classical forms. Therefore, this film score stands apart as the ideal founding model for third stream film scores for two reasons: its composition for quartet and orchestra; its distinctive interweaving of the Classical (Baroque) form of counterpoint with jazz improvisation.

> The Harry Belafonte film *Odds Against Tomorrow*, with a score written by Lewis and recorded by a 22-piece orchestra, was released October 1959. Gunther Schuller has summarized the importance of this score. "It utilizes jazz music as a purely dramatic music to underline a variety of situations not specifically related to jazz. . . . It can serve its purpose in the film but it can also stand as absolute music apart from the original dramatic situation."[9]

As Lewis previously stated, jazz in the movies before the 1950s was used for the most part as "incidental" or "situational" music—but that began to change with Alex North's score for *A Streetcar Named Desire* (1951).

While the music [for *Streetcar*] did not gain any great popularity away from the film (it was not suitable for pop market exploitation), it did open the door for the use of jazz in films. Indeed, the score is the first substantial use of stylized jazz in a film for anything other than source music. It would not be until 1955, with Elmer Bernstein's score to *The Man with the Golden Arm*, that stylized jazz "made the charts" and exerted any amount of pernicious influence on the type of scores being written for pictures.[10]

Elmer Bernstein's own analysis of his work for the Otto Preminger film is revealing: "The score for *The Man with the Golden Arm* is not a jazz score. It is a score in which jazz elements were incorporated toward the end of creating an atmosphere, I should say a highly specialized atmosphere, specific to this particular film." Critic Roy Prendergast: "One of the primary reasons it is not a jazz score is that the music is not improvised; improvisation is the lifeblood of jazz. What little improvisation does take place in the score is done by the drummer, Shelly Manne. The art of improvisation does not mix well with the split-second timing of a film score."[11]

The following year would find Lewis in a head-on challenge to the notion that "improvisation does not mix well with the split-second timing of a film score." The key for Lewis in constructing a jazz film score that relates to the expected aesthetic taste of the audience, and at the same time achieves the technically interactive relationship between score and film, would be found within the newly formed concept of third stream. Through the use of classical form—Baroque Counterpoint—Lewis is able to rein in the free form tendencies of jazz improvisation to form a cohesive structure which more readily enables the split-second timing of a film score. Here Lewis expresses his concern for form:

The audience for jazz can be widened if we strengthen our work with structure. If there is more of a reason for what's going on, there'll be more overall sense and, therefore, more interest for the listener. I do not think, however, that the sections in this "structured jazz"—both the improvised and written sections—should take on too much complexity. The total effect must be within the mind's ability to appreciate through the ear.[12]

In light of Lewis's statement, a very interesting comparison can be drawn between Lewis's approach to form and improvisation (content), and that of Abraham Polonsky, the composer of the film's screenplay. Lewis was experimenting with bringing classical form to the world of jazz, and jazz improvisation into the world of the classical, in a way which can relate directly to Polonsky's attempts to develop his own film style and content. Among Hollywood social activists in the 1930's and 1940's, any concern for aesthetics was expressed within the social content of a film, since stylistic experimentation for most artists was out of the question within the studio system.

> Polonsky was one of the few Hollywood leftists of this period who approached filmmaking in a systematic fashion. He placed as much emphasis on developing a radical film style as he did on creating radical content. Polonsky says that he is not absolutely sure there is such a thing as a "Marxist film aesthetic." But he does know that his films in some way reflect a Marxian concept of history. "The dialectical process as I understand it," says Polonsky, "means that we constantly have in motion, at all levels, uneven contraries which interact with each other, and this interaction creates the energy which is the nature of the world."[13]

A direct comparison with Polonsky's concept of the dialectic process can be made to Lewis's use of the form of counterpoint or fugue in the deliverance of his jazz content. As is Lewis, Polonsky seems to be in pursuit of new ways of interweaving form and content, appropriating some of the same concepts found in third stream music. Polonsky's interview with William Pechter concerning *Force of Evil* gives some insight to this comparison: "All I tried to do was use the succession of visual images, the appearances of human personality in the actors, and the rhythm of words in unison or counterpoint. I varied the speed, intensity, congruence and conflict for design, emotion and goal, sometimes separating the three elements, sometimes using two or three together."[14]

In view of this statement, a direct relationship can be suggested between Lewis's form of musical counterpoint and Polonsky's cinematic form of counterpoint. Each draws upon the use of similar aesthetic form to serve as the channel for content. Polonsky's response to Robert

Hatch's identification of the "presence of blank verse" in *Force of Evil* draws an analogy to Lewis's use of improvisation as content.

> As for the language, I merely freed it of the burden of literary psychology and the role of crutch to the visual image. Blank verse? No. But the babble of the unconscious, yes, as much as I could, granted the premise that I was committed to a representational film.[15]

Polonsky's description sounds very similar to Lewis's use of improvisation within classical form. Yet, as Polonsky shys away from the label of blank verse, Lewis likewise distances himself from overtly complex improvisation.

> When Lewis says that structured jazz should not "take on too much complexity," it is apparent that he believes that in some instances at least it has, and he speaks with authority. The complexity however is not, and has not been, the result of form, or frame; this has not become more complex. What has become more complex is the manner in which the musical material has been stretched over the frame, particularly in improvised music. While notated jazz has continued to remain foursquare, improvised music has developed a technique of what we may call "free phrasing" that is intended to escape the tyranny of the four- and eight-bar phrase."[16]

The literary idea of "blank verse" and the musical concept of "free phrasing" seem to have the same associative properties for both Polonsky and Lewis, and while both tend to maintain their distance in their compositions, they at times tend to lean out over the edge of the cliff just to see what's below. Indicative of Lewis's tendency to embrace improvisation only within a structured framework is the apparent tension which existed between Lewis and vibist Milt Jackson, who was more inclined to engage in "free phrasing" and more complex improvisational solos.

> Critics have argued that Jackson, the finest vibraharp player ever, is constrained in the quartet (Jackson himself doesn't hide his preference for the time he spent playing for Thelonius Monk). But Lewis's more formally inclined records are more lasting than the continual Jackson blowing

sessions. This tension between the two makes the group work. Jackson is a florid, romantic soloist, and Lewis, whose style derives from Basie and Kansas City blues (his is the piano solo on Charlie Parker's blues masterpiece "Parker's Mood"), often plays as few notes as possible, sometimes choosing to play counterpoint, rather than chords, behind a Jackson solo. The group is unmatched in its ability to derive varying textures from its limited instrumentation.[17]

The tension which exists in the music of Lewis and Jackson, and which Lewis attempts to bring forth in his film score, both within the quartet and the orchestra, and between the quartet and orchestra, can draw comparison to the dialectic tension to which Polonsky previously refers and tries to achieve in his films.

When listening to the score it is important to remember that tension is the axis upon which Lewis's composition rotates, and this underlying dialectic is accomplished through fugue or counterpoint. Through the film Lewis pairs varying instruments, or groups of instruments contrapuntally. Often guitar and vibes, or piano and guitar, will counter each other, while at other times the quartet will engage in a swing shuffle, with orchestral brass, strings and tympani sounding sustained dissonant progressions in opposition, at times resulting in a manic crescendo of despair. Lewis also, especially in the opening scene, achieves a quite interesting counterpoint pairing between wind machine, used for effect throughout the film, and a harp-like electric guitar. Throughout the film's score a certain coldness is also achieved due in some part to the dominating presence of the cool, steel-toned vibraphone of Milt Jackson. The overall achievement is one which reflects the intentions of the script in a build up of desperate tension, resolving in futility and hopelessness.

With the choice of John Lewis as the composer of this archetypal third stream film score, and by taking advantage of the Modern Jazz Quartet's cross-over popularity, the film's creators are able to gather blacks and whites into one audience through a common musical aesthetic, with the faint hope that some further unifying process can begin to take hold in people's minds as they are exposed to the film's message of the utter hopelessness and destruction which inevitably results from racial hatred and bigotry. Although there are film scores and composers associated with third stream which have gained more celebrity in the film world, such as David Amram's score for *The Manchurian Candidate*, and Lalo Schifrin's many scores for film and television, including the *Mission Impossible* theme, the score for *Odds Against Tomorrow* can be critically acclaimed not only as the prototype for third stream film scores, but as the very embodiment of what Gunther Schuller eloquently describes as the 'vision' behind the birth of "Third Stream."

> "The idea behind Third Stream is an extraordinarily important, profound philosophical one," said Schuller, "because what the world needs is not segregation and separation of cultures, of people, of countries. What we need is to bring people together. You can apply the same thing to music. To bring musics together. So it's not just a musical thing; this is a truly important social and you could even say political undertaking. . . . That was our vision. Quite apart from the fact that we loved both Mozart and Charlie Parker."[18]

NOTES

[1]*A Short History of the Cool,* file:C:\aol30\download\cooljaz.htm

[2]Owens, Tim. *National Public Radio Jazz Profiles: John Lewis.* file:///C/aol30/download/Lewisnpr.htm

[3]*A Short History of the Cool,* file:C:\aol30\download\cooljaz.htm

[4]Goldberg, Joel. *The Modern Jazz Quartet;* "Pyramid" 1960, Voyager Link, www.voyagerco.com/cdlink/voyager2/mjq/pyramid.htm

[5]Jazclass-*Profile of John Lewis,* www.elf.aust.com/~jazclass/lewis.htm

[6]Wynn, Ron, *All Music Guide,* Volume 1,#1, www.musicblvd.com/ cgi-bin/tw/16839...105_105467^TEMPLATE_PATH=/mb2/live/main

[7]JCS: *Third Stream, Jazz Journey,* www1.jazzcentralstation.com/newjcs/special/classical_1.asp

[8]Mark Evans, *Soundtrack: The Music of the Movies* (New York: Hopkinson and Blake Publishers, 1975), p. 126.

[9]Leonard Feather, *The Encyclopedia of Jazz* (New York: Bonanza Books, 1988), p. 312.

[10]Roy Prendergast, *Film Music—A Neglected Art: A Critical Study of Music in Films* (New York: W.W. Norton & Company, 1977), p. 104.

[11]*Ibid.,* p. 109.

[12]John Lewis, quoted in Leo Ostransky, *The Anatomy of Jazz* (Seattle: University of Washington Press, 1960), p. 292.

[13]Abraham Polonsky, quoted in Barbara Zheutlin and David Talbot, *Creative Differences: Profiles of Hollywood Dissidents* (Boston: South End Press, 1978), p. 82.

[14]Polonsky, quoted in William Pechter, "Interview with Abraham Polonsky," *Film Quarterly,* XV, No. 3 (Spring 1962), p. 392.

[15]*Ibid.*

[16]Ostransky, *Anatomy of Jazz,* p. 292.

[17]Goldberg, Joel. *The Modern Jazz Quartet;* "Pyramid" 1960, Voyager Link, www.voyagerco.com/cdlink/voyager2/mjq/pyramid.htm

[18]JCS: *Third Stream, Jazz Journey,* www1.jazzcentralstation.com/newjcs/special/classical_1.asp

John Lewis & the Film Score
for *Odds Against Tomorrow*: II

by Michelle Best

John Lewis has performed with almost everyone in the jazz community. His discography reads like a who's who of jazz royalty and represents an evolutionary chronicle of the jazz style from spirituals, bepop, swing, third stream, and cool. Lewis and Modern Jazz Quartet's own style can be characterized as controlled and refined, incorporating classical structure within the free form improvisational style of jazz. The Modern Jazz Quartet is comprised of John Lewis on piano, Milt Jackson on vibraharp, Percy Heath on bass, and Connie Kay on drums. Lewis, as music director, composed most of the music for the quartet, in addition to composing film scores, and a ballet.

Lewis composed music for five films. His first score was for a film by Roger Vadim, *No Sun in Venice (1958)*. The second was for Robert Wise, *Odds Against Tomorrow* (1959). Later films were *Exposure (1959)*, *A Milanese Story (1959)*, and *Cities for People* (1975). Comparing the first two scores, it is evident that Lewis is a masterful musician and composer. He picked up on the nuances of film scoring almost immediately. The characters were given motifs and themes, and he was able to compose music that played along with and sometimes against the action on the screen.

No Sun in Venice is a thriller with a love story. The music Lewis composed for the film is romantic, melodic, and even wistful at times. He wrote themes for the three main characters utilizing the instrumentation of the quartet. Michel's theme is heard in the vibraharp part, the bass plays the Baron's theme music, and Sforzi's motif is heard in the piano part. Lewis was able to interweave the three themes through the fugue, a classical composition form in which one to three themes are interwoven to create polyphony of sound.

> Lewis was approached by producer Raoul Levy, who . . . commissioned him to write the score for [this] new film by Roger Vadim. . . . Lewis tackled the assignment without ever having seen the film. He worked only with a script and timings. If the film is no great shakes (Lewis, who eventually caught up with it in Greenwich Village, says, "It isn't good, but it's very

beautiful, the photography was great")—the music he wrote constitutes an enduring milestone in the MJQ's repertory.
[Liner Notes, *40 Years of MJQ*, 1988.]

The jazz and blues score written by John Lewis for *Odds Against Tomorrow* adds to the noir mood and emotion of the picture through dissonant sounds and varied orchestration. Lewis's music incorporates many of the same elements as his first film score. He assigns a lead instrument to play Johnny and Slater's theme music and he uses classical forms like the fugue and counterpoint as the basis for some of his compositions. The music for the film has a hard and lean sound. Lewis uses standard jazz harmonies and dissonant tones to create tension along with note bending and shifting rhythms. There are no love themes in the score because there is no real love for anyone in the picture. Even scenes with children, parks, and zoos have a strange and twisted quality to them. Lewis's score is an integral part of the film and one of the many elements that people remember about the film.

Lewis has always credited Wise with showing him the proper way to score a film, which is to work with a "click track" [the clicking sound of a metronome set at the proper tempo played back through headsets worn by the musicians to help synchronize the music with the visual action], while actually viewing the scenes that are being scored. Their collaboration produced one of the finest film scores of all time. [Liner Notes, *40 Years of MJQ*, 1988.]

Source music is defined as music emanating from a realistic source either on or off the screen. Some examples are radios, record players, an actor singing and, in the case of *Odds* Against *Tomorrow*, Johnny Ingram's singing and the night club band. Lewis wrote two songs for the film: a blues song for Johnny and a swinging blues number for Annie that comment on the plot and society in general. Johnny's emotional subtext is conveyed through his music as a nightclub singer and vibe player. He is in the middle of his blues number when Bacco, the mob boss, shows up to collect a gambling debt that Johnny can not pay. Johnny glares at Bacco and his gang as he plays, seemingly aware of his desperate situation and how he was not able to keep Bacco away from his world.

"Johnny's Lament"

At night I tell you people when that cold, cold sun goes down
I cry, I sigh, I want to die 'cause my baby's not around.
What's the matter pretty baby, tell me what's your daddy done.
Won't you tell me pretty mama, what's your daddy done?
You've got to come and hold me for the morning sun.
Believe me pretty mama it's not just me I know
I just can't make that jungle outside my front door.

The last line of the song sums up Johnny's character. He has tried to make it in life, and on the surface seems to have accomplished some basic goals. He is employed, has an ex-wife and child, both of whom he loves, a car, and nice clothes. However, his inability to control his gambling is going to cost him everything, and he "can't make that jungle outside my door."

Annie's song is another interesting comment on the film and the assortment of characters in the underworld. The song's form is ABAB [rhyme scheme *aabb*], and it's a swinging blues song that incorporates some minor scat singing and improvisation. She sings "All Men Are Evil" directly following Johnny's confrontation with Bacco and his gang. Johnny confesses to Bacco that he doesn't have the seventy-five hundred dollars. Bacco threatens to kill Johnny's ex-wife and child. Johnny loses his temper, draws a gun, and Bacco hits him in the face with a string of pearls. Johnny leaves the office and hears Annie's song being performed.

"All Men are Evil"

Well it tells you in the good book and they teach the same in school
Let a man get his hands on you and he'll use you for a mule.
My mama gave me warning and now I know it's true
She said all men are evil. And daddy that's you.
All men are evil. All men are evil.
My mama gave me warning and now I know it's true.
She said all men are evil. And daddy that's you.
My mama used to tell me. Don't ever love no man.
He'll use you and abuse you, and that's something I can't stand.
My mama gave me warning, And now I know it's true.
She said all men are evil. And daddy that's you.
All men are evil. All men are evil.
My mama gave me warning
All men are evil and that's you.

Belafonte's character is a singer-vibist, and [Milt] Jackson found the task of dubbing his music virtually impossible: "They put that scene on the screen and told me not to concentrate on anything, just to look at the screen and, as he plays, play random, without thinking about the kind of notes I used. This was one of the hardest things I've been asked to do. My whole career, the basic lesson I learned from Dizzy and Charlie Parker is based on the idea that everything you do musically must make sense." [Liner Notes, *40 Years of MJQ*, 1988.]

Milt Jackson may have thought his solo was random and not musical, but the end result sounds perfect for Johnny's character and the film. This song is one more device used in the film to warn the viewer about the impending doom for Johnny—just like the whistling elevator, the popped balloon, and Bacco's visit to the club. The vibe solo sounds like church bells—open fifths—a funeral dirge that's an ominous premonition about Ingram's impending demise and a final visit to a church.

It is very hard to make the vibes sound bad; so while the violence and the meaninglessness of the playing that Jackson refers to may not be appropriate musically, they work within the generic conventions of film music. In a way, it is appropriate that the vibes sound good even in the middle of Johnny's violent playing. It is almost a comment on Harry Belafonte's character. Johnny isn't really bad, he just has a gambling problem and is not able to control it. He is nice to the elevator man, whereas Slater is not. He is pleasant to his ex-wife's friends, pays some neighborhood children to watch his car, and seems to enjoy himself at the park with Eadie. His friendliness and charm enable him to get people to lend him money, including his boss at the nightclub, and even Bacco, who says, "I stretched you six months with a debt someone else would be dead for." The vibe sound is smooth, melodious, and controlled, which fits Johnny's character. He may get angry and frustrated but, unlike Slater who will fight with a stranger over a perceived insult, Johnny only pulls a gun to defend his family and is caught up in something he can not control.

"Yeah, I got rid of the headache. Now I got cancer."

"No Happiness for Slater" is the theme for Earl Slater, a racist with a violent temper. All of the melancholy moments in Slater's life are reflected in his theme music that begins as he walks up the stairs into his apartment after Burke has shamed him. The music starts out using major second intervals, played in octaves which create a clashing dissonant sound that is held twisted to provide a sort of musical pain—and to create a feeling of violence, danger and menace. The music changes when Slater starts to act like a human being. The piano part is heard more clearly; the music is in a major key that provides for a brighter sound, and the tones are smooth, melodic and a little hopeful.

The orchestration of Slater's theme is never dense, but horns are used to increase the texture and provide more power to the evolving nature of the piece.

"No Happiness for Slater," a fine showcase for the quartet's decisive teamwork, is a 16-bar blues with a properly ominous theme; the title selection is a poignant, shimmeringly intimate mood piece, one of the most affecting Lewis has written, especially when Jackson "bends" notes over Lewis's repeated vamp. [Liner Notes, *40 Years of MJQ*, 1988.]

From the first sounds of tension in the overture to the film, one knows that nothing good is going to come to the characters of this story. When Johnny kisses and plays with his daughter on the carousel, the calliope music is overshadowed by horns playing dissonant notes, practically screaming of bad things to come. Lewis's music succeeds in adding to the complexity of each of the characters in the film. By adding a brass section and more percussion, he is able to manipulate the additional texture into his music to provide power and depth to the sound. A composer with only one previous film score to his credit was able to take his music—jazz and the blues—and weave their elements into a unified music score.

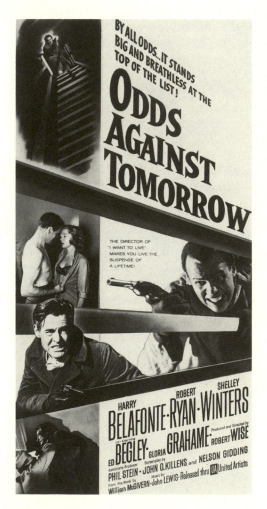

ACKNOWLEDGMENTS.
The editor needs to recognize the ineluctable contributions to this book by the following generous individuals:

Mark Schaubert, Sadanlaur Publications, whose relentless and indefatigable involvement in the creation of the "Film as Literature Series" makes him by any definition co-author of this project;

Dr. Judith Marlane, Director of The Center for Telecommunication Studies, whose personal salutary support, learned encouragement, and commitment to academic excellence continue to be indispensable components of the series;

Harry Belafonte and *Robert Wise*, whose personal graciousness supplemented that of their art;

Martin Myrick,
Michelle Best,
David Sconduto . . . all whose research and scholarship greatly enhance the worthiness of this endeavor;

Abraham Polonsky—Marcel Proust lent him a *madeleine* and a quill;

. . . and especially:

Flory, who, as from the beginning, continues to provide felicity, enchantment, and illumination to a noir world.

APPENDIX

Writers Guild of America List of Corrected Credits
for Blacklisted Writers

This published volume of Abraham Polonsky's screenplay of *Odds Against Tomorrow* is one component in the necessary and moral process of restoring legitimate film credits to writers who were denied them for political reasons.

In the 1940s and 1950s, Hollywood artists found themselves on a "blacklist" (an unofficial collection of hundreds of names) because—within the purview of the House Committee on Un-American Activities (HUAC)—they refused to discuss their political beliefs, refused to name others, were suspected as being Communists, or had been named by informers. The zealousness of HUAC extended beyond Hollywood to government, academia, and the unions—and destroyed the careers and lives of even non-Communist liberals and victims of mistaken identity. Some of the many writers who were blacklisted were able to work in some fashion utilizing "fronts" or pseudonyms.

The Writers Guild began correcting writing credits in 1986. The process involves replacing the front name or the pseudonym with the name of the authentic author, or instating a writer's name that was omitted in the original credits. The following is the list of corrected writing credits on 76 films, as of July 1998. The complete valid writing credits are given; the name(s) of the blacklisted writer(s)—the focus of the correction—is (are) printed in **bold**.

All Night Long (1961). Written by Nel King and **Paul Jarrico**.
Adventures of Robinson Crusoe (1952). Screenplay by **Hugo Butler** and Luis Buñuel.
An Affair to Remember (1957). Screenplay by Delmer Daves and **Donald Ogden Stewart** and Leo McCarey. Story by Leo McCarey and Mildred Cram.
Autumn Leaves (1955). Written by **Jean Rouveral & Hugo Butler** and Lewis and Robert Blees.
Boots Malone (1952). Written by Milton Holmes & **Harold Buchman**.
Born Free (1966). Screenplay by **Lester Cole**.
The Brave One (1956). Screenplay by Harry Franklin and Merrill G. White. Story by **Dalton Trumbo**. (Academy Award for "Motion Picture Story.")
The Bridge On the River Kwai (1957). Screenplay by **Carl Foreman and Michael Wilson**. Based on the novel by Pierre Boulle. (Academy Award for "Screenplay—Based on Material from Another Medium.")
Broken Arrow (1950). Screenplay by **Albert Maltz**. Based on the novel by Elliott Arnold. (WGA Award; Academy Award Nomination for "Screenplay.")
Cairo (1963). Screenplay by **Joan Scott**. Based on the novel by W.R. Burnett.
Captain Sinbad (1963). Written by **Ian McLellan Hunter and Guy Endore**.
The Careless Years (1957). Written by **John Howard Lawson & Mitch Lindemann**.

The Case Against Brooklyn (1958). Screenplay by **Bernard Gordon**. Screen Story by Daniel B. Ullman. Based on a story by Ed Reid.
Chain Lightning (1950). Screenplay by Liam O'Brian and Vincent Evans. Story by **Lester Cole**.
Chicago Confidential (1957). Screenplay and Screen Story by **Bernard Gordon**. Based on the book by Jack Lait and Lee Mortimer.
Circus World (1964). Screenplay by Ben Hecht and **Julian Zimet** and James Edward Grant. Story by Philip Yordan and Nicholas Ray.
Conspiracy of Hearts (1960). Screenplay by Robert Presnell. Story by **Adrian Scott**.
Crack in the World (1965). Screenplay by Jon Manchip White and **Julian Zimet**. Story by Jon Manchip White.
Cry, the Beloved Country (1952). Screenplay by Alan Paton and **John Howard Lawson**. Based on the novel by Alan Paton.
Custer of the West (1968). Written by Bernard Gordon and **Julian Zimet**.
The Day of the Triffids (1963). Screenplay by **Bernard Gordon**. Based on the novel by John Wyndham.
Deadly Is the Female [*Gun Crazy*] (1949). Screenplay by MacKinlay Kantor and **Dalton Trumbo**. Based on a story by MacKinlay Kantor.
The Defiant Ones (1958). Written by **Nedrick Young** and Harold Jacob Smith. (WGA Award; Academy Award for "Story and Screenplay—Written Directly for the Screen.")
The Detective [*Father Brown*] (1954). Screenplay by Thelma Schnee & **Maurice Rapf** and Robert Hamer. Adapted by Thelma Schnee. Based on stories by G.K. Chesterton.
Earth vs. the Flying Saucers (1956). Screenplay by George Worthing Yates and **Bernard Gordon**. Screen Story by Curt Siodmak. Based on a story by Major Donald E. Keyhoe.
Escapade (1955). Screenplay by **Donald Ogden Stewart**. Based on Roger MacDougall's play.
Escape from San Quentin (1957). Written by **Bernard Gordon**.
Five Branded Women (1960). Screenplay by **Michael Wilson & Paul Jarrico** and Ivo Perilli. Based on the novel by Ugo Pirro.
Friendly Persuasion (1956). Screenplay by **Michael Wilson**. Based on the novel by Jessamyn West. (WGA Award; Academy Award Nomination for "Screenplay—Adapted")
The Giant Behemoth (1958). Screenplay by Eugene Lourie & **Daniel James**. Story by Robert Abel & Allen Adler.
G.I. Jane (1951). Screenplay by **Henry Blankfort**. Story by Murray Lerner.
The Girl Most Likely (1957). Screenplay by **Paul Jarrico** and Devery Freeman. Story by **Paul Jarrico**.
Go Man Go (1953). Written by **Alfred Palca**.
Gorgo (1960). Screenplay and Screen Story by **Robert L. Richards and Daniel James**.
A Hatful of Rain (1957). Screenplay by Michael Vincent Gazzo and Alfred Hayes and **Carl Foreman**. Based on a play by Gazzo.
Hellcats of the Navy (1957). Screenplay by David Lang and **Bernard Gordon**. Screen Story by David Lang. Based on a book by Charles A. Lockwood and Hans Christian.
The Highwayman (1951). Screenplay by **Henry Blankfort**. Screen Story by Jack DeWitt and Renault Duncan. Based on the poem by Alfred Noyes.
The Horror Express (1972). Screenplay by Arnaud d'Usseau and **Julian Zimet**.
Inherit the Wind (1960). Screenplay by **Nedrick Young** and Harold Jacob Smith. Based on the play by Jerome Lawrence and Robert E. Lee.
The Indian Fighter (1955). Screenplay by Frank Davis and Ben Hecht. From an original story by **Robert L. Richards**.

The Intimate Stranger [*Finger of Guilt*] (1956). Written by **Howard Koch**.

Ivanhoe (1952). Screenplay by **Marguerite Roberts** and Noel Langley. Adaptation by Aeneas Mac Kenzie. Based on the novel by Sir Walter Scott.

Joe Palooka in the Square Circle (1950). Screenplay by **Henry Blankfort**. Screen Story by B.F. Melzer. Based on a character created by Ham Fisher.

Joe Palooka in Triple Cross (1951). Screenplay and Screen Story by **Henry Blankfort**. Based on a character created by Ham Fisher.

Kenner [*Year of the Cricket*] (1969). Screenplay by **Robert L. Richards** and Harold Clemins. Story by Mary P. Murray.

The Las Vegas Story (1951). Screenplay by **Paul Jarrico** and Harry Essex and Earl Felton. Story by Jay Dratler.

The Law vs. Billy the Kid (1954). Screenplay and Screen Story by **Bernard Gordon**. Based on a play by Janet & Phillip Stevenson.

Lawrence of Arabia (1962). Screenplay by Robert Bolt and **Michael Wilson**. Based on the life and writings of Colonel T.E. Lawrence. (Academy Award Nomination for "Screenplay—Based on Material from Another Medium.")

Little Giants (1958). Written for the Screen by **Hugo Butler and Edward Huebsch**.

Malaga [*Moment of Danger*] (1962). Screenplay by David Osborn and **Donald Ogden Stewart**. Based on a novel by Donald MacKenzie.

The Man Who Turned to Stone (1957). Written by **Bernard Gordon**.

A Matter of WHO (1962). Screenplay by Milton Holmes & **Harold Buchman**. Adapted by Patricia Lee. Based on a story by Patricia Lee and Paul Dickinson.

The Miracle (1959). Screenplay by Frank Butler & **Jean Rouverol**. Based on the play by Karl Vollmoeller as produced on the stage by Max Reinhardt.

The Misadventures of Merlin Jones (1964). Screenplay by **Alfred Lewis Levitt & Helen Levitt**. Screen Story by Bill Walsh.

The Monkey's Uncle (1965). Written by **Alfred Lewis Levitt & Helen Levitt**.

The Naked Dawn (1955). Written by **Julian Zimet**.

The Naked Earth (1958). Written by Milton Holmes & **Harold Buchman**.

Odds Against Tomorrow (1959). Screenplay by **Abraham Polonsky** and Nelson Gidding. Based on the novel by William P. McGivern.

[In light of director Robert Wise's comments regarding the circumstances of Nelson Gidding's involvement with this film—and the *lack* of justification for his screenplay credit (see Annotation #1, p. 137 in this volume)—the presence of Gidding's name in the official Writers Guild list represents an anomaly, which has the following explanation. When the Writers Guild notified Abraham Polonsky of his restored credit, Polonsky, "as a matter of courtesy" (because Gidding had been graciously willing to act as a front), called Gidding and asked him whether he wanted to continue to have his name included in the credits. Gidding said he did. Rather than initiate an arbitration process to have Gidding's name removed, Polonsky decided to accept the wording of the screenplay credits as specified above. (Polonsky Interview with Author, 13 December 1998.)]

Operation Eichmann (1961). Written by **Lester Cole**.

Pancho Villa (1971). Screenplay by **Julian Zimet**. Story by Gene Martin.

Passage West (1951). Screenplay by Lewis R. Foster. Story by **Alvah Bessie**.

A Place for Lovers (1969). Screenplay by **Julian Zimet** & Peter Baldwin and Ennio de Concini and Tonino Guerra & Cesare Zavattini. Story by Brunello Rondi.

Psyche 59 (1965). Screenplay by **Julian Zimet**. Based on the novel by Francoise des Ligneris.

Revolt in the Big House (1952). Written by **Daniel James** and Eugene Lourie.

The Robe (1953). Screenplay by **Albert Maltz** and Philip Dunne. Adaptation by Gina Kaus. Based on the novel by Lloyd C. Douglas.

Roman Holiday (1953). Screenplay by Ian McLellan Hunter and John Dighton. Story by **Dalton Trumbo**. (WGA Award; Academy Award for "Motion Picture Story.")

Shark River (1954). Screenplay by **Louis Lantz** and Lewis Meltzer. Story by John Rawlins.

The Sheriff of Fractured Jaw (1958). Screenplay by **Howard Dimsdale**. Based on the short story by Jacob Hay.

Short Cut to Hell (1957). Screenplay by Ted Berkman & Raphael Blau. Based on *This Gun for Hire* (1942) screenplay by **Albert Maltz** and W.R. Burnett. Based on a novel by Graham Greene.

The Sleeping Tiger (1955). Screenplay by **Harold Buchman and Carl Foreman**. Based on the novel by Maurice Moiseiwitsch.

Torero (1956). Adapted for film by **Hugo Butler** and Carlos Velo.

The Tunnel of Love (1958). Screenplay by Joseph Fields & **Jerome Chodorov**. From the stage play by Joseph Fields & **Jerome Chodorov** and Peter De Vries. Based on the novel by Peter De Vries. Presented on the stage by The Theatre Guild.

Under Ten Flags (1960). Based on original diaries by Bernhard Rogge. Screenplay by Vittoriano Petrilli, Duilio Coletti, Ulrich Mohr and **Leonardo Bercovici**. Additional Dialogue by William Douglas Home.

We Joined the Navy [We Are in the Navy Now] (1962). Screenplay by **Howard Dimsdale**. Based on the novel by John Winton.

The Young One [Island of Shame] (1960). Written for the Screen by **Hugo Butler** and Luis Buñuel. Inspired by a story by Peter Matthiessen.

Zombies of Mara Tau (1957). Screenplay by **Bernard Gordon**. Story by George Plympton.

BIBLIOGRAPHY

Andersen, Thom. "Red Hollywood." In *Literature and the Visual Arts in Contemporary Society*, ed. Suzanne Ferguson and Barbara Groseclose, 141-196. Columbus: Ohio State University Press, 1985.

Ansen, David. "The Neo-Noir '90s." *Newsweek* (27 October 1997): 68-69, 70.

Appel, Alfred. *The Art of Celebration: Twentieth-Century Painting, Literature, Sculpture, Photography, and Jazz*. New York: Alfred A. Knopf, 1992.

Armes, Roy. "Jean-Pierre Melville." In *The St. James Film Directors Encyclopedia*, ed. Andrew Sarris, 336-338. Detroit: Visible Ink Press, 1998.

Asselineau, Roger, ed. *The Literary Reputation of Hemingway in Europe*. New York: New York University Press, 1965.

A.W. "Richard Wright Plays Hero in Movie Adaptation of His Novel, 'Native Son.'" *New York Times* (18 June 1951).

Bailey, Frankie Y. *Out of the Woodpile: Black Characters in Crime and Detective Fiction*. New York: Greenwood Press, 1991.

Baldwin, James. *The Devil Finds Work*. New York: Dial Press, 1976.

_____. "Everybody's Protest Novel." In *Bigger Thomas*, ed. Harold Bloom, 5-6. New York: Chelsea House, 1990.

Balio, Tino. *United Artists: The Company Built by the Stars*. Madison: University of Wisconsin Press, 1976.

Bazin, Andre. *What Is Cinema? Volume I*. ed., trans. Hugh Gray. Berkeley: University of California Press, 1971.

Bergan, Ronald. *The United Artists Story*. New York: Crown, 1986.

Biskind, Peter. *Seeing is Believing: How Hollywood Taught Us to Stop Worrying and Love the Fifties*. New York: Pantheon, 1983.

Bobo, Jacqueline. "Black Women in Fiction & Nonfiction: Images of Power & Powerlessness." *Wide Angle* 13, No. 3 (July 1991): 72-81.

Bogle, Donald. *Blacks in American Films and Television: An Encyclopedia*. New York: Garland, 1988.

_____. *Toms, Coons, Mulattoes, Mammies, and Bucks*. New York: Continuum, 1989.

Borde, Raymond and Etienne Chaumeton. *Panorama du Film Noir Américain, 1941-1953*. Paris: Editions du Minuit, 1955. Their chapter, "Towards a Definition of Film Noir," Trans. Alain Silver, reprinted in *Film Noir Reader*, ed. Alain Silver and James Ursini, 17-25. New York: Limelight Editions, 1996.

Bordwell, David, Janet Staiger and Kristin Thompson. *The Classical Hollywood Cinema: Film Style and Mode of Production to 1960*. New York: Columbia University Press, 1985.

Bordwell, David. *Filmguide to La Passion de Jeanne d'Arc*. Bloomington IN: Indiana University Press, 1973.

Bradbury, Richard. "Sexuality, Guilt and Detection: Tension between History and Suspense." In *American Crime Fiction: Studies in the Genre*. ed. Brian Docherty, 88-99. New York: St. Martin's Press, 1988.

Brinnin, John Malcolm. *William Carlos Williams*. University of Minnesota Pamphlets on American Writers 24. Minneapolis: University of Minnesota Press, 1967.

Brun, Joseph. "*Odds Against Tomorrow*." *American Cinematographer* (August 1959): 478-479, 510.

Brunette, Peter. "Two Wrights, One Wrong." In *The Modern American Novel and the Movies*, ed. Gerald Peary and Roger Shatzkin, 131-142. New York: Frederick Ungar, 1978.

Buss, Robin. *French Film Noir*. London: Marion Boyars, 1994.

Campbell, James. *Exiled in Paris: Richard Wright, James Baldwin, Samuel Beckett, and Others on the Left Bank*. New York: Scribner, 1995.

Chabrol, Claude. "Little Themes." *Cahiers du Cinéma* 100 (1959). In *The New Wave*, ed. Peter Graham, 73-77. Garden City NJ: Doubleday, 1968.

Chase, Donald. "In Praise of the Naughty Mind: Gloria Grahame." *Film Comment* (September-October 1997): 50-58.

Coursodon, Jean-Pierre. "Robert Wise." In *American Directors, Volume II*, ed. Jean-Pierre Coursodon, 367-378. New York: McGraw-Hill, 1983.

Cripps, Thomas. *Black Film as Genre*. Bloomington IN: Indiana University Press, 1978.

_____. *Hollywood's High Noon: Moviemaking & Society before Television*. Baltimore: The John Hopkins University Press, 1997.

_____. *Making Movies Black*. New York: Oxford University Press, 1993.

_____. *Slow Fade to Black: The Negro in American Film, 1900-1942*. New York: Oxford University Press, 1977.

Dargis, Manohla. "N for Noir: *Sight and Sound* A-Z of Cinema." *Sight and Sound* (July 1997): 31.

Davis, Mike. *City of Quartz: Excavating the Future in Los Angeles*. New York: Vintage, 1992.

Derry, Charles. *The Suspense Thriller: Films in the Shadow of Alfred Hitchcock*. Jefferson NC: McFarland, 1988.

Diawara, Manthia. "Noir by Noirs: Toward a New Realism in Black Cinema." In *Shades of Noir*, ed. Joan Copjec, 261-278. London: Verso, 1993.

Dixon, Wheeler Winston. *The Early Film Criticism of Francois Truffaut*. Bloomington IN: Indiana University Press, 1993.

Durgnat, Raymond. "Paint It Black: The Family Tree of the Film Noir." In *Film Noir Reader*, ed. Alain Silver and James Ursini, 37-51. New York: Limelight Editions, 1996.

Dyer, Richard. "Entertainment and Utopia." *Movie* 24, (Spring 1977): 36-43.

Edelman, Rob. "Abraham Polonsky." In *The St. James Film Directors Encyclopedia*, ed. Andrew Sarris, 393-394. Detroit: Visible Ink Press, 1998.

Eliot, T.S. *Selected Poems*. New York: Harcourt, Brace & World, 1964.
_____. *The Waste Land*. New York: Harcourt, Brace & World, 1962.
Ellison, Ralph. "The Essential Ellison (Interview)." *Y'Bird* 1, No. 1 (1978): 130-159.
Fabre, Michel. *The Unfinished Quest of Richard Wright*. Translated by Isabel Barzun. New York: Morrow, 1973.
Farber, Manny. *Movies*. New York: Stonehill, 1971.
Farrell, James T. *The League of Frightened Philistines*. New York: Vanguard Press, 1945.
Gates, Henry-Louis. "Belafonte's Balancing Act." *The New Yorker* (26 August & 2 September 1996): 133-143.
_____. *Figures in Black: Words, Signs, and the "Racial" Self*. New York: Oxford University Press, 1989.
_____. "Preface to Blackness: Text and Pretext." In *Afro-American Literature: The Reconstruction of Instruction*, ed. Dexter Fisher and Robert B. Stepto. Modern Language Association of America, 1978.
Gayle, Addison. *The Way of the New World: The Black Novel in America*. Garden City: Doubleday, 1975.
Gelfant, Blanche Housman. *The American City Novel*. Norman: University of Oklahoma Press, 1970.
Gifford, Barry. *The Devil Thumbs A Ride & Other Unforgettable Films*. New York: Grove Press, 1988.
_____. "The Godless World of Jim Thompson." Introduction to *The Getaway* by Jim Thompson, v-vii. Berkeley: Creative Art Book Company, 1984.
Gow, Gordon. *Suspense in the Cinema*. New York: Castle, 1968.
Gray, Herman. "Television, Black Americans, and the American Dream." In *Critical Studies in Mass Communication* 6 (1989): 376-386.
Grebstein, Sheldon Norman. "The Tough Hemingway and His Hard-Boiled Children." In *Tough Guy Writers of the Thirties*, ed. David Madden. Carbondale IL: Southern Illinois University Press, 1968.
Haut, Woody. *Pulp Culture: Hardboiled Fiction and the Cold War*. London: Serpent's Tail, 1995.
Highsmith, Patricia. *Plotting and Writing Suspense Fiction*. Boston: The Writer, 1966.
Higgins, William H. Jr. "John Oliver Killens." In *Dictionary of Literary Biography: Afro-American Fiction Writers After 1955*, ed. Thadious M. Davis and Trudier Harris, 144-152. Detroit: Gale Research, 1984.
Hillier, Jim, ed. *Cahiers du Cinéma: the 1950s*. Cambridge MA: Harvard University Press, 1985.

Himes, Chester. *A Case of Rape*. New York: Carroll & Graf, 1994.
_____. *Conversations with Chester Himes*, ed. Michel Fabre and Robert E. Skinner. Jackson: University Press of Mississippi, 1995.
_____. "Dilemma of the Negro Novelist in U.S." In *Beyond the Angry Black*, ed. John A. Williams, 51-58. New York: Cooper Square Publishers, 1966.
_____. *The End of a Primitive*. New York: W.W. Norton, 1997.
_____. *If He Hollers Let Him Go*. New York: Thunder's Mouth Press, 1986.
_____. *A Rage in Harlem*. New York: Vintage Crime/Black Lizard, 1991.
Hirsch, Foster. *The Dark Side of the Screen: Film Noir*. San Diego: A.S. Barnes, 1981.
Hogue, Peter. "Melville: The Elective Affinities." *Film Comment* (November-December 1996): 17-22.
Houston, Penelope. "Uncommitted Artist?" In *Focus on Shoot the Piano Player*, ed. Leo Braudy, 138-140. Englewood Cliffs NJ: Prentice-Hall, 1972.
Howe, Irving. *A World More Attractive: A View of Modern Literature and Politics*. New York: Horizon Press, 1963.
Jarlett, Franklin. *Robert Ryan: A Biography and Critical Filmography*. Jefferson NC: McFarland, 1990.
Johnson, Albert. "Beige, Brown, or Black." In *Black Films and Film-Makers: A Comprehensive Anthology from Stereotype to Superhero*, ed. Lindsay Patterson, 36-43. New York: Dodd, Mead, 1975.
Kael, Pauline. *The Citizen Kane Book*. Boston: Little, Brown, 1971.
_____. "Notes on Black Movies." *The New Yorker* (2 December 1972). Reprinted in *In Black Films and Film-Makers: A Comprehensive Anthology from Stereotype to Superhero*, ed. Lindsay Patterson, 258-267. New York: Dodd, Mead, 1975.
_____. "Trash, Art, and the Movies." In *Going Steady*, 103-158. New York: Bantam, 1971.
Kaminsky, Stuart M. *American Film Genres: Approaches to a Critical Theory of Popular Film*. New York: Dell Publishing, 1977.
Keenan, Richard. "William P. McGivern." In *Critical Survey of Mystery and Detective Fiction*, ed. Frank N. Magill, 1154-1155. Salem Press, 1988.
Killens, John Oliver. "Hollywood in Black and White." In *The State of the Nation*, ed. David Boroff, 100-107. Englewood Cliffs NJ: Prentice-Hall, 1965.
Krutnick, Frank. *In A Lonely Street: Film Noir, Genre, Masculinity*. London: Routledge, 1991.
Leab, Daniel J. "Blacks in American Cinema." In *The Political Companion to American Film*, ed. Gary Crowdus, 41-50. Lakeview Press, 1994.
_____. "A Pale Black Imitation: All-Colored Films, 1930-1960." *The Journal of Popular Film*. IV:1 (1975): 56-76.
Leeman, Sergio. *Robert Wise On His Films: From Editing Chair to Director's Chair*. Los Angeles: Silman-James Press, 1995.

Lehan, Richard. *A Dangerous Crossing: French Literary Existentialism and the Modern American Novel*. Carbondale IL: Southern Ilinois University Press, 1973.

Lott, Tommy L. "A No-Theory Theory of Contemporary Black Cinema." In *Representing Blackness: Issues in Film and Video*, ed. Valerie Smith, 83-96. New Brunswick NJ: Rutgers University Press, 1997.

Lowry, Ed. "*Madigan.*" *CinemaTexas Program Notes* 9, No. 3 (30 October 1975): 47-54.

Macgowan, Kenneth. *Behind the Screen: The History and Techniques of the Motion Picture*. New York: Dell, 1965.

Madden, David. *James M. Cain*. New York: Twayne Publishers, 1970.

Malle, Louis. Foreword to *Blues for a Black Cat* by Boris Vian, vii. Lincoln: University of Nebraska Press, 1992.

Maltz, Albert. "Moving Forward." *New Masses* (9 April 1946): 8-10, 21-22.

_____. "What Shall We Ask of Writers?" *New Masses* (12 February 1946): 19-22.

Mapp, Edward. *Blacks in American Films*. Metuchen NJ: Scarecrow Press, 1972.

Margolies, Edward. *The Art of Richard Wright*. Carbondale IL: Southern Illinois University Press, 1969.

Marling, William. *The American Roman Noir*. Athens GA: The University of Georgia Press, 1995.

McArthur, Colin. *Underworld U.S.A*. New York: The Viking Press, 1972.

McGivern, William P. *Odds Against Tomorrow*. New York: Dodd, Mead & Company, 1957.

Melville, Jean-Pierre. *Melville on Melville*. Rui Nogueira, ed. New York: The Viking Press, 1972.

Merritt, Bishetta and Carolyn A. Stroman. "Black Family Imagery and Interactions on Television." *Journal of Black Studies* 23, No. 4 (June 1993): 492-499.

Morrison, Toni. *Conversations with Toni Morrison*. Ed. Danille Taylor-Guthrie. Jackson: University Press of Mississippi, 1994.

_____. *Jazz*. New York: Penguin, 1993.

Moullet, Luc. "Sam Fuller: In Marlowe's Footsteps." *Cahiers du Cinéma* 93 (March 1959). In *Cahiers du Cinéma: the 1950s*, ed. Jim Hillier, 145-155. Cambridge MA: Harvard University Press, 1985.

Muller, Eddie. *Dark City: The Lost World of Film Noir*. New York: St Martin's Press, 1998.

Naremore, James. "American Film Noir: The History of an Idea." *Film Quarterly* (Winter 1995-96): 12-28.

_____. *More Than Night: Film Noir in Its Contexts*. Berkeley: University of California Press, 1998.

Oates, Joyce Carol. "Man Under Sentence of Death: The Novels of James M. Cain." In *Tough Guy Writers of the Thirties*, ed. David Madden, 112-113. Carbondale IL: Southern Illinois University Press, 1968.

O'Brien, Geoffrey. *Hardboiled America: Lurid Paperbacks and the Masters of Noir*. New York: Da Capo, 1997.

Older, Julia. Introduction to *Blues for a Black Cat & Other Stories* by Boris Vian, ed., trans. Julia Older, IX-XXIV. Lincoln: The University of Nebraska Press, 1992.

Ottoson, Robert. *A Reference Guide to the American Film Noir: 1940-1958*. Metuchen, NJ: The Scarecrow Press, 1981.

Parish, James Robert and George H. Hill. *Black Action Films*. Jefferson NC: McFarland & Co., 1989.

Pasternak, James D. and F. William Howton. *The Image Maker*. Richmond VA: John Knox Press, 1971.

Pines, Jim. *Blacks in Films: A Survey of Racial Themes and Images in the American Film*. London: Studio Vista, 1975.

Polonsky, Abraham. "*The Best Years of Our Lives:* A Review." *Hollywood Quarterly* II: 3 (April 1947): 257-260.

_____. "Une expérience utopique." *Présence du Cinéma* 14 (June 1962): 5-7; English text in *Force of Evil: The Critical Edition*: 186-188.

_____. *Force of Evil: The Critical Edition*. Northridge CA: The Center for Telecommunication Studies, California State University, Northridge, 1996.

_____. *A Season of Fear*. New York: Cameron Associates, 1956.

_____. *The World Above*. Boston: Little, Brown and Co., 1951.

_____. *You Are There Teleplays: The Critical Edition*. Northridge CA: The Center for Telecommunication Studies, California State University, Northridge, 1997.

Porfirio, Robert. "No Way Out: Existential Motifs in the Film Noir." In *Film Noir Reader*, ed. Alain Silver and James Ursini, 77-93. New York: Limelight, 1996.

Pudaloff, Ross. "*Native Son* and Mass Culture." In *Bigger Thomas*, ed. Harold Bloom, 90-102. New York: Chelsea House, 1990.

Reid, Mark A. *Redefining Black Film*. Berkeley: University of California Press, 1993.

Richardson, Robert. *Literature and Film*. Bloomington: Indiana University Press, 1972.

Roffman, Peter and Jim Purdy. *The Hollywood Social Problem Film: Madness, Despair, and Politics from the Depression to the Fifties*. Bloomington IN: Indiana University Press, 1981.

Rohmer, Eric. "Rédecouvir l'Amérique," *Cahiers du Cinéma* 54 (Christmas 1955). In *Cahiers du Cinéma: 1950s*, ed. Jim Hillier, 88-93. Cambridge MA: Harvard University Press, 1985.

Rose, Vattel T. "Afro-American Literature as a Cultural Resource for a Black Cinema Aesthetic." In *Black Cinema Aesthetics: Issues in Independent Black Filmmaking*, ed. Gladstone L. Yearwood, 27-40. Athens OH: Ohio University Center for Afro-American Studies, 1982.

Rudelic, Zvjezdana. "Boris Vian." In *French Novelists 1930-1960, Dictionary of Literary Biography,* Volume 72, ed. Catharine Savage Brosman, 384-396. New York: Gale Research, 1988.

Ryan, Robert. "I Didn't Want to Play a Bigot." *Ebony* (November 1959): 68-72.

Saada, Nicolas. "In the Mood." *Civilization* (February/March 1998): 76-81.

Sallis, James. Introduction to *A Case of Rape* by Chester Himes, v-ix. New York: Carroll & Graf, 1994.

Schlondorff, Volker. "A Parisian-American in Paris." *The Village Voice* (6 July 1982).

Schrader, Paul. "Notes on Film Noir." *Film Comment* (Spring, 1972): 8-13. Reprinted in *Film Noir Reader*, ed. Alain Silver and James Ursini, 59-61. New York: Limelight Editions, 1996.

Schultheiss, John. "*Force of Evil:* Existential Marx and Freud." In *Force of Evil: The Critical Edition*, ed. John Schultheiss and Mark Schaubert, 151-198. Northridge CA: The Center for Telecommunication Studies, California State University, Northridge, 1996.

_____. "A Season of Fear: The Blacklisted Teleplays of Abraham Polonsky." *Literature/Film Quarterly* 24, No. 2 (1996): 148-164.

_____. "A Season of Fear: Abraham Polonsky, *You Are There*, and the Blacklist." In *You Are There Teleplays: The Critical Edition.* Ed. John Schultheiss and Mark Schaubert, 11-37. Northridge CA: The Center for Telecommunication Studies, California State University, Northridge, 1997.

Selby, Spencer. *Dark City: The Film Noir.* Jefferson NC: McFarland, 1984.

Shaw, Arnold. *What Is the Secret Magic of Belafonte?* New York: Pyramid, 1960.

Silver, Alain and James Ursini, eds. *Film Noir Reader.* New York: Limelight Editions, 1996.

Silver, Alain and Elizabeth Ward, eds. *Film Noir: An Encyclopedia of the American Style.* Third Edition. Woodstock: Overlook Press, 1992.

Sitney, P. Adams. "Robert Bresson." In *The St. James Film Directors Encyclopedia*, ed. Andrew Sarris, 59-61. Detroit: Visible Ink Press, 1998.

Slide, Anthony. *The American Film Industry.* New York: Limelight, 1990.

Smith, Darr. "Native Son." *Los Angeles Daily News* (13 August 1951).

Snead, James. *White Screens/Black Images: Hollywood from the Dark Side.* ed. Colin MacCabe & Cornel West. New York: Routedge, 1994.

Soitos, Stephen F. "Crime and Mystery Writing." In *The Oxford Companion to African American Literature.* New York: Oxford University Press, 1997.

Springer, John. *Forgotten Films to Remember.* Secaucus NJ: Citadel Press, 1980.

Starr, Cecile. "Dede Allen." In *The International Dictionary of Films and Filmmakers: Volume IV. Writers and Production Artists*, ed. James Vinson, 9-10. Chicago: St. James Press, 1987.

Stephens, Michael L. *Film Noir: A Comprehensive, Illustrated Reference to Movies, Terms, and Persons*. Jefferson NC: McFarland, 1995.

Truffaut, François. "Should Films Be Politically Committed?" In *Focus on Shoot the Piano Player*, ed. Leo Braudy, 133-137. Englewood Cliffs NJ: Prentice-Hall, 1972.

Unger, Leonard. *T.S. Eliot*. University of Minnesota Pamphlets on American Writers 8. Minneapolis: University of Minnesota Press, 1970.

Vian, Boris [Vernon Sullivan]. *I Shall Spit on Your Graves*. Paris: The Vendome Press, 1948.

Walker, Margaret. *Richard Wright, Daemonic Genius*. New York: Amistad Press, 1988.

Warren, Virginia Lee. "Argentina Doubles as Chicago Locale for 'Native Son.'" *New York Times* (21 May 1950).

West, Nathanael. *Miss Lonelyhearts*. New York: New Directions, 1962.

Williams, William Carlos. *Collected Poems*. New York: New Directions, 1951.

Wilson, Edmund. *The Shores of Light*. New York: Noonday Press, 1967.

Wood, Robin. "Servants and Slaves: Brown Persons in Classical Hollywood Cinema." *CineAction* 32 (Fall 1993): 81-88.

Woods, Paula L., ed. *Spooks, Spies, and Private Eyes: Black Mystery, Crime, and Suspense Fiction of the 20th Century*. New York: Doubleday, 1995.

Wright, Richard. "How 'Bigger' Was Born." 12 March 1940 lecture at Columbia University. Printed as addendum to all subsequent publications of *Native Son*.

_____. "The Man Who Killed a Shadow." In *Spooks, Spies, and Private Eyes*, ed. Paula L. Woods, 89-101. New York, Doubleday, 1995.

_____. *Native Son*. New York: Harper Perennial Edition, 1993. Includes "How 'Bigger' Was Born," 503-540.

_____. *The Outsider*. New York: Harper Perennial Edition, 1993.

_____. *Savage Holiday*. New York: Award Books, 1965.

Wu, William F. *The Yellow Peril: Chinese Americans in American Fiction 1850-1940*. Hamden CT: Archon Books, 1982.

Yearwood, Gladstone L. "The Hero in Black Film: An Analysis of the Film Industry and Problems in Black Cinema." *Wide Angle* Vol. 5, No. 2 (1982): 42-50.

Zolotow, Maurice. "Harry Belafonte." *The American Weekly* (10 May 1959): 9-14.